NO LONGER PROPERTY OF
SEATTLE PUBLIC LIBRARY

D0978615

"Getting Back To Me"

from girl to boy to woman in just fifty years

Scottie Jeanette Madden

Copyright © 2015 Scottie Jeanette Madden

Cover painting: "The Endless Raspberry Queen" Sally Park Rubin
artistsparkrubin@gmail.com

Cover photography: Malcolm McVickar

All rights reserved.

ISBN: 0692541772
ISBN-13: 978-0692541777

DEDICATION

To Mylove - the light, the heat of all that I am, and all that I will ever be.

Zuzubean Press
www.zuzubean.com

Contact the author for questions, booking and appearance
schedule (or trading recipes) at scottie@zuzubean.com

REFLECTION

Okay, you're right, I'm not the first girl to walk this path, but when I found myself at the edge of the abyss called "unknown" with vertigo pulling me ever forward, I still believed I *had* a sworn duty to skirt the edge. Even when I saw others defy gravity, I felt grounded. My path just wasn't as obvious as theirs. I didn't have a "hell" to leave.

Until I'm honest with myself.

Which is hard for me to do. It's what got me in trouble, deep trouble. I'm compelled to tell my story for that one person who finds herself (or himself) like me, lost in a house of mirrors of her own making. The kind of girl who, instead of searching for a way out, just makes another mirror; the kind of girl who didn't trust herself *to trust herself.*

This is for the girl or boy out there who has convinced themselves that they aren't worthy of going from "there" to here. The kind of girl who learned never to trust that mirror, but never stopped *praying to it everyday.*

Because one day, the mirror answers...

CONTENTS

ACKNOWLEDGMENTS

There are countless (countless? Really? stop with the exaggerating girl!) okay *many* great souls to whom I am grateful: David who asked that question that launches almost every book, *"have you written any of this down?"* To Eileen for her generous time, her diligent proof reading and her commentary, to my reader team, who braved a weighty read, rife with typos (before Eileen) Melissa, Sally Joy, Brent, Paige and Danielle, to Valerie who is a patient and generous mentor, colleague and trailblazer, Merrie Lynn for her publishing handholding and much needed *"atta*-girls," all the wonderful people who touched my heart on my journey (though your names were changed in this account for privacy – you and I both know who you are), and most of all, to my beloved wife; who held me, supported me, coached me and cheered me on, even as we went *back* through the confusion and heartache of our past, turning each memory into a joyful moment of love, understanding and growth.

INTRODUCTION

I knew being who I really am wasn't in the cards for me. So I came up with a noble plan. I would earn my womanhood _next_ lifetime by being everyone's best man _this_ go-around.

Which almost worked.

It all started with a simple question – How could my life be so wrong? I was known for being not only happy but "too god damned exuberant!" Well, if that was true, then how could those thoughts and feelings that stalked the "happy" – constantly hanging over it, like bats in a cave – be so consumed with "it?"

If I closed my eyes "it" was there.

When I opened them, "it" was still there.

When I was happy, "it" was there to dim the light.

When I was sad, "it" would seize the moment and blow up my depression to epic proportions.

Nothing could ever dispel the darkness when "it" descended. Despite all I did to hide "it," run from "it," and keep "it" behind fortress walls, "it" became stronger. "It" was the terminal denial I learned to use to imprison myself, a choking black smoke so thick it drowned out the pounding of fists pleading for release from the dungeon:

I am, and always have been, a woman.

But the above statement means nothing, certainly not worthy of the crushing weight described, _unless_ you know that my body had been born a boy, forced to live a boy's life, destined to die a false and ultimately lonely death. This crime was perfect in its undeniable plausibility: I was the firstborn, my father's only son, my mother's "baby," and my three little sisters' "big bro." I cherished my position, loving the responsibility of caring, watching over and protecting them more than oxygen.

Life kept trying to affirm the mirror's male reflection. I was all boy: good at sports, a leader, captain and coach. As I grew older, I found true love and heavenly marriage.

As a filmmaker/television producer in the adventure-documentary world, "success" was my armor of choice and I hid myself behind a carefully constructed "dude" who was at home in the gritty outdoor arena of remote mountaintops and dense jungles. I developed a hard-won reputation for leading my crews into some of the most dangerous places in the world and then home again safely, and military alpha-wolves to places not even they dreamed of conquering. And they all trusted me as the one who has been there, done that, with heavier equipment.

I had built a great guy named Scott.

He was a good man, damnit, and I was killing myself to insure that.

He wasn't a lie, a fake or an imposter, but steward and stand-in for the me locked away by my own hand.

It took until this past year to really accept that. But it's one thing to accept the cause of the suffocating veil that hung over my life, sticking to every thought, prayer and feeling. . .

And quite another to do something about it.

When "it" didn't go away, never got outgrown, became harder and harder to ignore, and I still didn't do anything about it, Grace had to take over for me. And for once, I was smart enough and strong enough to get out of its way.

But I'm getting ahead of myself...

Scottie Jeanette Christine Madden, Summer 2015

a journal is a funny thing...

CHAPTER 1
DUDE, YOU'RE SCREWED

From my journal – written at 35,000 feet, between sleeping strangers:
Exhausted. . . been on the road for almost 3 years straight . . . not freakin' kidding! When we tabulated my "days out of town" for our taxes last year, it was easier to add up the days I was home, fifteen! This year we're on track for even fewer. I did eight countries on four continents in three months. It's not a record we can be proud of; my crew is toast, and I'm feeling like I barely got them out alive. Tempers are frayed, and our sense of accomplishment is more like survivor's guilt. It's not how I like to run a show.

Feeling defeated when I should be elated: a hit show! Broke my second season curse and the shows are going to look amazing. We hit that magic point in a TV show's life when the cast is getting recognized in airports – we almost missed connections as they signed autographs and posed for pictures in JoBurg (South Africa), Norway and Romania. As we say on my crew, "First world problems!"

Heck yes, I'm proud of what we built, but I can't help feeling like this is the end. The network is in turmoil (they never knew what to do with us), and they have a problem making "intellevision." (Shows that require an IQ higher than a network suit.) We are one of the most expensive shows they have. My cast has not been treated well by our overlords and our pride of ownership is all we've got left; it hurts my heart that we are living up to our name.

I say "my," as in my crew, my cast, my show because, even though this show was not my idea, I can say without reservation or challenge that I am the mother bear of our little cub. I will confess that I had nothing to do with the title, "Dude, You're Screwed," but I was the one who made sure that a show where "boys will be boys" would not only redefine the survival genre, it would make for a fun ride. As comes with the territory, I take responsibility for the things that didn't work (there were a few) as much as the things that did. I also confess to pushing, pulling, dragging and nagging, and when required, being such a pain in the butt there was no choice but to grant our wishes, so we could make a show that would be worthy of the insane effort my cast and crew put into every moment. As my dad would say, "Lead, follow or get the hell out of the way." So, I fostered a take no prisoners, us against the world, give us what we want and no one gets hurt, environment.

7

Did I say I was the showrunner? This is technically a nickname for my position. I am a Co-EP, which in reality television is the title for the one Executive Producer who is actually *producing* the television series. At the top of every show (the beginning) there is a list of Executive Producers who made the deal that made the show you are watching. These people are my bosses; I'm the one who is making the show they all promised to deliver.

I'm both the lead storyteller (creative) and business person (management) on the set. As my friend John Hudson RAF says, I'm "the adult." It's my name that gets approved by the network, a name built in the adventure doc-reality sect.

This is probably the most übermale of the genres with remote, harsh locations and conditions that stretch personnel and equipment to their limits. In my career, I've led crews into the amazon jungle (gold mining), the South Pacific (surfing), Iceland, Chile, Alaska, Nicaragua, the Arctic Circle twice (survival). I've spent a summer chasing catfish noodlers (believe me they're not hard to catch, the noodlers I mean) in Oklahoma's Red River, and a hurricane season with shrimpers on the Gulf of Mexico.

Not bad for a girl.

Wait. That was a cheap shot. I guess I'll leave it in, because it illustrates what's going on. . . I'm changing. I can't even say the same jokes anymore. Count me in the-best-man-for-a-job-is-a-woman club. As cool as this whole life sounds, the glory is dimming. I don't feel comfortable even seeing pictures of myself as a "dude." I haven't referred to myself as anything male or masculine for the past year. What's odd is that I don't seem to have any control over what's happening to me and, stranger still, is that:

~ I don't want control over these changes.
~ I like what's happening.
~ I won't do anything to stop the flow.

I will say it hasn't been easy these last few months. The schedule was brutal and I shined because of it in some areas, taking care of my crew (as Tezzer says, "Nobody got hurt, nobody got pregnant, nobody went to jail, it was a successful mission.") But there were more than a few "explosions" and despite the fact that not a jury in the world would convict me (the above itinerary, plus a wife going through chemo for the second time, and oh yeah, my gender dysphoria – the cool medical term for the psychological distress and trauma that occurs when your biology and your identity don't match), I'm not proud of the times where I lost my shizz. My rep as an unflappable Zen master; cool in the chaos, fun to be with and, more importantly, the one who brings home the story and a happy crew, was in jeopardy.

I am the showrunner for arguably the most testosterone fueled, alpha-male-fest on TV. The only thing more masculine than us is the NFL. I've got an active duty, Green Beret Master Sargent, an RAF Elite SERE Instructor (Survive Evade Resist (as in torture) & Escape) and a former Navy SEAL turned college football coach, *plus* a revolving cast that includes a grizzly bear tracker and other outdoorsmen.

I wish I could tell the world that this Ultra Boys' club is run by a girl.

I wish I could tell my cast and crew.

And I feel like I need to hurry. My body is trying like hell to out me. My hair is past my shoulders and I get daily flak from the "dudes" for my girlie earrings (okay, everyone gets flak from them for anything). I've had to wear a jog bra all season long because "the girls" have grown two cup sizes (this is without hormones) and I can't go swimming without a shirt. The SEAL noticed and announced at every watering hole, "Why does the boss-man always wear a shirt in the swimming pool?"

At this point, I had no clue what was about to happen. I didn't know it yet, but a lifelong struggle was ending and happening so quietly, so gently, that there was nothing to resist. Oddly, in the same way that I have been complicit in my own imprisonment, I'm looking the other way as the She in me files the bars of her cell for the jailbreak.

All I do know, as I feel the airplane cabin pressurize, is that I'm going home. Finally. It's bitter sweet. I'm so homesick, I miss Mylove so bad, I'm literally walking into walls; you know that feeling you get when you haven't eaten in so long that you don't even know you're starving? I'm numb. I'm so mentally fried, I can barely function, and I'm so sad. We're not even through post, the shows haven't hit the air yet, and though I have nothing to base it on, I can feel it all ending.

As I sit on the plane (I've lost track of how many times I've made sure my seatback and folding tray table were in the full and upright positions) my head is spinning. Numb as I am, I'm also oddly disoriented. A mental picture haunts me as I close my eyes: warning lights blink dully on the control panel of a ship already underwater. . . a ghostly warning that the ship went down before anyone could respond. . . I'm drifting as the bridge fills with cold murky ocean, I can sense I should care, that something vague is wrong, but, I'm lulled. . . the sense of falling, slowly, into intense silence, threatens to. . . SHIT! I sit bolt upright. It's freakin' true! It really happened! Courtney outted me! WTF!

Courtney is my dear friend and the Line Producer (she's the money girl) on my show. We've become very close over the last three years. I call her "Mom" and even though she works under me, she's the inside girl for the production company. She keeps track of the money I decide we're spending. We are a great team. She's the one who has our backs back at HQ, while I'm running through malaria, customs and freezing cold.

But as we sat waiting for our wrap party to begin last night, enjoying a margarita and a brief moment of quiet before our crew arrived, we recounted the year that just streaked past us both; Robin Williams had just passed, (among other real events) and Courtney lamented that "The World According to Garp" was her favorite Robin movie, that she could totally relate to it. Now maybe it was the margarita talking, but I replied, "Me, too." (And, of course I pictured John Lithgow's portrayal of the NFL tight end turned transsexual, Roberta Muldoon.) What the hell am I doing? Warning lights! Sirens! Deflector Shields impotently sliding down their tracks, too late to stop the launch!

Courtney smiled as she sipped and said, "Oh I bet you did."

GOD SHE. . . KNOWS!

DIVERT ALL POWER TO THE FORWARD THRUSTERS, REVERSE ENGINES!

I tried to be cool, but I was trapped, or was I? Is this really happening, I asked myself? Or am I freaking out for nothing. Calm down!

I croaked, "What do you mean by that?"

Courtney is a gentle soul, never confrontational, I'm the passionate one, I have to coach her to stick up for herself. She leaned in, eyes unwavering and whispered, "What do you mean, what do I mean?"

I tried to shake it off. Was I making this up? Why was the air being sucked out of my lungs?

"I mean. . . Courtney, what are you saying?"

She gently grabbed my trembling hand, "Sweetheart, I know."

Time stopped. The shattering sound of cosmic airbrakes arresting the planet's orbit. In an instant, everything would be flung into space and chaos.

My life had begun to revolve around this company, my new Denver family, and I loved them and loved being in charge of their most challenging, highest profile show. Only recently had I begun to feel my place there was wobbly. I would always be the outsider; a "Hollywood" philosophy was a gamble in the Mile High City (as it is in any city outside the 30 mile zone) and I couldn't afford to make any mistakes. Because of my take no prisoners ethic, I could be more trouble than I was worth to some, and who wouldn't want to step into my place, take over the coolest show in house, the crown jewel of the company, especially now, that I had figured it out for them, if I gave them half a chance?

It turned out that Courtney had always known I was transgender. She thought it was obvious and never thought she knew a "secret" about me, just who I was. Just Scott being Scott.

She said that every time she booked my air travel, it broke her heart to check the "M" box (under Gender) because it had to match my passport, even though it wasn't true. I started to cry, which made her tear up, too.

God bless this woman, I was going to miss her terribly. She snuck one last comment in before the rest of our crew arrived. . .

"Besides, I thought your Google Plus announcement confirmed it."

"What are you talking about?"

"When you changed your gender on your profile to "Female" Google Plus sent out an announcement to all of your contacts. I thought, good for her, she's officially coming out."

This is so not good. Could it be true? Why would she lie? As I sat with the shrapnel of this bomb all around me, the crew started filing in, and we had to shelve this for now.

I snuck into the bathroom and feverishly checked on my iPhone sure enough, of the ten or so fields under profile, I had filled in only two: my birthdate & my gender: FEMALE!

I had unconsciously "outed myself." After almost 40 years of clandestine spycraft worthy of CIA deep cover to conceal my true identity, I had outed myself with one keystroke. Seriously? Really? Seriously. Really.

As alarming as that should have been, I was excited and... SCARED OUT OF MY MIND! I tried to talk it away, nobody pays that much attention to lil ol' me, right?

Courtney had.

That was last night, and now I'm on this plane. . . buzzing, sinking, too tired to fight and too anxious. It feels almost like excitement, but without the adrenaline. What now?

I will dive into home. Time to be with her. Time to rest & heal. Time to... Time to... be me?

That's right, I've been promising myself that I would have "it" figured out by now. I have been dodging Mylove's inquiries for months. And to keep both our sanity, it is time.

Even if I'm not ready, I don't have a choice anymore. As we say on DYS, "That train left the dock."

2
MYLOVE

Ugh!! Still on the plane. . . The unfortunate woman next to me just woke me up. Apparently, I was taking my half out of the middle of the armrest, or I was just drooling. I'm too baked to read her lips and too rude to take out my ear buds. After a 3:00 a.m. frantic packing job, plowing the extra stuff into a friend's garage with promises to call for them, dropping off the rental car and getting dinged for <u>hail</u> damage, really? (I had nothing left to fight.) Then an extra charge for two bags to bring everything dirty home to wash. I'm still sweating, and we've been in the air for hours.

Yes, Mylove, I made it. By the skin of my chinnie-chin-chins and within hours, we'll be back in each's arms. I've got that deep exhaustion that only your love will be able to cure.

And after that?

Mylove is my wife. It's my name for her, and her title. Technically, it's my name too. We call each other "Mylove," so our friends refer to each of us (when the other is not present) as "Herlove" and "HisLove."

Like I said, we've got some things to work out. Like life. Our life. And our marriage. A marriage of twenty-five years.

One of the best ways to be the best man ever is to make one woman's life special. Just one woman. Make her life the most special of all.

"Mylove" (truly love at first sight) inspired that in me.

I don't want to tarnish my actions; but if I was forced to do this life thingy trapped in a boy suit then I was going to enjoy it. Loving someone with all your heart – what better way could you spend a life? With Mylove it was as effortless as breathing. Between you and me, of course I know everything a woman truly wants. I am one!

It's important before we go any further for you to understand what I mean by Mylove. It's how I will refer to the reason I am living, the life force that animates me, the love of my life, my lover, my companion, my best friend, and my bride.

To understand me, you have to understand that Mylove is a dream come true (really, I prayed for her every morning for three solid years). When I try to describe what she means to me and how important she is to me, you have to promise that you will not view my words as romantic rhetoric, or just poetry, or the ravings of a school girl gushing with her first crush. My words must be heard with all of the gut-wrenching, heart-aching frustration that comes when you try to describe the force of a hurricane, the thunder of a tidal wave, the blessed reassurance of a spring breeze and deep affirmation of the summer's morning sun; a desperate attempt to encapsulate the cry of the heart, the feeling of love.

The easiest way to insure Mylove's life was special, was to treat life and our marriage as if it was the only marriage in the history of the "institution." It worked. Celebrating it everyday with romantic acts and simple gestures made our marriage the "gold standard" that other's sought. We were credited with restoring everyone's faith: an amazing marriage was possible. So, you can bet that I was loath to put this into jeopardy.

The love we have inspired our family, friends, and acquaintances. It's the bar couples use to measure their relationships and the North Star for lonely singles.

I'm not joking. I've never cared what others think, but if I were going to start – it would be here. Yes, our marriage is *that* marriage.

That I love her isn't the half of it. I'm a basket case when we're apart. I mean, a walk-into-walls-blithering idiot. I truly cannot exist without her. Trust me I know. I had just tried and though I ran a hit show for two seasons, I was too "dead" to know even that I'd died.

Every good story has *stakes*. My stakes were not just a marriage, but *the* marriage, the most epic, romantic union in the history of love, and with it, my entire life and identity.

Now, I never said, implied, inferred, nor thought for even a moment that what I needed to survive "the total identity breakdown" that had stopped the planet from spinning on our axis five years ago would require a quantum shift in our love and life. If I had, I would've never had the courage, clarity or faith to put it all on the line.

I was either cavalier or naïve. Mylove would, I told myself, only want my happiness and fulfillment which would only mean *together*. She knows better than I that I would cease to exist, if "we" couldn't be. I had already confronted this possibility many times in the long dark hours in a hospital room holding her hand and wiping her brow with a schmatta. (Her surgeon used the Yiddish word for any cloth I used to cool her fever.) The answer was always the same: without her, I am not.

I don't say this lightly. She is the center of my universe. I tried, God I tried, for as long as I could, to keep the real me, the me with an "it" ruling my life, from rocking her world. Until I just couldn't do it anymore.

I'm sorry Mylove. I'm truly, truly sorry for all of this.

This fear of hurting her, even more than hurting us, was the fire-breathing dragon that barred my escape from the hell of my own creation, a fortress, I had built with my own fear to keep that dragon caged.

But five years before, the dragon had escaped and almost burned it all down. . .

To Mylove, it must've looked like this: It's five a.m., and Mylove can tell by an absence in the air that her husband is not in bed. In the dark of morning, she can barely see anything, and but for the snoring of Zuzu & Aria (the dogs) that share the bed, there isn't a sound.

The smell of coffee gives away her husband's position. Whew, he's just upstairs in the kitchen, making "fawkey"(our pet name for our morning libation. Mylove's lil brother could never pronounce coffee, so the name stuck.)

Minutes later there he is, two cups of steaming fawkey, a typical Saturday, except:

"It's still dark out," she says, brushing her hair aside as she sits up in bed, "you are so lucky I love you."

He stands for a moment as if frozen in midair. His lip trembles. A tear crawls from one eye, catches the faint available light, runs down his cheek. "Mylove," he stammers, "I. . . don't know who I am. . ."

That was the last coherent sentence I uttered, as a tsunami of over 40 years of confusion, pain and what I would later learn as denial, flooded from my mouth, threatening to wash away Mylove, our marriage and hope forever. Tears, fear, compassion and anger, and still more tears swarmed around us for what would be the next six months as we tried to make sense of the tidal wave that rocked our world.

I tried to make her understand what was happening, but the truth was I didn't really know. I knew the cause, of course, because for the two weeks prior to this, I had "it" really bad; I hadn't slept for two weeks – I never ever have trouble sleeping, I can sleep standing up. Something was really, really wrong. I had a monster pain in my chest as if an elephant was standing on it. I was hyperventilating. I was cold.

I wasn't sure what a nervous breakdown was. All I knew was that I was broken and down.

Something I do know about myself is that I have a tendency to physically "spit-up" the truth whenever I try to stifle it. But it's never been about something dire before. Usually, throughout the twenty years of marriage to this point, when I had tried to stifle anything, it was beautiful, like declaring my love for the first time or the special birthday surprises I had for her. My body just couldn't keep even a lighthearted truth from her. Mylove treasured this – a sign of true love.

But a dark truth, well, until this morning that had been a different story. I had learned to keep dark truth imprisoned in the deepest dungeon of my mind. And it would have to resort to drastic measures for a jailbreak. . .

It went nuclear.

My beloved wife tried to understand what the fuck was going on. . . her husband, her knight in shining armor, her best friend, companion and soulmate was literally melting down before her eyes, spinning a crazy yarn about an alternate universe that was not the marriage she had just devoted 20 years to. Nuh uh, no sirree bob, because after three marriages, she had finally gotten it right. She always knew she could have it all; a man who loved her beyond all time and space and who shared everything: likes and dislikes, philosophy, spirituality, worldview and chocolate. . . and, he cooks! The fourth time for her was the charm.

All of her friends were envious of his clever and thoughtful gifts and shows of affection. Every holiday was another chance to shower her with romance. There were lavish art installations on Valentine's Day (handmade as valentines should be). Don't believe me? Try these:

*The first thing she saw as she opened her eyes on the first Valentine's Day was a canopy of a hundred velvet hearts strung on golden cords over her bed,

*a field of 300 paper heart "flowers" secretly planted overnight in the lawn for her to discover,

*a giant Cupid's arrow (12 feet tall) was stuck in the yard,

*mailing himself home in a box to be unwrapped as a birthday gift,

*the weekend getaways for no reason other than pure romance, not to mention the days where he would simply pass out if he didn't get a kiss, her kiss.

But in the parallel universe being laid before her by the husband described above, this man was not a man at all, but a woman trapped inside a cruel joke. A woman who confessed to feeling this way since childhood. A woman who had no answer when asked why "she" had willingly entered into marriage, her marriage, if this was true and known.

How could I say that all my life, all I could do was deny the existence of these feelings, hoping they would "just go away" when I grew up? How could I say that I thought it had worked?

This is how you learn to cope with something this big: you keep the secret even from yourself.

In this world, the person Mylove thought she knew, had no idea who he/she was.

Which, I know now, was not exactly accurate. It's sort of how this whole thing works: you kind of learn to sneak up on the truth, to ease into reality without scaring away your fragile courage. Done right, you can, if you strike quickly before the drawbridge is raised and battlements armed, look the dragon in the eye.

Yes, I knew I was a woman. Had always been a woman. But I had no idea how to live like one. I certainly hadn't even mustered the tools to say any of this out loud, least of all to the woman I loved.

But something inside me glowed bright – I knew that this had to have happened, painful as it was, for a reason. This faint glow was faith that God doesn't do mistakes. And we were in love, and we did have something so strong that we could weather any storm together. But I also knew that this was about me.

With as much faith as I had in her love, I knew I had to have at least equal faith in myself that I could figure it out. I owed her the happy person to whom she had committed body and soul.

It's this woman I thought, who will teach me what love really is, what commitment to one's self really is. Relentless in her pursuit to have and maintain the love she wants (ours) she will stop at nothing, including her own fears, to get it.

It's been five years since the morning I came out to Mylove over fawkey, but I'm not out in the world, our world, at this point, by any stretch of the imagination. This is our secret. We've told no one. And we discuss it only under duress, because I haven't been around for a long enough period to control the fallout. It's irresponsible to set the house on fire if you're not going to be around to put out the flames. Nothing worse than trying to console your love on a satellite phone. . .

Because it will happen. When she's alone. While I've been traipsing around the world in the name of "reality" television, Mylove's demons have had their way with her. And I've had to quell more than a herd of both rational and irrational boogiemen. There are few things worse than hanging up after our calls, knowing she's alone and still afraid.

But that doesn't mean she's been sitting around waiting for me. I will learn that she too has had time to work on us. That she puts in that much effort for this love is beyond humbling. Lord knows, I've never made it easy on her but when I, her husband, declared that I'm a woman, neither of us knew how far down the rabbit hole went.

There was a flicker of hope that shined through the fog of fear and confusion. Love. Our love. It had to amount to something. It had to stand for something besides a good time. I had to believe in us. I had to be able to trust in the love we were famous for. I had to trust that it would be the beacon it was legend to be.

The bounce, shudder and pressure of the reverse thrusters wake me from my prayer. Reverse thrusters? Really God? As I'm violently shoved backward into my seat, I realize. . .

God has such a great and playful sense of humor.

16

3
IT'S LIKE DÉJÀ VU ALL OVER AGAIN.

I'm home. I call it airplane stink. No matter how long the flight, you feel like you've been hermetically sealed in your own sweat for weeks. I had to shower!

After 27 years together, 25 of them married, one thing that's defined our relationship is that after our first date, we have been inseparable (work notwithstanding) and we have seen every square inch of each other. When we say we know each other inside-out, we're not being poetic. (Hospitals will do that.) So, when you hear me say I have never been self-conscious around Mylove, you know that's not just talk. We practically live naked around each other. But right now, as we stand in the bathroom, catching each other up on the mundane (even that's interesting to lovers) I have to take off my shirt. And I'm hesitating. She's going to see me for the first time in weeks and will see my, well, I like to call them the "girls." She notices them, instantly. It's gone beyond obvious; I still try to act surprised, "I know, right? Isn't it strange what's happening to me?" (Talk about insulting her. Who do I think I'm kidding?)

But - she shouldn't be surprised. I tried to prepare her for the "girls'" arrival by telling her that I had a bra fitting weeks ago in Denver, even called her after it was done to "report in." She says, "No you didn't," and before we know it, it's on. Like four year olds. Nuh uh? Did not! Did too! Did not!

I fall prey to my own ego in these situations. What galls me is I know the exact point each time where I am to blame for sending the conversation skidding sideways, and it's this:

I obscure the news (or information) by a fear that if it is heard (and truly understood) I will be in trouble. My fear is a cloaking device rendering the news/information invisible.

The worst of it? I know it's happening <u>as</u> it's happening, and I'm too chicken (why does poultry get the bum rap anyway?) to repeat the news/information to make certain it's heard. It's like I'm hoping that "the truth" occurs anyway (by what? Osmosis?) and I'll dodge the consequences (sigh).

Like here. To plead my case, I did tell Mylove on my way to Nordy's, which had taken me an hour to psyche myself up to do. But still I had to endure the interrogation: "how long had I been planning this?" (Answer:

months). And after I had the fitting, I forced myself to report back that I had bought not one but, two bras. I did this, and wanted credit for doing it despite the resentment for <u>having</u> to do so.

I can also understand why she's blotted this out of her memory, which makes right now that much harder. As I've said, I <u>know</u> it's not easy for her to watch her white knight ride side-saddle.

Complicating this round of "here-we-go-again" is that I'm also feeling something new. Modesty? I don't know if it's an adolescent thought (I am at this point emotionally about 12 years old, on the verge of puberty; seriously, look it up). But I am feeling more than a little self-conscious standing here before Mylove, naked, with more breasts than a man should have, and I'm no good (having no experience with this) at defending my body.

Because I love them. If I had been a man, I would understandably be freaking out. Boys have all kinds of derisive, fun names for this "situation": Moobs, Man-boobs, Mits (sigh again). All of these imply that they are just not cool to have. I know, because I have researched this phenomenon online; it's how I learned that it's common, especially with men over 50. It's so common that Nordy's expects men to call for help getting a bra. You can schedule an appointment with a specially trained expert. It's safe. They are very professional.

I am shy yes, but I have wanted these all my life, and though I don't have medical evidence to support this, my body is done waiting for my mind to get its courage on. Whatever the reason, my mom's genes, or my dad's, I got 'em. YAY!

But none of this explains the self-consciousness I'm suddenly feeling. It's like a feeling of modesty came with them.

But for Mylove, it's not new at all, in fact. She's having an ugly case of Déjà vu. And rightly so.

This isn't the first time I've bought a bra. . .

When I first came out to Mylove five years ago – I did force myself to get real and knew that it would take a professional. I knew I was a woman, but with a man's body. I'd be lying if I didn't have questions. I had to be courageous enough to ask them and then stick around for the answers.

Was I a woman born into a man's body or just a crossdresser?

I'm not judging here, there's differences between someone dressing for sexual gratification, someone who identifies as transgender, but doesn't feel a need to do anything but dress, and someone who identifies as the opposite sex of the biology they were born into. And a whole lot of variations in between.

I have to confess here that every time I heard the old joke, *"what's the difference between a crossdresser and a transsexual? Answer: About three years."* It took my breath.

I went to see a therapist who was a well-known gender specialist here in LA LA Land. In addition to her practice, she ran support groups and sat on several councils. I was in good hands.

But the truth was, I didn't need a therapist to tell me. I knew I was a woman. I needed to know what to do about it. Or bluntly, I needed to know a way around it.

Because, I reasoned, if I was *just a crossdresser*, I could manage it, like, I dunno, maybe a hobby, and get back to my life. (See how fast this denial cloud can spring up like a thunderhead?) Sure I could, if I was willing to, once again, sell myself short, *"Fourth floor: lingerie, ladies shoes, denial, and broken dreams."*

I gave her a schedule. Six weeks. The therapist took the challenge. We started with a word that had been my constant companion since puberty:

Inevitable.

And only now, five years later, do I see "inevitable" as the light at the end of the tunnel, rather than the headlight of an oncoming train.

My therapist had me journal between weekly sessions. That week, I wrote that I had a dream where I was heartbroken; I would never have breasts (at least my subconscious was stepping up, we've got a schedule to keep). When I woke, I realized that it was not a dream. Was this the source of the deep sadness that had been my constant cloud? The profound loss of a life as a woman? We would test and my therapist assigned me a follow-up exercise: buy a bra and wear it.

I went right to the store and bought two, put one on in the car in the parking lot, and wore it home, ecstatic! I wore it under my clothes as soon as I left the house every day after that (and would take it off at the end of each day, when I got home to my neighborhood). She was surprised – she hadn't thought I would jump on it. Noted. We dove in deeper.

My past was a trail of *heartbreak*. I was in agony whenever I saw a woman pull her hair back into a ponytail. Growing up, my breath would catch in my throat when I saw girls approaching the milestones of womanhood. I would revel in the significance of these moments, then crash to the ground in despair when I knew it would never be for me. I was watching life lived at a distance like a ghost.

I would come home and recount each session with Mylove. I knew I was soft selling each discovery, trying to be truthful, while still painting a coat of whitewash over so they didn't seem as scary. I was trying to have my truth and eat it too. I wasn't learning anything new (I was just saying it out loud for the first time) but now, it existed beyond my fantasies and imagination. It was getting real. And nothing could cover that.

I was seeing my story reflected in my Beloved's face, it stung her and it made me feel incredibly mean. I was the one knocking her white knight off his charger with each revelation; I was killing the man she loved.

It wasn't entirely easy to accept a version of my life that had never been outside my own brain pan before. As a professional storyteller (and a reality show producer at that) this may seem strange, but I don't trust real life thoughts that can be compressed into a single kernel.

Maybe it's because I know how effortlessly I do this with someone else's story, that I don't trust myself to be complete with my own. I know what parts to leave out.

But we were getting somewhere. Each week with the therapist, I watched as the definition of "it" changed:

At first, "it" looked like this: I was three-and-half or four years old. My father was a charismatic icon of a man. I loved him dearly, as did everyone else. When we lived not a stone's throw from the Ontario Motor Speedway, my pop sold cars on weekdays and raced at the drags on the weekends, a mid-sixties version of the cool, hip, ultimate man. Enter "Mark" my babysitter. (He's still known in our family's oral tradition as "Mark, the/my/our babysitter.") My pop hired him as a "lot boy" (the foot soldiers of a car dealership). Mark was a teenager in a turbulent time – his father was a steel worker at Kaiser Steel. I can't say exactly what was going on with Mark and his father, but let's say that when *my* father would come home from work (usually late 9:00 - 10:00 p.m.) Mark and his friends would race over to hang out – my dad was a cool father-figure.

Mark would also make extra cash babysitting me and the little girl who lived next door. One rainy evening my friend came over and had the cutest pink rubber rain boots. Mine were the classic fireman's galoshes complete with "safety yellow" stripes at the top. It wasn't too long before I had talked her into a trade. We exchanged boots in my bedroom, just two very happy 4 year-olds, basking in the glow of a win-win situation.

When the door opened, I still had my back to it. I heard Mark gasp out, "Scottie what the hell are you doing?" I wasn't sure what we had done wrong, but my friend shoved her feet under the bed to hide them; I instinctively followed her lead. Still not sure, what was wrong, I only felt the heat of bad, wrong, and awful.

The next thing I know, Mark grabbed me around the waist, yanking me backward. I tried to resist but he was too strong, and before I knew it, I was standing. "Did you take her boots?" Mark screamed.

Take? "No," I protested, "They're mine. Fair and square."

Then the hammer came down, "You can't wear those, they're for girls!" He started to yank them off my feet, getting frustrated that I wasn't cooperating – now she was scared, and we both were crying as Mark was yelling, "What's your father going to say?" That's where the memory ends – a hard cut to black.

I don't blame Mark for his intentions. My Pop was a huge persona – as I said, a "man's man," and Mark probably thought he was just protecting "Big Jim," the man he idolized.

This is the problem with processing these forty-some-odd years later; but I would be surprised if my dad would have had a problem with it at all.

Maybe I've got a rose colored lens on my hindsighter; sure, there were times he goaded me whenever I cried as a child, which was a lot.

"What's with the waterworks, Mary Jane?"

"You run like a girl."

"You're not gonna let a girl beat you, are you?"

"If you're gonna whine, go put on a dress."

I can't blame my father. In his defense, I have to say that my friends' fathers said similar things to them growing up, and they are cis-gender heterosexual men.

Whereas, I am not.

So, it was deeper, way below blame. How did I get this way? Some believe that a hormonal flood in the womb at some stage of my development gave me the mind/awareness of a woman, and a second (hormonal flood) the biology of a man. This makes the most sense from my experience, but whatever the cause, does it matter at this point? Because, that's the not what I'm fighting. . .

The rain boot experience cut me so deep that at a very young age, I knew one thing to survive:

I had to keep "it" a secret. It really freaked people out and I would be in trouble with my dad.

Flash forward to the puberty years. Now, I'm the babysitter. But nothing like Mark; I loved children, I was always left in charge of my sisters, so when I got the chance to do it for money, I was in heaven.

My mom's best friend, Geri (who was beautiful), had two daughters my sister's age, and I was already like their big brother. They were easy-peasy to look after, but it gets better. Geri was not only beautiful, she was my size. And she was young and hip and I was free to try on pretty clothes and be a girl, if only for an hour at a time.

It was crazy, a blazing hurricane of adrenaline that would settle down into the most amazingly quiet shower of happiness, and a fresh breezy freedom.

But it had a soul crushing crash at the end, every time. Like Icarus falling from the sky, each time I had to take my wings off, I slammed into the earth. It became more unbearable the more I dressed. It was so distressing that it almost made me never do it again. *Almost.* Here's where I develop another superpower: I could "disappear" the memory of last time's fiery crash to open that drawer again. It's utterly amazing to me that I would willingly endure that level of suffering for a few minutes of freedom.

Then, it stopped. The opportunities, but not the desire. I grew out of babysitting. And tried to with the feelings. They made me feel hideous. Guilty. Confused. But instead of digging into the why, I chose a quick fix; denial's obscuring fog.

So my therapist made me dig, but I knew the answer without even picking up the shovel. Dressing up wasn't the "it."

To recount, "it" had already gone from:

1. Starting happy and free, then suddenly treated as something I wasn't, to:
2. Being overpowered, shamed and threatened for trying to be myself to:
3. Never telling anyone that I was really a girl – even thinking I was a girl was the most wrong thing I could ever do, to:
4. The actual crash that came when I realized I had to stop being a girl, to:
5. Realizing that I would never get to be a real girl.

And this was just the puberty years.

To prop-up Denial's stone walls, I would use this boy's life as cement. I knew that to achieve the things I wanted in life, I would need to get really good at them, and that took focus. I was popular, creative, and active in student government. You would never know that I had to build a huge dungeon in my mind.

It seems so plain now that I was growing up on two parallel tracks. My true female self was straining to blossom without sunlight, watching everything with an insatiable hunger; while the boy trudged on knowing his sister was languishing.

I had to grab my mind with vise-like claws as I watched girls my age showing signs of the women they would become, the woman I would never be. And that became the next iteration of "it:"

The blinding fog that came from suppressing my growing female identity. This version of "it" became the version that would rule my world for the next thirty years. I even gave it a name: Hijacking.

This was a scary mental state, a "bout" that was akin to sleepwalking. It would be so strong that for decades it thoroughly confused the whole issue of who I was. It made me think it was "the bouts" that were the issue, instead of digging into what caused them. I had an adversarial relationship with my female self. I hated her when she seized control of my life.

"It" would happen about once a month for 3-4 days, sometimes longer. I would have to "pull into myself" when I felt it coming, literally duck deep into my psyche and brace myself for the Hijacker. "It" was relentless; all-consuming feelings of being a woman would overwhelm me. Like phantom injuries, I could feel the breasts I was supposed to have, the curves of my hips that were "supposed" to be there, the long hair that had been mutilated. All of this making me *grieve*.

During these episodes, every sense was at full alert, my blood pressure had to be spiking, my breath would be shallow for days and my skin burning/tingling, it was almost impossible to get anything done.

The only thing I could do was ride these times out, actually step into twilight imaginings of what life could be. These surprised my therapist; they were never big sexual fantasies, just little things like getting dressed for the day, or meeting friends and family as my true self. Every once in awhile, I would allow bigger feelings to come in, like having a baby, but these were the most dangerous of all. The mourning, and suppression of it, left me almost suicidal.

Afterward, the days of the "guilt cycle" would kick in, how could I be so powerless? How could I let my own mind take me as hostage? What was wrong with me?

I never had the courage to really find out. I would be so anxious to get back to my life that I would forget – more like ignore – it ever happened. My ol' friend Denial never let me down.

It wasn't until therapy that I realized I never allowed myself to sew these hijackings together into a pattern. I was so scared by the power of each bout that I could not accept them as related events.

Because that would make "it" a "something."

Six weeks of gender therapy was ending, I need to get back to my life to repair the damage I had done to my marriage.

When I climbed the stairs to my therapist's second floor office for the last time, I wore a skirt and heels and a little bit of make-up, that I had put on in the car – I was getting good at it.

She gave me her diagnosis: I was a "high functioning" transsexual.

Now this was only five years ago and the term "transgender" was used by everyone, already accepted as the politically correct way of describing "anyone on the spectrum." And yet, here was a gender therapist saying I was transsexual. Maybe she was using the term because that was the way I had worded our mission together. The term was oddly comforting, quietly exhilarating, but SCARY AS HELL!

"What does that mean?" I asked. She took a breath, this wasn't easy for her. She set her notebook down, she too trying to understand how I could come to this. I wasn't prepared for her answer – it had a tinge of admiration: "I can't believe you have gotten this far without being a woman."

Okay, so, I'm not crazy. I am not making this up. I was…

WHAT I KNEW, AND HAD ALWAYS KNOWN! I AM A WOMAN.

She went on to say that I could "manage my condition" like a chronic disease or a birth defect: living in a man's body.

Or, I could live. I could flourish. I could even blossom.

That was five years and a lifetime ago. I'm back home in Mylove's arms and it's really strange how this has come around full circle:

It could be five years ago all over again. We sat just like we are now, legs entwined, stroking each other's hair. Dealing with mind-blowing news, holding onto each other for dear life. Back then, I had been recounting the therapist's diagnosis. Right now, I'm recounting Courtney's admission. I've been outed. And that means — we've been outed.

We've been ignoring this for five years, and it took Courtney to let us both know, I wasn't fooling anyone. We were the last to our own party. Separately, we've been doing some thinking. But those chickens had come home to roost. Time to work together.

I'm hearing "inevitable" echo off the hills like distant thunder. I had always had this feeling. It had never gone away: some day I would live my life as I am. A woman. It was inevitable.

Inevitable had finally come home with those darn chickens.

4
MAKE-UP WORK

If I'm not fooling Courtney, then am I fooling anyone? Mylove and I never moved from the couch, we didn't even get up to turn on the lights. We keep talking into the night – we'll need food soon, but first, we need to get real. Mylove was patient, trying to understand what the heck I was saying. I knew I was babbling. A thousand wishes and thoughts and fears tumbling out as I tried to make her understand that I just can't bear to wear boy clothes anymore. Mylove promised she wants the best for me. Which may fly out the window as soon she sees me in a dress.

Okay – a brief pause here – I have to stop this – I have to trust that she is capable of this. Cynicism will kill us both.

Mylove has had time to not only search her own heart but to do some research of her own. She knows that I'm in turmoil and hugs me and tries to comfort me. How had I survived this long? How badly had I been scarred, who could've done this to me? We agree. Tomorrow, no more boy clothes.

This is how love works. Our love anyway. It's best when it's point blank range; when we're tied in a love knot on our couch. As we stare into the quiet darkness of the evening, it dawns on us – even though this phase started five years ago, both of us have taken until just this past year to shake off the initial shock. And now our life is on the verge of a page-one rewrite.

In our defense, we've been. . . well, going through some things these last eight or so months that may have competed for our attention:

It was our 25th year of marriage – our silver anniversary – and I'd been on the road for 625 days out of the past two years.

Mylove had been going through chemo <u>again</u>. I was in the arctic circle (Finland) back in March when I first got the news. She had been cancer free for almost four years. Neither of us was ready to face the beast again; we had been living on the island of hope. After all, 10% of the women who get ovarian cancer are free after the first course of treatment and we're always in the top percentile of things like this. So we're good, right?

I flew home immediately. I wasn't half as cold in the Arctic Circle as I was in that doctor's office, again. AGAIN? It's weird how reality can push your identity problems into the background. For both of us, it was not the time for me to be she. We swung our every waking thought and prayer to her healing.

The doctors would "just be going in" to look around (the first time they "just went in" ended in a full hysterectomy and a year of chemo). But this time we had a brilliant surgical oncologist whom Mylove loved and a new protocol that was just as effective – and we wouldn't lose our hair this time.

I could willingly put myself on hold, again. I was put here on this earth to love one woman and tell stories. I would come to know that both of those required me to be *only* who I truly was. In the meantime, I scrambled back and forth between Mylove's care and running a show.

Yes. It was a freaking gnarly year.

Which brings us back to the here and now. Reunited. WHEW!

The next morning, I go through my closets, anything boy-like? Out! Sorta. It's a little harder than I thought. I've tried to ignore my clothes the same way I've tried to ignore my reflection in a mirror. But some clothes are sentimental – the shirt Mylove bought me for my birthday when she came to New Orleans to visit while I was doing a show on shrimp fishermen, or t-shirts I designed. But as hard as it is, I. . . just don't, I just can't wear any of them.

In the end, I'm more brutal than I thought – but there it is; terminated with extreme prejudice. Three bags filled; one to give to my brothers-in-law and nephews, one to give to Goodwill and one to just throw away.

It's funny, during the next couple of weeks Mylove and I flow as if nothing has happened, yet everything is happening. I'm starting to feel more comfortable around her as me. I'm getting a little braver with my wardrobe (it's in the upper nineties here in LA LA Land, so it's shorts and tanks. True, they're girl's shorts and tanks, but still not a threat). More importantly, there's a blossoming in our marriage – we are getting comfortable, with only a hint of tentative, with "She" or rather. . . me.

I would love to take any "ray of daylight" from Mylove as a green light to go full-on girl, but let's be real, it's not her. Am I capable of stepping out as a respectable woman?

Which let's face it, I have no idea what that means. But it's not for lack of trying. Mylove is actually helping me to put on make-up – just a little mascara and a touch of eyeshadow. But the fact is:

SHE IS HELPING ME WEAR MAKE-UP!

I never saw this coming. I never thought she could be okay with her king being a queen. (Okay let's not get crazy, a princess at best.) But the stakes are suddenly higher. We laugh as she stares at me, trying to get the lines right – it's WEIRD we know, but it's also kinda fun. And we're doing it together and that makes it easier for her to take. We even worked in some brown eyeliner "to make my blue eyes pop." This is a HUGE victory! The woman I love was joyfully helping me! It was dream a come true.

It's not like I haven't worn make-up before. But it is way better this way. Before, whenever I was "exploring" (a stupid euphemism for dressing up and going out while I was on the road), my approach was to camouflage. I could dodge scrutiny because they didn't know Scott from Madam. I was just another "girl" among "girls" inside the t-community. Outside the community, most would just look away from whatever that was.

But it's different when you're no longer hiding. Back then, it was a "persona" that I was trying on, but now; it was *me*. And it's Mylove. And I'm not hiding behind the make-up. I'm enhancing what and who I am.

But let's be real, Mylove isn't fooled either. She knows I know more about make-up than I'm letting on, and there's only one way this is possible.

My shadowy past.

This is still a sore subject. The one step forward ten steps back thingy – even "not talking about it" is a corrosive agent in a marriage. Being away for almost three years, I made use of the time for my "explorations" and she knew it. Back to not wanting to start a fire, I never ever admitted to dressing up and going out when I was away. I just didn't answer the phone. I couldn't lie, so I would try to stop the questions before they even started.

Mylove confesses that the mere fact that I was keeping details from her is crime enough in her book. (RATS! She's on to me) I knew this, and try to light a backfire (check out my language – am I hiding something?). So I wouldn't have to deal with this in the future. I confessed (back then on the phone) to doing a little exploring. But it doesn't matter that I told her; she hadn't told <u>me</u> yet how she felt about it. And they're a package deal. Without her response, it wasn't done.

And here it comes, between swipes of mascara on my lashes. She let's me know that she is still "smarting" from me even being able to go out, or do anything without her.

Okay, some context here: Mylove hasn't had a drink since before we started dating almost 30 years ago. It was a personal decision (history in her family). So, I stopped drinking and getting high after our second date, because I was horrified when I couldn't find her on my "radar." She of course, cherished this and celebrated this to any who would hear. Another feather in the King's cap.

But the truth was, I actually still liked drinking, I was never afraid of my relationship with it, though with both Irish & Finnish blood in these veins, I probably should be.

In my defense, she mixed her feelings (about me doing something she vowed she would never do) with being alone, tying in "being honest" and tangling the whole knot together with a string of barbed wire labeled: "I thought that's what we both wanted," which was then nailed to door with an iron spike of, "I guess I was wrong."

I confessed to my own picking at the festering scab of resentment called, "stop telling me how to live my life" which would grow into "I have every right to live my life, my way," spreading to "haven't I sacrificed enough for everyone else by now?" So, feeling quite justified (don't we always) I decided to live by Road Rules – what happens in Reykjavik stays in Reykjavik.

A recipe for disaster, it turns out, because it had me hiding from her. Normally, if she called while I was out, I could be in a burning building, dodging bullets and stampeding unicorns, and I would still "pick-up" if only to tell her I'd call when I could talk. But if I was "out" (exploring) I would let it go to voice mail, or worse, step outside and have our "goodnight phone kiss" without mentioning I was dressed as a woman having a cocktail with the girls.

If a tree falls in the woods and nobody is there to interrogate you, were you really wearing heels?

It's a deflection technique that every TV person has tattooed on our hearts: "It's better to beg for forgiveness, than ask for permission." Cuz if we move fast enough, we won't even be around for the begging part.

Otherwise, life right now is good and though I surprise Mylove with my wardrobe choices, she's giving me room to stretch a little. But it's frustrating, I'm reluctant to "commit" fully (clothing-wise) and nobody besides Mylove and my therapist knows my true identity (soooo Diana Prince!). So I'm still feeling like I have to blur the lines here between "isn't that a woman's blouse?" and "Creative people wear such interesting things."

As a woman, I'm neither a novice nor fashion-challenged. I do actually own a decent (if small) female wardrobe, but it's back in Denver in Paige's garage. I know how to look good, but this "caught-between" look is neither comfortable (too boyish!) nor flattering, (too, too. . . Oh, I don't know what!)

Okay on a positive note? I'm trying to be realistic. Mylove is starting to grasp that this can be a joyous change, and I don't want to screw that up!

But I'm also becoming aware of a gnawing hunger: despite not being fully confident about going "full-on girl" I'm feeling that going this slow is also killing me. I can't blame anyone for this. I'm losing control.

And just when it looks like I may explode in a supernova of conflict, sabotaging a really good thing, I got a gig! And it's Alaska! Now watch carefully folks as denial gets to masquerade as action, and another can gets kicked down the road by yours truly.

I can focus on making television instead of re-aligning my life. It'll be great!

I have a few weeks of prep here in town, then north to Alaska till the end of the year! Okay, on the bright side – that brings my showrunning season for the year to three shows.

Career-wise, I'm on fire!

5

WHAT NOTHING SOUNDS LIKE

With a gig coming in, summer vacation is over before it started – so when the going is going to get tough – the tough bar-be-que! Mylove and I decide to slam everything we wanted to do this summer into one party, and throw it on my sister Kimm's birthday. Which means. . . Shit! Coming out to her!

I'm, um well, actually accepting myself as. . . as. . . what the hell do I call myself to explain myself to Kimm?

I've known all my life that I'm actually a woman. BUT try to tell that to your sister, the one you're about to forever change the concept of your shared past, present and future, the one that has no idea this is coming. Thank God I didn't put this much thought into it before I sent out the invitations, I would've "tharned." (Watership down anyone? Anyone?)

However, if anyone is cool, it's Kimm, the oldest of my "three little sisters." She is the best mother on the planet, she has all of my mom's best qualities and I'm closest (of my three sisters) with her. We had to step in as surrogate parents for Keira and Shane when Mom passed and Dad went into mourning (from which he never recovered) and I worship the ground Kimm walks on.

Of course, my two other sisters, Keira, the mid kid, and Shane, the baby, will also love and understand my new me. I've been pretty low-maintenance during our adult years, and this will be low on the wow factor compared to climbing Chilean volcanos and gold mining in the Amazon. I've never even wondered if they'll have a problem with my news, even in my darkest moments; if anyone understands me, it's they.

But for now, I'm starting with Kimm, I can't wait to see her. Her daughter, sixteen-year-old Hana (the youngest of Kimm's three), and her husband, Mikey, will be making the two-hour trek from San Diego.

And I'm going to gamble on the color purple. Toenails to be exact. Mylove and I just got back from a pedicure, and I went wild while she went classic (scarlet red).

So, yes, I am super naïve at this point. Even the tiny changes I've made to my appearance don't seem that obvious to me. I have been hiding behind the human phenom that people see only what they want or expect to see. And nobody *expects* to see me like this. And as I pass around the bbq turkey molé and grilled tortillas, my family and friends are just plain happy to see me in the same area code, let alone, in person.

So, do they notice? If they do, they ain't talking. We talk about everything, except my nails, earrings and hair. Until Hana, stares at my toenails. Here it comes. . . she says, "Uncle Scott, that's the wrong shade of purple."

Not that having painted toenails is wrong, but if you're gonna do it girlfriend, represent! This opens the door a crack for everyone to "join in" and my nails get their 15 minutes.

Is this the time? Do I "read in" my sister now? How? Will I take her for a walk? Maybe find a quiet corner? Will there be tears? I'm only halfway in my body, half listening to dear friends and family having fun, eating good and enjoying each's company, and it hits me, this is how "it" has been, behind my back, filtering everything, letting in only half the available light of life.

But I never get that chance to talk to Kimm, or rather I won't let myself. It's her birthday, getting serious never felt right. Am I ready to do this? Inside the bubble of my marriage, all secrets are protected, but outside, we can't control how people think.

And it hits me: of course I'm no good at this. I've spent a lifetime creating the Aegis Missile Defense System, an advanced distant early warning battery to protect me from outing myself. I only know how to NOT tell anyone who I really am!

This is so bad, so deep, it even prevents me from relating to the words and phrases used to describe a "me." Yes, I've known since I was four; never tell anyone I was girl ever. Ever. Holy shit! I was reaping what I had sown as a child.

Where was that when I was on the therapist's watch? But hang on, I can do this. Let's see, I'm not sure what happened after the rain boot incident, I can't imagine much, and nothing of note seems to be until the second grade.

I built a fort with my friend Kenny out of a derelict camper shell in our backyard. In my second grade mind, this would be an oasis and I had it all worked out. A place to be me. A place to be safe, a place where no one could make me be what I wasn't. A place to be a girl.

So, if I could borrow a little make-up from my mom, I could wrap a towel around my waist and be transformed, *back into me.*

First, I had to "suss out" my co-conspirator Kenny. Oddly, Kenny was in. We made a plan – tomorrow we'd meet in the clubhouse. He'd bring the towels.

That night my job was to make the heist.

This had to be the birth of my "spycraft" superpowers.

I learned to shut-off the part of the brain that keeps you from taking chances (a huge firewall with many moving parts, this would take the most effort to tear down later).

My seven-year-old mind was surprisingly crafty. I pretended to go to sleep, stashing a flashlight and plastic bags for the loot under my pillow.

It's after midnight, my dad's snoring is my "alarm clock;" and it's time. Creeping down the hallway, holding my breath, past my sleeping parents into their bathroom. Even in the dark, I could see it, my prize; lime green canvas with white daisies on it. It practically glowed in the dark! *My mother's make-up purse.*

I had it in my hands when I heard my father's voice, "Punky, what's going on?" I had to think fast, and I wish I could remember the excuse I mumbled out, whatever it was got me back to bed. As I lay in bed HEART POUNDING, I tried to calm down. I knew I needed to wait until my parents fell back asleep before chancing the rest of the plan. Finally, I could stand it no more, with the covers "tenting" over my head, and flashlight to illuminate the magical bag, I stared at the treasure: lipstick, eye shadow and mascara. I even tried the lipstick. But I heard my father again, "Punky?" I panicked, too committed, too exposed, a fatal error as I snapped the case closed. It sounded like a GUNSHOT!

"What was that?"

Time froze, icy deep space, black hole frozen froze.

"Punky? I said, what was that?"

Words failed. I'm dead. "Nothing."

"Didn't sound like nothing."

Silence.

"We'll talk in the morning about what nothing sounds like."

In the morning, hoping it a bad dream, I felt my mom's purse under my pillow. My life flashed before my eyes. I was too young to die. And then the hangman reared his head, "I'm running out of time to have a proper discussion about last night, so we'll talk when I get home."

In my seven-year-old mind, you could substitute the word "talk" with "hanging," "firing squad" or "gas chamber." He pulled his Windsor Knot tight with a final deft yank, my sentence delivered without so much as a jury trial: "And I better have an answer for what nothing sounds like."

31

That's it. It's official. I'm doomed.

That day Kenny was absent. (Weird. I would never see him again. Ever. He stayed home that day from school and for the rest of that week. Weeks turned into a month and we were told later that he moved.) It didn't matter, all it meant right now, was that I would carry out my sentence alone. I had cement shoes and a noose around my neck all day. What was I going to say? If I lied, I would be found out, my parents were mind-readers, that much I knew.

But if I told the truth, they would try and stop me from being a girl. I wasn't sure which was worse (I hear ya, this should've been a sign!)

When I got home that day, I was told to go wait in my room, Dad would talk to me when he got home from work. I sat in my cell, out of options, this was it. Been nice to know ya. The Grim Reaper was due and I still had no clue how to defend myself. I fell asleep.

It was his "old spice" that I remember hitting me first. He sat on my bed – I felt chilled as he wiped the sleep from my eyes – he was pensive and calm.

I felt my eyes fill with tears. I choked back a sob. This was not the time to cry. "What were you doing in the bathroom last night?" I couldn't make my mouth work. He took that as defiance and filled in the gap. "Your mother says that the 'sound of nothing' was her make-up purse closing."

Dead. Done. Over. You could hear the guillotine sliding down its tracks, gaining momentum, cutting edge glinting, the killing blow imminent.

My dad had this predator's stare, the pupils of both eyes would dart side to side, but *just* the pupils, as he probed my mind, like a tiger deciding if I was worth the bite. It usually worked; I would crack under his stare and confess to a million crimes I hadn't committed.

"Well, Punky?" He waited for his answer, letting the silence step on my chest. Yes, it's only obvious now, why I would not surrender. That girl was tough, is all I can say, finding a strength that didn't exist in any other part of my seven-year old life. That little girl was going to go down swinging here, standing behind her cover story under pain of death. Nobody was going to tell her what to do. She looked her father right in the eye and without flinching said, "Kenny and I were going to be. . . clowns."

She doubled-down! He released me from his stare, sat back and looked at me, x-raying me from head to toe.

"Clowns, huh? Well, you've been waiting for the other shoe to drop all day, you've been punished enough. Get some sleep."

Whaaaa? Was this a stay of execution? He kissed my forehead, "You should probably stay out of your mother's bathroom, eh?" He turned out the light.

Did he know what I was? There's no way he bought the clown line, I told it and I didn't buy it. I've asked this a million times; did my parents know I was their girl trapped in this boy's life?

I never got the chance to ask. My mother passed when I was 20, and my father when I was 32. Well before therapy.

And, here I am today, the party's been over for hours, Kimm is gone, I survived but failed in a huge way. Maybe I'm not ready. Maybe I don't know how to do this. Maybe I won't ever know how to do this.

6
CODE PINK PROTOCOLS

I'm walking into a new office, a new company, and. . . a new me. I know I'm taking a chance, but I just can't bring myself to put this genie back into her bottle. I'll be meeting the president and I'm wearing a cute sailor t-shirt with a very flattering low-cut collar and women's jeans; casual, yet professional, sporty yet feminine. I've surprised even myself, I can only imagine her reaction.

But right now my resume is my shield. I'm highly recommended by the network, and if this (meaning me) is what one of the most respected showrunners in adventure reality looks like, well, who are they to question? Cuz we've got a job to do.

Which will be huge. I'm doing my best to prepare this new company for the reality of shooting in Alaska, which means take your budget and triple it, then triple it again. Your profit margin evaporates the moment the ink dries on the deal.

The president is a lovely woman, who gets me set-up quickly and heads back to NYC where her real headquarters are. She accepted me as her newest showrunner, and left her show in my capable hands. "Me" never came up. Which is how it should be, right? I don't have the bandwidth to wonder. It's show time.

Mylove and I will be apart yet again with chemo still in progress. The company has agreed to help me return from Alaska for her treatments. These guys are incredible. But first I gotta get there.

Once again I'm on a plane. My third trip. It dawns on me that Alaska is the first place I worked when I finished my gender therapy 5 years ago.

This feels embarrassing, even horrifying to admit, but five years ago, after my diagnosis, Mylove decided to take matters into her own hands: we were going to "fix" my gender thing.

I can't blame her. As cruel as it seems for my wife, who loves me, to even suggest "curing" the one she loves, remember this: she was fighting for her husband, lover, and soulmate. She would do anything not to lose me. I had detonated her world. I would do anything to make her happy again.

I went to see her homeopath, he prescribed (after weeks of tests and research – yeah, they're like that) a cure for "transsexualism." And I swallowed the medicine and my pride and used denial to keep me from feeling crushed and rejected by the woman I love, for being *me*.

Mylove would check in on me from time-to-time, "How are you doing?" a shorthand that really meant, "How is your sense that you are really a woman? Is it gone yet?"

It felt unbelievably cruel (for both of us) but I wanted to reassure her. And the truth was, there were times when I actually thought I might be able to find a way to make it all work. But maybe I should be thankful for that homeopath, who couldn't cure what ain't a disease. And she learned.

But let's face it, there's no way I was ready to live as a woman back then. You can give me all the excuses you want, but I know better: I was using life as an excuse to back down from the fight. And. . . I was sacred straight – this was our *first* cancer diagnosis. (It's how we got so good at it the second time around.) If Mylove had not survived while I was selfishly trying to be me? No way. Forget about it – I could never live with myself.

Good news? Our life did get better, Mylove got through her cancer regimen; it took a hysterectomy, chemo, loss of hair and energy, but she bounced back like a champ. This was "all her" – a positive attitude and warrior spirit that made it happen. I, on the other hand, was scared out of my mind. Remember, this is the woman that I was willing to sacrifice EVERYTHING for, including my own soul. Every breath was a gift.

We had weathered the financial storm of 2008.

My career picked up with the economy. It was the first time I was sent off to Alaska to prove myself in the Superbowl of outdoor survival, then on to The Gulf to cover the demise of the small shrimpers' fleet during hurricane season, then three months in the Amazon following redneck numbskulls as they raped the jungle for gold. It was harsh in harsh conditions, but I was rising as an adventure documentarian, earning my stripes.

I was "the man." And I continued to put myself on hold. BUT, "She" would sneak out whenever I had a chance.

I hadn't dressed since high school, but I got up to speed instantly. However I had forgotten that I faced a monstrous crash every time I put on lipstick. Did it stop me? Heck no. Remember, I've had a black belt in denial.

I had been under its thumb for thirty years. Still, you are probably saying to yourself, she should know better by now. I know I am. And soon the cure for the crash was "more."

Since I was always a stranger in a strange land, I was invisible. I buy a few things to make me feel better. A few hours as a woman felt like a vacation.

It started in New York (post production for the jungle gold mining show). I looked up LGBT and got a "Meet-Up" group, run by a woman named "Rita." This was it. I couldn't believe I was doing it – but the superpower that had propelled me to open that lime green make-up purse so many years ago had me saying yes to a girl's night out.

Seeing yourself as beautiful is a lot easier in your mind then it is in, *gasp*, real life. In your mind, your make-up is flawless, your body shapely, your legs are damn good in four-inch heels. But in reality, learning to draw a straight line with eyeliner is not something for amateurs.

Finally, I was released from the mirror's tyranny and made it to the club to meet the lovely Rita. She was a conscious and loving guardian who worked as a social worker by day. Tonight she was my tour guide, and the gay club we had picked that was supposed to be friendly to girls like us had decided that Saturday nights were boys only. 'Scuse me? We're being discriminated against at a gay club? Welcome to the community, united we divide. Discrimination breeds more discrimination.

Rita was incensed, but I was not into fighting tonight, so we hopped a cab to her old stand-by, the Stonewall Inn, a storied landmark of the LGBTQ Movement.

It was fun, a little loud for chatting, but it felt good to be seen. I didn't look half bad (thank gawd there's no evidence to destroy my rosy memory) and the big headline was:

I survived. I had stepped out into the world and I hadn't been stoned. Rita and I made empty promises to get together soon, but the truth is, I haven't been a party girl since college; and after 20 years of marriage and outdoor life, the idea of sitting in a bar was not really for me.

But I did begin to discover some things about myself.

For example, as much as I thought I wanted to dress – well, there's no easy way to say this – slutty, when I actually did, it felt *not real*. It was creepy, weird and uncomfortable.

And I simply did not look good with a lot of make-up. (Heartbreaking cuz I love it!) I could see instantly what most women learn as girls: the best cosmetics are health, happiness and . . . pride. (Now, don't get me wrong, I said a lot of make-up.) Still, I was learning to paint by numbers and trying for the first time ever, to stay within the lines.

I become *enthralled* with my new activity. I had a safe place to practice, thanks to my recently passed aunt. I was staying in her vacant house in Brooklyn. This amazing woman who made the effort to watch over me while she was alive was still looking out for me.

One day off, I was looking fine in heels and a thrift store dress, my make-up better than ever. I started down the stairs when I heard the front door open! It was my cousin and a realtor!

What the hell should I do? I bolted for the bathroom and hid, smart enough to turn on the shower. I started to take off my make-up immediately sad at destroying an hour's work, but ready to do anything to avoid being caught.

My cousin knocked on the bathroom door and I yelled that I was in the shower. He apologized, saying that the realtor had what she came for, so they were leaving, sorry to bother me. I mumbled something, promised to call him later and finally exhaled! I had half my make-up off, and the steam from the shower destroyed my curls, but disaster had been averted.

So I thought. When I got downstairs, I saw that I had left my purse by the front door (where it belonged if I was supposed to have a purse). And did I mention that my cousin is a retired NYPD detective? He never misses a trick. I was certain this would come back to bite me.

But he never said a word. I walked on eggshells for the next few months, waiting for this shoe to drop. I should've seen this for what it was: exhaustion at keeping up the walls that were closing in, of subconsciously trying to get caught. But I was not ready to see that. My Aegis radar swept the skies.

I trusted the security apparatus charged with protecting me from outing myself was on duty. Even the simplest question was made to pass like lightning through an incredibly efficient and intensely focused "office of security" (on the same base the Aegis crew was stationed) to make sure the answer would pass the CODE PINK protocols of which there were:

DEFCON 1. The simplest threat: "Of course we don't wear pink." It seems silly, and yes, boys wear pink all the time, and now that I'm a liberated woman, I love pink and wear it all the time. But according to Code Pink Protocols, the notion that admitting that you like pink, either in clothing or in general, attracts scrutiny too close for comfort, thank you very much. "We do not, nor have we ever liked pink," is the proper denial when questioned.

DEFCON 2. Mid-level threat: "Long hair and earrings are very fashionable for all genders. After all, everyone in LA does it – it's "the biz." Like Neo dodging bullets in the Matrix, I learned to "juke and jive" around, over, and sometimes through, scrutiny about my appearance. Code Pink Protocols call for you to play off all appearance choices as nothing special. Anytime someone questioned my earrings, the length of my hair or even my new manicure, I had an amusing anecdote that would playfully stake my ground as male, entitled to wear what ever I wanted. It made those outside the biz jealous as they muddled through casual Fridays and other workplace bullshit that we in the arts usually scoff at. As a "creative" (a species classification in my world of TV & Film, in which there are "suits," "creatives" and "techs"), I was merely expressing myself. And I was quick to add, if nothing else, I was tame compared to some of my pierced, "tatted," neon haired, combat boot wearing, sports-jersey clothed, colleagues.

DEFCON 3. RED ALERT – HIGHEST IMMINENT THREAT – COMPLETE SELLOUT: "Deny, deny, deny. Make counter accusations," say the Army's manuals on survival. The military translation of *"Hell no, that's not mine, it must be yours!"* These denials hurt. Because when that faint glimmer, of what most call "the truth," appears, it's a chance to stop lying forever.

"Is this, YOURS?" You're caught, a fake fingernail stuck in the carpet, a pair of undies you forgot to purge, or that darn purse by the door.

And time stops. Your breath catches in your throat.

But you see a faint ray of light out on the distant horizon. If you could just admit it, say yes, say it, "YES! IT'S MINE! YOU CAUGHT ME, I AM A WOMAN!" It would be so simple! Clean. DONE! No more hiding, no more lying, life could actually start right here. Right Now. But no, you are at DEFCON 3, ALL GUNS LOCKED ON THE ENEMY! AWAITING CLEARANCE TO ENGAGE. PERMISSION GRANTED, TAKE THE SHOT.

Because like Judas selling out his Christ for 30 pieces of silver, Code Pink protocols demand that you *deny, deny, deny, make counter accusations,* and you do.

And hope dies. And that light on the horizon is instantly obscured by clouds.

And what's most corrosive about Defcon 3 is that it takes so much firepower to obliterate all traces of the energy signature that there's nothing left but a smoking crater where the truth had been, and a hole in the ozone between you and someone you love.

I thought I had gotten good at sewing that hole back together with misdirection, cool, calm demeanor and total psychic washing of my own auric field of any negativity. My Aegis Missile Defense System sweeping the skies, gauging the threat's deterioration.

Or so I thought. Cuz as anyone who tries to hide something from their loved ones eventually discovers, it only ever works because your loved ones <u>allow</u> themselves to <u>appear</u> to have bought your excuse. Even if your loved ones don't admit it aloud, their own Aegis System detects a threat to their truth field, and the missiles stay primed at the ready.

Left unchecked, this corrosion will cause irreparable damage.

Geezus Criminy! All that in five years? No wonder I'm exhausted. I need a gig just to get some rest. From myself.

And that's where I am. At the beginning of a coming out that the referees would argue should be marked back at the pink rain boots incident. But we're being marked "half the distance to the goal line" (we're inside the ten). I guess if I need me some location, the 57th parallel, is as good as it gets.

I'm strangely giddy. It's not lost on me that God, the Universe or whatever you want to call it, has sent me here. Not only was this the first location I shot at after I came out, years later, it's where I shot the pilot for what is now my signature show, "Dude, You're Screwed." Why is Alaska being so nice to me? Hopefully, I'll have time to find out, But we're about to land, and I've got a show to figure out.

7

THE ONLY WAY AROUND IS THROUGH

Been in Alaska for a month and half. Show's a beast, a logistical nightmare: four locations spread across the state with over 800 miles between the northernmost location (30 miles shy of the Arctic Circle) and the southernmost location, the infamous Kodiak Island, 150 miles off the coast of Alaska proper. Trying to physically be in all places at once is the challenge of a lifetime (how much Alaska can one girl take?). But it's made bearable by a new crew who is magical, youthful and crazy enough not to ask why we're doing this in the first place.

I'm basically flying in a giant circle over Alaska, landing to jump on either a snow machine (don't call them snowmobiles up here) a float plane, or four wheeler to keep four locations, crews and casts on track to make a show about homesteading in the most remote areas of our wildest state.

We've set up a production office in Anchorage, and I roll back to home base every four weeks or so to physically check-in with Brent, my number 2 (second in command, known in our game as the Supervising Producer) and Ivy, the woman who's keeping us on track as our UPM or Unit Production Manager. I say physically, because every second of every day I'm in close contact with both of them – either on the phone or texting – as the three of us keep this mad circus (commonly known as an adventure reality show) from suddenly bursting into flame.

Anchorage is the place to wash my clothes, eat a good meal and sleep in a real bed for a week or so. It's also a place to be my girl self. A tent in the wilderness is no place for mascara, I know the rules: no self-respecting woman wears make-up when she's roughing it. My sisters would be so embarrassed if I turned out to be *that* girl.

At this point, all of my adventure clothing is feminine, but even though the colors and some fabrics are girlie, a parka's a parka. I'm still blurring the lines rather than defining them. I'm still not brave enough to try to wear make-up around my production staff. But I'm sporting classy feminine mocha and pink-framed glasses (still ambiguous) and when I can, non-adventure clothing (athletes wear tights, right?) but I'm still running this show like the guy on my resume.

However, something is changing. I'm discovering that *any* little feminine touch gives me joy, because now they're real. I call each of them my "one little victories[1]."

It used to be all or nothing. As I started to "explore," I wouldn't be satisfied with just a single thing. I had to dress from head to toe or it didn't count. Merely "under-dressing," as I had done during therapy (wearing a bra and panties under your boy clothes) came to feel like cheating. A lot of us girls do that or have done that, but it always made me so sad to be hiding who I was. It had to be visible or it didn't work. I know, I know. Crazy dichotomies. Welcome to the zany, madcap world of "trans."

I splurged on a few pairs of earrings, always a nice touch, and I'm getting bolder with the size and style. Suddenly, I'm not trying to hide behind a perception that I'm "like a pirate" or some other creative "guy explanation," I want a girlie hoop, darn it.

I'm still hoping no one will ask or comment on them. I'm brave enough to wear them, but not sure what will come out of my mouth when I try to defend them.

When I conduct business with the subcontractors in town, I can dress a little more stylishly than the bulky parkas and snow boots of production. I figure that I can wear sensible tights and big sweaters and pretty knee boots – a standard uniform for outdoorsie people whatever the gender, right? But only a woman would wear these things together. Chalk up another "one little victory."

If I start to waiver, worried that I might start getting looks, I tell myself that I can get away with pushing the envelope a little, without jeopardizing anything – *it's Alaska.* Hey, they'll just say, "The Showrunner's a little weird, but aren't they all like that down in the lower forty-eight?"

And so I can step out of the apartment without selling myself short. It's my story and I'm sticking to it. The joy of one little victories is magic and I feel myself lightening up. I am forcing myself to expand on this joy.

A song comes on in my play list, and I realize that without really acknowledging it, I am using the song's chorus as the banner I'm carrying to embrace my identity. . .

Wait? Did I just say embrace? What just happened? I did say embrace, didn't I?

Holy, shit! "it" just morphed again, evolved really, to embrace who I am. This isn't airy-faery new age "love your self" crap ("Loving myself" has never been an issue, too big an ego!) but embrace, hug, hang onto, live. . . myself.

This is the first time that "it" has felt good! It still has a weird air of. . . urgency? Anxiety? Fear? I'm not sure, but – it's still a quantum leap from hijacking!

Embrace? Like how?

---

1 One of my favorite songs by Rush on their "Vapor Trails" Album.

Here's the thing that anyone who hasn't gone through this might have a problem understanding: it's not about the clothes and it is about the clothes. A disclaimer here, I'm going to use the binary gender structure (only male & female) to describe my situation only. Gender, as we've discussed, is not binary, but rather a spectrum.

Gender roles and how they're expressed (or "presented," to be academic) are the basis for my inner turmoil. This is how we define what we are and how we want to be. *And want to be treated.*

I was brought up with the binary mirror, staring out from a woman's view at the reflection of a man. Admittedly, there are countless variations in between and on both sides, I'll grant to those who identify, but it is not how I view myself.

At the core of fashion (for anyone) is the appeal of wearing it and the desire of being seen in it. For girls like me, the focus is on the latter, because we seek validation that what *you* see on the outside, matches the way *we* feel and think on the inside. Yes, we know that others cannot define us. But oh, others try all the time. Others try to make laws against us, discriminate against us, and just plain judge us, and we would all rather avoid that, thank you very much. Your judgment won't make my feelings go away, but they will make my life harder and sometimes, dangerous. So yes, we seek validation. Call it reassurance. Better? Okay good. Now as I was saying…

If you've never questioned who you are, you can't imagine the havoc that that question wreaks. Cisgender women (Mylove for sure) always ask, "why would you want to dress this way," or "You would hate (panty hose, high heels, make-up, etc. insert your favorite fashion requirement here) if you <u>had</u> to wear them." But that's the key, Mylove and her cisgender sisters have a choice to wear or not wear. The choice has been taken from me. It's not only that I can't, it's a huge and potentially *dangerous* can't, a full-on red-light <u>should-not</u>.

Make no mistake, what clothes you wear is a charged issue. And society has always made it a big deal. There are laws that made it a criminal offense for a man to wear a women's clothes. These aren't societal mores, these are criminal acts!

The question is why?

Why would people get so freaked out that they would write an enforceable law to punish someone for doing what we all do everyday. You dress the way you think, feel, or don't care about, everyday. So why does it matter what the other girl or guy wears?

Because it speaks to our roles in this society. More directly, our expected "appearance" (not just clothing but manner and actions) confirms the role and it's appropriate expectations, responsibilities, and behavior.

When I know in my heart that I'm a woman, I want to dress like one.

I'm not a freak; I <u>want</u> to conform to society's expectations regarding my appearance. As a woman. Not just for me, but for everyone.

Not every woman wants to have society make her wear a dress to be formal, and certainly, that's not what makes her a woman. Every trans woman KNOWS THIS!

None of us can deny that any dude, especially a leader, who wears women's clothes, makes people uncomfortable. It's why "Tootsie" is funny, "The Crying Game" was creepy, and "Transparent" is fascinating – on their surfaces. It's the enlightened souls who transform that uncomfortable feeling into openness and acceptance, and reality.

Trust me, I have to do this for myself as much as I want it of others.

It's October and I am not quite there yet. I can dress fully when I'm alone and be comfortable with what I'm wearing, but despite all I am doing here in Alaska, despite my one little victories, I have to admit to myself that <u>I'm</u> still holding back. It's exhausting to wrestle with my own psyche and rationalize and chide, and sometime out-and-out accuse myself of letting myself down.

So I says to myself: Who am I living this life for anyway? Do I want to die before I ever really live? I didn't ask for this! It's not easy! What moron would choose this scrutiny? Who wants to live knowing that others talk about you behind your back with derision?

So, I keep working on it, even developing a muscle that gets more okay rocking pink acrylic nails around my crew. But make-up? Uh, we're not there yet.

I've never backed down from any challenge, which seems to be a weird way to handle one's own identity. It should be, literally, a no-brainer. Meaning that it is never even thought about, it just is. But it wouldn't be the first time I faked it till I "maked" it.

So that's why that song in my playlist is so important, it's a battle cry to myself from myself.

"The Only Way Around is Through."

Words to live by. Words I have lived by – just ask my parents and every coach or teacher that ever had me. I don't take no for an answer on anything, so why would I here?

Embrace. Embrace. Embrace. It's not going away.

Okay, I get it… It's time, and the next thing I know, my cellphone is in my hand, and I'm calling my sister Kimm. Time slows. I'm aware that this is a significant turning point. I thank my body for once again being the courageous one; it dialed before I could chicken out, again.

Kimm answers, but I'm stuttering, aware that I'm breaking a family rule to NEVER beat around the bush – we've been through the deaths of both parents and life threatening illnesses, the imagination kills you a thousand times in one "um." So, I let it fly without a spoonful of sugar, or even an adjective:

"Hi, it's me. Um. . . I. . . was born in the wrong body."

Silence. Did my heart stop?

In truth, she probably spoke immediately and said all the right things: "I love you no matter what. I only want you to be happy, etc. etc." I think I came back into my body as she started to ask questions. Her first:

"I mean... are you... do you... well, what about... boys, or Yourlove?"

"Well, if you're asking if I'm gay, then the answer is technically yes; as a woman, I am only attracted to, and in love with Marcy. So, I'm a lesbian, I guess."

We hung up, and I realized I had just crossed another barrier – strange, I know. I stare at her face on my caller ID as it winks off. I felt the sky open and the northern lights ripple across my heart.

I'm... out. Now.

And, as I stare into the sky, the world has shifted on its axis. I call Mylove to tell her that it's begun. "I'm out to my family... well, I started anyway – one down, four to go."

And we both take a breath.

8
LOBSTER ROLLS WITH A SIDE OF DIGNITY

I'm on a plane again, heading back to Alaska. Yes, I said back to Alaska. Thank God, I still love flying, I have to! I've clocked almost 100,000 air miles this year alone. I'm about to land in Anchorage airport for the seventh time in just the last month, but that's not the weird part. I boarded this plane in Boston – Logan, MA – after a two-hour taxi ride from Rhode Island.

This is something I've never done; take a break in the middle of a show. Not since our honeymoon during the production of "Surfer Magazine" (I was DP, AD and editor, ah the good ol' days, where I actually was superhuman). The truth is I never believed I could switch off my production head to turn on my fun head, genetic mutant that I am.

But this is a special trip for Mylove, her "Girls Weekend" (a note here, I use the word girl for anything good in life, from my breasts, to our two dogs, to here) where Mylove connects with three of her best friends from, wait for it, elementary school, and the husbands tag along for the ride. These girls take turns hosting it every two years, and with two girls on the West Coast and two on the East Coast, it's a great way to have an incredibly sweet and warm dose of fun in a place you might not think to visit. This time, it's Christie's turn in Rhode Island, practically on the campus of Brown University.

I really enjoy these special friends, joined together by almost nothing other than a shared childhood. I would never be friends with any of these people had fate not intervened.

Mylove, Bunny, Mitzi, and Christie pick up exactly where they left off, sixty years ago, and we, their spouses, Greg, Mark and Jeff, sit back and laugh for three days solid. With a conservative republican (Greg), and three liberal democrats, Mark, Jeff & moi, it's safer to keep the conversation on our wives. We each share a profound love for our girls and the "pinch me" disbelief to be loved by amazing women.

They already know I'm weird and the conversations always steer toward my adventures in television. I try hard to avoid the spotlight, because I know my life; I wanna know what these guys are up to. They are successful, accomplished men: a retired communications/IT entrepreneur, a retired social worker/counselor turned stockbroker turned poker dealer, and a retired postal worker; they have what I will never have. Retirement! They each have that relaxed demeanor that comes when men reach the end of middle age, where each has nothing more to prove, only more to enjoy.

But, with long hair and earrings, this is where I first got accused of being "a mad pirate," pillaging the world for television. I will confess, I hadn't wondered how pink acrylic nails would go with lobster rolls and reminiscing, until now.

I don't have Alaska's parkas and mittens to hide in here. It's an unseasonably warm fall on the East Coast, and shorts and tanks are the order of the day.

Okay, stop beating around the bush, I purged all my boy clothes and I'm not wearing anything remotely manly. I've got pink running shorts and a racerback tank, which requires that I wear a matching sports bra.

Mylove and I have been able to fly together (I'd flown home from Alaska and we turned right around and boarded for Logan.) She's so excited! She really needs this; we're still in the middle of chemo (literally between appointments) so she'll have time to be with her chums, rest up, then head home for another dose, but for now, it's fried clams and Girl Talk! I let Mylove get down to socializing and volunteer to unpack for us both.

I kick off the airplane clothes and change into something more comfortable. I've not only got pink fingernails, I've got crimson toenails. Are they ready for them? To show or not to show. . . should I ease into this or come out toes blazin'?

Ten minutes into "no decision," Mylove suddenly comes in, "What's taking so long?" I explain my hesitation, "I'm not sure if they're ready for red toenails."

She looks at me, with dumb-struckery flashing briefly through compassion before alighting on impatience. "Really?"

This is what I'm taking about: I'm brave, until I'm not. "How silly is this? You're afraid of what they may say about your toenails, but those pink fingernails are just screaming he-man right now!"

Ah, my mind. I shrug and Mylove shakes her head, tells me to decide either way, I'm missing all the fun.

Which is what it is and will be for the next three glorious days: dorky touristy outings that we all would never allow ourselves normally, more lobster, clam chowder and – even a ferry ride to Block island and island corn!

I notice a few whispers (about me?) when I join conversations late, but for the most part, it's all good. The days are filled with talk of retirement plans and realities, aging and more reminiscing, and then it's over faster than it began.

Mylove has arranged an extra two days to hang with her bud, Christie. They were closest growing up, and both women share a special spot in the other's heart and history, having gone on together from their elementary school to a famous girl's boarding school. We've just waved good-bye to the other two couples and catch our breath in the foyer. The door has barely shut behind us, when Christie says: "So, Scott… are you… well, are you getting in touch with your feminine side?"

I look to Mylove. And there it is. We smile.

Christie has just retired from over 30 years as a family counselor/therapist. She knows the answer to her own question before asking, but she also knows to give me the courtesy as a friend and her guest to be the one who drives this conversation whichever direction I choose. And so, I choose, "Well, Christie, that question has a long answer."

She smiles compassionately and we all head for the dining room for, "the chat."

With two social worker/family counselors in this house, I know I'm on safe ground. Mylove and I (we've got this down to a duet now) tell <u>our</u> story.

Christie and Jeff listen to everything. I am, of course, dying to know how the other couples felt. Christie indulges me by saying that I, and more importantly, Mylove were *the* topic of the weekend, but everyone wanted to respect our space. Of course, they were all worried for Mylove, worried that she would be okay, worried what this meant for our future.

Then Christie confesses as a friend, that when I got out of the car at the beginning of the weekend, she was taken aback when she realized I wasn't some other woman, that I was, in fact Mylove's husband. She says, "I felt the ground shake beneath my feet."

Christie is not a dramatic person. I can only imagine having her as a therapist: grounded, calm, intelligent and insightful, but never dramatic. So, I take her words to heart seeing the "scene" from her point of view. Her old friend Marcy bounds out of the car into her open arms while this other, vaguely familiar, woman unloads suitcases from the taxi – a woman with a side ponytail, hammered silver cuff, silver hoop earrings, black tights, and a light woman's jacket over a black tank top (I thought I looked quite cute, despite eight hours of plane and taxi travel). Cute or not, I was a bit of a shock.

Christie goes on to say that she had to work at allowing me to change in her mind. She fought through the disorientation (I know that one, sister) and she could see that the love between Mylove and me hadn't changed, it felt stronger. But here's where she blows me away: "If you both live your life with dignity, you will be better than okay."

Dignity. I let her word wash over me. Dignity. I need to live with dignity. I think I want a "dignity," but it's not a word I have ever sought before. I have never even looked for any words that go with that word. My words came from the server marked, "Incorrigible": Brat? Hell yes. Immature? I wore it like a badge of honor. Bull in a china shop? My middle name.

But as a woman, I realize that yes, I want dignity. Dignity is not respect from others. I have that respect. Dignity is respecting yourself. And acting accordingly; it's knowing to the fiber of your being that you really do belong. I start to cry. Mylove starts and Christie joins in. And Jeff. . .

I want to know what is going on in his mind. Jeff and I have been close when we shared these weekends. I love his sense of humor and wisdom. We're the two liberals of the group, but he's the one mature enough to know what a liberal is, having fought the actual fights for social and civil rights the first time around. He smiles, as all three women blow our noses, "You might not like what I'm thinking." I assure him I still want to hear it.

He takes a sip of his coffee and lets the air clear for his opinion. "Are you both prepared to fight for your rights?" Am I prepared for discrimination? *Is* Mylove?

Are we prepared to stand and fight together?

Thanks for the buzz kill, Jeff! But he is spot on, and if anyone knows what is out there, it's Jeff. He never really stopped being a social worker. He would know it ain't easy out there, and what guiding light would be better than Dignity?

We have another day and half to work this all through, enjoying each other's company, laughing about how funny and rich life is. And then, we hug goodbye. I have to get Mylove home and get back to Alaska. I have a show to run.

On the drive down to Boston, Mylove and I cuddle in the back seat of the taxi; the driver occasionally asking us ladies if we need anything, which always gets a quiet giggle. We are fine, we say, content to whisper to ourselves things we want the other to know from Christie and Jeff's intervention, the gratitude for their wisdom and friendship and the great good fortune to be loved.

At the airport, I get another tickle that this has been more than just a good talk. Mylove and I arrive earlier than expected, and feeling indulgent, have time for an airport chair massage. As I lean forward into the chair, the therapist gently stops me and puts a "breast bolster" on the rest for my comfort, a wedge shaped cushion that fits between your breasts so you don't have to press them against the rest. Putting to rest the question, "does anyone else notice my chest?" Mylove, sees this happening and whispers, "You Madden Girls and your chests."

I whisper, "Don't hate us because we're pretty." We can joke with each other, love each other and be envious of each other. What a life!

After a cross-country flight and switching back to my cold weather gear, we kiss each other goodbye (again). It's getting harder, rather than easier, which we both agree is as it should be. We're half way through this show.

So much to chew on, as I line up this show for an elegant landing. Dignity, huh? I can do that. Wait, can I do that? I'll practice till I get home. Mylove and I both have a lot to think about in the next few weeks.

What's just dawning on me is that while my back was turned, the "She" in me started coming out. Christie saw it immediately. Now Mylove, my sister and my wife's best friend are "in the know." Christie was given the greenlight to tell the other girls, which will bring the total to a baker's dozen. Without any official announcement, warning or fanfare, I'm stepping out into the world, (being pushed from within is probably more accurate) whether I'm ready or not.

Buckle up girlfriend, it's going to be a bumpy ride.

9

TURKEY & DRESSING

As I write, the Alaskan snow is knee deep outside and we're all dealing with the realization that we will be orphans for Thanksgiving once again. I am bummed to not only be missing Mylove, but to be stuck in a rented apartment. There's nothing else to do but cry "potluck!" and unleash the dogs of food!

I never schedule my crews willingly into the holidays, they're that important to me — both crew and holidays. But this year, I've got no choice. We're all thousands of miles from family, so biting the bullet will have to be just another side dish. My Anchorage Production office crew has put everything they have into this show, including working seven days a week. It's not that I make them do it, they just won't/don't stop. Life on the road will do that to you — strangers in a strange land, work is all you know. But, I put my foot down — It's Thanksgiving, damnit!

In my world, the holiday season (which to cooks and foodies is sacred), starts at Halloween, the gateway to the playoffs of food that leads through league championships at Thanksgiving and on to the Superbowl at Christmas (which is a week long ending at New Years Day). This is where the best of your kitchen gets tested, bested and enjoyed! No matter where I am, or what I'm doing, I will figure out a way to not only get some cookin' done, but to show my love and blow some minds!

Everyone is game and we divide up the chores. I will bring the Turkey, which has been brining for three days in hard apple cider, spices and onions. But it's the dressing that I am the most excited about, artist that I am. It's inspired by Alaska: sourdough bread as the base, boasting three pounds of king crab, plus wild blueberries – absolutely amazing – playing with the usual suspects: onion, celery, herbs and broth. The irony of *dressing* is not lost on this girl because today, I am "going for it," in more ways than one. I am "dressing for the occasion," and my crew will see me looking even more feminine than before. I am throwing caution to the winter winds and dressing the way any sophisticated, mature, happy woman would for a holiday with people she loves. Within reason.

In other words… real-ish.

As I chop onions, I drift . . . this isn't the first Thanksgiving Mylove and I are spending apart; it's the third time in a row we've spent it on a phone from separate gatherings. The last two for me were in Denver, and though I was able to dress up, there weren't any stakes. In Denver I was with two dear friends, my big sisters in the Mile High transgender community. But today, I'm going for it head to toe with people who aren't expecting me to look like, well. . . me. I'm not sure how or if my crew will welcome the complete feminine form of me. I'm not sure how, or if, *I* will be okay being me with *them*.

Last year at this time, I was sitting down to a Denver Thanksgiving with Green Chili dressing (see what I mean? I can't help it, I'm that way). I am so thankful for Denver and its loving embrace. It gave me strength and confidence to be who I am; and even if only in controlled settings, it was more than enough. It had started two years before, and in my diary I wrote:

I got really lucky, this time. My own show. After three shows where I ran the production but didn't get the title, this one came with no apologies or compromises. The concept was great, the people greater! Smart, savvy, committed, conscientious professionals with only one drawback, they were in Colorado.

Now, at first this wasn't a problem. It was just a pilot. One episode. No biggie. I had started to make a name for myself in adventure documentary/reality, survival world, having done three shows. Which was appreciated by the Denver company. They listened to me when I asked for more safety and security measures than anyone had thought necessary. At a significant budget increase, mind you. I had been in some really sketchy situations (almost lost one of my best friends) and this was in the wake of a series of horrendous safety breaches on other shows where crew did die, because of hubris. (The networks are doing everything they can to divert blame, but they are the most responsible, culpable and criminal in all of the recent accidents. We now return you to our regularly scheduled story…)

The pilot episode would be shot in Alaska and then post back in Denver. Post (editing) is essentially an office job for a showrunner. Indoors with running water. This phase of any show always starts with sane "bankers hours" – and this company placed home and family life at a premium, so unless your show was up against itjs air date, you left at 6:00 PM like a <u>normal</u> person…

… Giving me time to explore this thing called *me* and my gender identity. I was away from Mylove and my home, and when I went back to the long term corporate housing each night, I had no one but myself waiting. This was the first time since New York that I was able to open the gates of the dungeon and examine the feelings that I had put off working with for a year. I was still trying to figure out what to do with my diagnosis as a "high functioning transsexual," and one word that haunted me was "full time."

In the transworld, this is the holy grail. It means:

A. You're serious. This is you and this is how you live your life. Or...

B. You're retired, rich and don't have to interact with the outside world.

C. I'm kidding about B, this is something transgender girls tell themselves when they haven't figured it out yet.

D. You live 24/7 as the woman that you are. You don't take "boy breaks," you don't dress like a man for work and a woman when you come home at night. It means you wake up like everyone else, get dressed like everyone else, and no one questions whether this is a strange phenomenon or not.

Welcome to our world, defined by how close we are to the "real world." Even when the real world isn't looking, isn't checking up or couldn't care less.

I discovered that I had no clue how to fit my "diagnosis" (the latest definition of "it") into my life. How had others done it?

Again, I turned to the "Meet-Ups" and Denver's was the "Mile High Meet-Up." (Clever.) I corresponded with the moderator and she suggested the Denver GIC, Gender Identity Center. They had weekly meetings and always posted a group photo of last week's attendees, all dressed very nice, dresses and heels. They looked harmless enough. But it would mean showing up. Which at this time, a mere three years ago, was still scary. As bold as I was in New York, I was still able to hide in the anonymity of a public place where everyone was taking the same anesthesia. But a support group? I could keep my mouth closed and have people wonder about me or open my mouth and remove all doubt. *And what would I wear?* These girls were not fetish or playacting, they were dressed up. Call it date night formal. Some beautiful, others almost tragically "fashion challenged" (lest you think we're all love and roses in the trans community, many of us haven't matured as women and we're judging/comparing ourselves to each other's appearance as much as any teenage girl you know).

I had to overcome this or I would never get out the front door. This isn't all ego, it's also a safety issue. The specter of hate crimes hangs over our head whenever we walk outside our homes. But even more than my own safety, was a bizarre form of vanity, which was a weird mix of equal parts of low self-esteem and high standards. It wasn't helped by fashion choices I made from lack of experience, knowledge and more importantly, access. There's only so much you can find at a thrift store that's fashionable.

But! They (the GIC girls) professed not to care. So I mustered up the courage one Wednesday night and got "dolled up." I looked downright respectable – of course, a dress and heels were in order. I had to show them

I was serious after all. They didn't care. They were warm, loving, diverse and some were a bit sad. I wasn't prepared for that.

There were girls who only dressed as a hobby, fully committed to being a Transvestite. Crossdresser. Tranny for short. (A bit pejorative, yes, but some wear it as a badge of honor.) These gals love their male lives and like appearing when they can as women. They adore women and have various reasons for why they do it, but, make no mistake about it, they do not see themselves as women in the least. After a night with their "feminine side" they put their pants on the next morning and go back to the man's world. This is not the same thing as Drag Queen. These gals may or may not have feminine leanings, but are all about the "commentary" on and of femininity, from the guy's point of view. A sure way to spot a Drag Queen (other than foot-long eyelashes) is you'll never see a Drag Queen at a support group. At least not one for gender identity issues. They have no issue. And they'll tell you that, usually with a mic in their hand and your dollar stuffed into their bra.

There were girls here tonight who were confused. And their lives showed it. Some were sure what they wanted, but not willing to find out how to get it. Some weren't sure what they were, but were sure what they were not. And others weren't sure of anything.

Then there were the women who were sure what they were, what they were doing, and where they were going. That night, two of them came to the center to "give back" as big sisters in the community, and they stood as living examples that it can get better.

They would become trusted and cherished friends. Danielle & Paige.

I realize between bastings of the bird, that I need to give thanks for two amazing women on this journey. So I leave voice mail hugs for both, having to stuff two years of growth into a thirty-second recording. Both have a simple theme, "Who would've guessed that I would be here?" Emotionally, socially, and physically, and all because of them.

But where exactly is here?

Here, for now, is a happy moment out of time, a day where I'm stepping out in a small way to a still "safer" group. I confess that my crew has to respect me. But I don't want to take anything away from them, they are lovely people, even if it is a calculated risk.

I am singing and dancing as the bird begins to sizzle, time to turn the bird right side up – you always start with him down. Yup, it was just last Thanksgiving, when Paige loved learning tricks like this, and cooking together became a cherished weekend thang. But, at Thanksgiving, we pulled out all the stops and she got to break out her family's heirloom china – strange that her mother knew (at least in her heart) that one of her "boys" might one day appreciate what would normally be a daughter's birth rite.

Now to be clear, these women, Danielle & Paige, were on two very

53

distinct frequencies of the spectrum. Danielle was the "smooth jazz FM," to Paige's "24 hour news radio AM." Danielle was on the fast track. She knew she was a transsexual, was doing thoughtful research for a successful transition and had the resources to do it. Though she was a woman on a mission, impervious to the challenges, Danielle had a messy, in-process divorce and two daughters who hadn't quite been able to process mommy and daddy splitting after thirty plus years. Both believed that "daddy's confusion" was to blame for the break up. Neither grown daughter had any idea that Danielle had come out to her wife, well over a decade ago.

And Paige, "Paigie" (she hates when I call her that), is a different story. Some people were just born to be an older sister, and Paige's life is all about service, looking after people the same way others look after a career. A twenty-five year plus veteran of AA, Paige's daily routine and reality is guidance, support and giving. Between caring for her sponsees, going to meetings (four a week) and volunteering for the Denver AA community, she has just enough time to work as a social worker in a hospital helping Transgender patients navigate health care.

I sought out both ladies after the GIC meeting. Our conversation continued in the parking lot for two more hours (see what I mean? Sisters at first sight) and though I couldn't bring myself to blurt out my story back at the formal meeting, neither Dani nor Paige would let me off the hook now, and it seemed safe outside under the stars and in the darkness. My story was similar to Dani's, down to knowing who we actually were since childhood.

After I poured out my life under the prairie sky, I trailed off. And in the silence, Danielle cleared her throat and whispered words that would rock me to my core.

"I wish you well. I. Wish. You. Well."

I felt the earth stop. It was delivered like a sentence. There was "inevitability" in her tone that shook the mountains. Paige broke the silence by making plans for dinner the following Friday at a "real" restaurant. It's common language among "girls in the community" that a real restaurant is one that normal people go to, as opposed to a Transgender friendly hang-out. There it is again: the trans experience is defined by degrees to the left, right or center of "normal."

The next week, I got my first taste of being at a real restaurant. Through the friendship of these two women I would start to develop a fearlessness to step out into the real world where normal people would be, head held high. It wouldn't be easy, I would still have to clothe myself in out-and-out chutzpa. Danielle is Jewish, Paige is Jew-ish (her ex wife is Jewish and for 20 years Paige was very active in her temple) so I was in good company. Even so, I was always tense because a brittle veneer of confidence was merely sprayed over a roiling self-consciousness. It can be scary "out with normal people," if you allow yourself to be an outsider.

The most dangerous shield girls like us pick up is a feeling of being "not normal," as if normal was the baseline of worthiness. It's a fine line that separates self-determination, and self-consciousness; the former knows it's worthy of all things, the latter believes that since it is not really worthy, it will end up taking what it wants, sometimes by force, and rarely graciously.

I would go through the latter to develop the former, as my big sisters held my hand to navigate the Denver trans scene, or "the community."

This loose collection of girls and boys who make up a good portion of the frequencies along "the spectrum" meet regularly at four of Denver's restaurants and saloons, and I got a good look at all things trans. And like the GIC of Denver, some stories were inspiring and other's downright scary.

All served to put me on notice – I knew nothing about life.

There were truck drivers who, even with a tight silk dress stretched over a beer belly and a six foot frame, couldn't give up telling actual war stories, or how they had to fix (with excruciating detail) their diesel four by four to get to the club that night, as if they were staking their masculinity, lest "we" girls get the wrong idea. And sometimes, they were just genuinely into trucks as much as the next girl.

There were the straight-up floozies who thought the affections of an "admirer" (cisgender men who want a trans women) were because the floozy had fooled the admirer. (BTW a trans woman would never think this.) And there were cisgender women who were there for a safe time, maybe a little curious, but interested in why girls like me exist. I loved these women, talking with them was magical, because I would eventually, after the interview portion of the conversation, win their sisterhood, at least for another hour.

Then there were just great girls. Our circle of three opened to six and when it was girls' night out, we were like the varsity cheerleaders. Oddly, this had nothing to do with our stages of self-acceptance or transition; in fact, four of us are on this side of the river now, one will never come across and one may find a comfortable blend. We were all successful in our lives in our very different careers, had great connections to our families, and shared a love of community.

As I read back over the last paragraphs, I realize I may not have said what I was feeling as I stepped out into the world with these friends, dressed as a woman, dressed as me.

I just *felt*. I was lighter (no armor, but still a coat of chain mail under my dress). I felt great, wonderful, real, and relaxed… and just… right. That it wasn't a big deal was the key. No fireworks, no waves of excitement, just calm and peace.

And yet, I detected a small splinter, a growing sense of dread. It started whispering as I grew to be a part of the girls' club. A growing sense of disquiet that even told me its name. A dark dangerous whisper called *not enough*.

It wasn't about clothes and make-up, and looking the part. It was about being. I could see from my Mile-High view that my feelings, emotions and thoughts about the things that we all call "character" were those of a woman. I could see why I always understood my mother and her fears, trials and joys, or my grandmother, or my sisters, aunts and female cousins; whereas I had to try to figure out what my father, uncles, and boys were thinking.

Looking the part is where we all start, but the path to *being* is as long and as uncharted as anyone's life. How to get to "enough?" How to get to "be?" How to grow into a woman? With my life thus far: successful showrunner, captain of a five million dollar ship called a TV series, and with all the respect I've painstakingly described, it looked like it might be easier to sprout wings. Looking the part might have to be the only way I could alleviate the pain long enough to keep the dragon in its dungeon. I hadn't really progressed since my diagnosis. I was essentially still trying to make crossdressing work. And it would always be. . . not enough.

But it would have to do. Paige and Danielle were patient, but they were changing, too. Paige was formally coming out at her law firm; she was doing it textbook style, developing a formal relationship with a therapist who took the lead presenting Paige's case to her firm (only after Paige had met with the partners one-on-one). On Friday, "Page" (with no "I") said goodbye, and on Monday, Paige (with an "I") said hello. Smooth, like buttah, it was over in a matter of days.

Danielle's divorce got nasty as soon she started taking hormones. Her sixty year old, soon to be ex-wife, no skills and scared about her future (justifiably so), got a lawyer who smelled blood. Luckily, Danielle is a blissfully resilient, addicted runner/marathoner (fifteen miles a day, rain or shine). She would convalesce from her trench fight with us.

Eventually my time in Denver came to an end. Thanksgiving at Paige's house was the celebration of a year's growth that broke down the main fortress wall and I couldn't be more thankful. I had been wished well. And, well, I got it.

The turkey's almost done, and I've still got my "round" of holiday calls to my sisters. Cooking is a passion for my whole family and with three sisters and their families, they've usually got their hands full. Which I'm counting on, because who has time to listen to their brother "come out" as a woman while you're up to your elbows in turkey and punkin' pie? I left messages for Kimm. Next up: my baby sister, six hours ahead in South Carolina – I've been bracing myself for this, and it could get interesting. But the tryptophan had taken its toll, so another message left. I turn my attention to our token

Brit, my middle sister, Keira.

Keira has been living across the pond. She came out to us as a lesbian at the same time she announced that she was moving to England with a woman she met over the internet. That she was gay was no surprise to any of us. We wanted her to go back to the part where she was moving to England with someone she met on the internet! But after ten years, Keira and Jordyn (we love Jordyn!) are still together.

I wipe the grease and flour from my iPad: time to come out to the Brits. I check my make-up in the Facetime window as I wait to connect.

Jordyn is answering. Keira is horrendously sick. I stammer out "Should I call back?" But Keira bucks up (stiff upper lip and all, she's becoming so British!) And then, ta da, we're face to face over the internet.

"Oh my, you look, wow... girly?" I stare into the tiny window and sneak a look at myself – yikes! I move the iPad to a more flattering angle.

I look great, they say and both are happy for me. Keira is no stranger "to the community," and knows the right questions to ask, namely, "What's your girl name?" I explain that I have used one but don't like it. Keira volunteers to conduct a Girl name contest. I would really like that. As I try to elegantly wrap up this "holiday call," I apologize for using technology for something so important, saying I had planned on saying this face to face when she came for Christmas, but couldn't wait any longer. Keira has bad news, they won't be able to come for Christmas after all, they have to postpone their vacation until the spring. So it's better that it worked out this way. Love you Bye!

I get back to my dressing (the crab kind). But I have no idea I had lit a fuse across the pond, and it's gonna take roughly three weeks from now to detonate. Ignorance is bliss, I'm so happy now... and out to her.

The turkey's done. Dressing is perfect and I'm heading over to the production HQ/apartment. Ivy gives me a heads up – two of her friends are Thanksgiving "orphans" as well (friends on other productions up here in Alaska who can't get home either) will be joining us. I'm not sure what my Ivy thinks of me, so I have no idea if the orphans have been prepared for a "me."

My make-up, despite sweating in the kitchen is fine, my tunic and tights elegant enough, and off I go.

It's awesome. Dinner is great, the orphans fine and interesting. We're all good cooks and I'm surprisingly comfortable and . . .

My crew. How amazing are they? I did manage to send my number 2, Brent home to be with his wife, but the rest of us are hunkering down together. Ivy, big surprise, is absolutely lovely. Almost, but not quite treating me as if I've come to work this way everyday. I say almost because she does compliment me, and admires my earrings. The orphans are friends of hers and follow her lead. The woman has blue hair and nose piercing, and her eyeliner is better than mine. Her date is a musician, and I get a dose of how a lady graciously listens to someone, helping to draw them out to make them feel comfortable. This is a new skill for me, as Reality Show Showrunner, I'm used to listening for weakness to exploit for dramatic effect. But today I'm relaxed and enjoying his take on things. He seems to be happy to have someone listen, but now I'm trapped. I'm his "go-to face" for acknowledgement as the conversations swing this way and that, what to do now? Hey guy, leave me alone! I want to chat with my Ivy. She must be able to sense my longing, because she swoops in like a perfect wing-woman. Well, if that don't say sister, I don't know what would. Ivy's so cool with me; I'm wondering why I even allowed myself to be anxious to begin with. Her brother Phillip, our office PA, and Ivy's mentee, is also surprisingly cool. He's a Michigan country boy, who's just happy for the chance to be in Alaska. If anyone could have an issue with me, it would be Phillip, but even he accepts me as if nothing is special. My dressing(s) it seems are a hit!

Like Cinderella, I don't want the night to end. But it finally does. I floated across the parking lot as the November wind pecked my cheeks. I wish I could say I knew why I chose to "go all in" today – but I'm so glad I did. I think it's because I have an aversion to regret – it's gotta be what makes me always go the extra mile. I already have a tough enough time with mirrors, I for damn sure don't need that reflection shaking her head at me.

Back alone in the apartment; the destruction of the kitchen is. . . grim. But it will wait until tomorrow. (In fact, maybe we should just condemn the place.) I'm calling it a day. A perfect day! Tonight I go to bed complete!

And tomorrow, I go back to blurring lines.

10
OUT IN THE COLD

December already? We have survived. The show looks pretty good, and despite the brutal schedule, I continue to blossom. It's not like I'm learning anything new about myself, more like letting my guard down.

Once under the northern lights, I walk away from the camp to pray to the intense rippling ribbon of magic snaking through the night sky and hear my safety officer step up from behind. Respectfully, he asks if he could pose a personal question. I only know him from this job and as I'm the moving target, I never developed more than a working dialogue with him. But I say, "Pose away!"– Pinks and lime greens shimmering against an indigo ceiling, take both our breaths away. He finds his first, and asks if he had offended me when he called me "sir."

Before I go on: Heck yes! Pronouns (and titles) matter! But he asks this without any official discussion, and whether he is smoking me out with one deft line of questioning or has truly figured out who I really am beneath the air of authority and goose down, doesn't matter. I open up completely. No it hasn't offended me, but, yes it did still hurt.

But as I finish, I still feel compelled to ask that he keep this between us. To which he, of course, agrees. Bizarre, really, that I had thought I was so clandestine up here. I still believed that I was good at keeping "it" under wraps.

I know, of course, that he will not honor our agreement. Any intel about the showrunner is the coin of the realm, and it's only a matter of time before it is common knowledge. Still, when I return to Anchorage, I am curious what has gone through the ranks about me. The trick will be to do it without looking like Captain Queeg. (Caine Mutiny anyone?)

I put this question to my number 2 and to my UPM. They're both savvy and they got my back. I confess, at least with Ivy, I feel, I dunno, sorta stupid? She was so amazing at Thanksgiving (and I know that Brent and she had to have talked when he got back). It's like I'm fishing for something we already silently agreed was cool.

This is, I know, a trap for girls like me. We've spent an entire lifetime worrying what others would or might think if they "only knew" that we either develop calluses overcaring, or will weaken in our ability to trust. I cannot let this happen. I won't. So I force myself to err on the side of clarity.

I take them to dinner and it is a learning experience for me. Shocker! They have no issue with me, or my clothing choices, or even my manicures. They both think I am a little bit crazy that I worried about it all, thinking *they* might have an issue with it. This is the half-generation behind me, but light years ahead in maturity.

Brent (My No. 2) is so damn cute and newly married and he shakes off my query with nothing more than an eye roll; but catches himself and suddenly realizes he is talking to a woman, and says, "Unless, you need to talk about it." Good boy, he's learning his lessons well.

Ivy catches my smile and winks. She has always let me know what was what, and here she assures me that there is no what. I am as natural as the next girl, and her favorite showrunner to work for so far.

Okay, I now feel more embarrassed than relieved that I could think this of them. It seems silly to press any further. Does it matter if they see me as a woman? Impossible at this point. They aren't blind. My reputation alone is shouting, "Dude." Dude who dresses pretty femmie, looks decent in make-up for special occasions, and can talk about hair and nails with Ivy when we both have the time (which isn't much these days). And the truth is, only I know at this point that I'm a work in progress.

My number 2 does confess that Jim, our location manager, called a "fixer" – or as I call them, the unfuckers (they unfuck logistics, nothing ever really gets fixed) – did confide that I had the biggest balls to dress the way I do in Alaska (gross, but I get the point). Which, until I hear this, hasn't occurred at all to me. This place makes Alabama rednecks seem liberal. He's right, but it speaks to my swaggah; as I said, I can not only hang with the boys, but I lead 'em and they respect me.

So the answer is "yes," my crew does know, but what they know is up for debate. It seems, in many cases (just like my northern lights moment) that I am the agent of my own destruction. Hmmm, that was a pithy phrase to write but if I let it linger, it's accurate. Destruction can be a good thing … like the demolition of an abandoned building so a new park can be built in its place.

I know psychologists have a name for this, but my friend Dani calls it "polling." You are trying out this thing called honesty about yourself in small doses, on certain groups of people to test the waters of acceptance. I'm not sure I agree with that. To me, it feels like her "Sheness" is running around like a pyro, lighting fires to all the bridges in my life. Soon, she'll torch the drawbridge. Probably her plan.

And I am her half-witting accomplice. As we wrap the first of four locations here in Alaska and sit around the campfire, I toast the crew for a job well done. We have violated a cardinal rule by letting one of the cast members join us (we rarely "fraternize" with the subjects of our video scrutiny, but this is Alaska and survival dictates decorum). BJ is a gem and so over the top polite (like good southern boys, but even nicer). I am painstakingly trying to express my deepest gratitude to my crew for a job well done, and I beg BJ to stop calling me "sir." He uses the usual response of "But this is the way I was raised, etc." I have no idea why I persist. To compromise, he asks what he can call me to convey respect for my leadership. I hear myself say, "I prefer ma'am." He must be responding to the authority in my voice, because he switches gears without hesitation, and then, before you know it, I've now expanded the circle of those "in the know" with one command.

WHAT IS THIS LITTLE PYRO DOING???

So there it is: my first gig as a different me is in the books. And the results are in: my crew knows I'm like no other showrunner in the biz (the adventure reality tribe) and though I am not ready to say they regard me as a woman, I can say that they will all be able to say: "Yeah, I know this transgender showrunner…"

I guess it's time to have "the chat" with my agents.

11
VISIONS OF SUGARPLUMS

I'm home again. And it's the countdown to Christmas! I only have three days before I take off for Canada to get my last project of the year started, only to turn right back around and race back for the biggest Christmas of our lives. Mylove's brothers (two of three) and her baby brother's daughters will be here for the "Empress of holidays," Christmas Eve. I've got cookies to bake and candy to make. Mylove has already gotten the tree (first time in 25 years that she did it by herself). She wanted to have it waiting for me.

We sit by the fire and the tree, and it's time once again, to talk about "it."

I wasn't "going out" in Alaska, but rather living more as a "guyish-girl" than a "girlie-guy" (okay, this was more like surviving – my last week was in a tent 300 miles from the closest habitation, and minus 20 degrees). I'm stronger than before. And, as we sit to sip tea after putting the last ornament on the tree, I am able to let Mylove all the way "in," much to her surprise.

We decide that we've got work to do (along with baking and preparing). First are "the boys." Her brothers will be here in less than a month and they need to be told about me.

Oh, and did I mention that Mylove's big brother, Macky, will be coming to live with us? Christmas is the beginning of a six-month stay to help him get on his feet.

Macky has just finished a stint in the pokey, the hoosegow, the slammer, for a white-collar "indiscretion." But since he'll soon be a "roommate," it might be helpful if he knows.

A quick snapshot of my brother-in-law: all three are amazing guys, but Macky has always been a little, well, how to put this, *lost?* He's wicked smart, funny and loving, the guy who always makes sure everyone *else* is comfortable. Warm and generous of heart and spirit, he is utterly harmless. His little stunt that got him in trouble was well intentioned, if not silly and, okay, let's be real, stupid. He's also a gullible person, and the only one (of the group) left holding the bag of a ponzi-esque scheme. But this sorta sums him up, he wants to believe in people; his light at the end of the tunnel *has always* been the oncoming train.

He is so sweet, cries at episodes of the "Dog Whisperer" and "Long Island Medium," and asks the most embarrassing questions of complete strangers, genuinely interested in making new friends. I'm sure he drove his daughter (Acey, the Jewel of the family) completely nuts when she was a teen.

But I love him dearly, and this will be interesting.

Today's the day, the circle widens. It's almost time and Mylove has been quizzing and coaching me with my spiel. I have to be careful with Macky, I'm not sure what he thinks of the transgender thing. He's picked up a few surprising opinions in the pokey, but that may be just leftover male "posturing" or "frontin" (he even knows what that means). I have to remind myself that life in federal lock-up ain't a picnic, and he was bunking with lifers and manslaughterers. I'm sure his gentle nature, imposing size (at six two), and guardian angel got him thru without incident. Still, he's seen a lot more of life then he ever dreamed. So, without further ado, I tell him my story.

Macky's amazing with the news, compassionate and a little blown away (okay, a lot blown away. I've rocked his world and I know it). My life, until this, might be one he would trade for, as he's always been fascinated with my adventures in television. And he was a huge help when I shot my first feature film; the set of a horror movie, like nothing he had seen as a Marin County architect. "Dude, You're Screwed" and his "brother-in-law," the executive producer, gave him some prison yard cred, or at least something other than shitty food to talk about.

But he does get teary, which makes me teary. He hugs me tight. He begins what becomes a mad war with pronouns whenever he talks to me or about me, that usually ends with "Shit! Sorry! God!" But hey, at least he knows why it's important to me. The point is, he's trying. He of course is smart enough to check in with his sister, Mylove. I'm happy that he's starting to treat her the way I always insisted they treat her. "Marce, hon, are you as okay with this as you seem?"

It's a point blank question, and though it's a bit harsh to be sidelined (I can't influence her answer), she chews a bit and says, "Well, I love her, and it's as odd for me to say this as it must be for you to hear it, but... when I look at her, I don't have to go through Scott, to see her."

Now, we're all teary.

My days home are a turn & burn operation. I leave in two days to prep the biggest project of the year for me. I've got to get it "pushed off from the dock," then fly home for the aforementioned biggest Christmas of our life, only to head back to Canada to produce the project. Yes, my other car is an airplane...

I've starting packing for the trip... and wardrobe... ah, yes wardrobe.

Even I'm getting tired of thinking about it. Because, I'm not settled. I can't get away with outdoorsy clothes. This broadcast is very formal, and I'll need to dress it up.

But I still worry that I will look silly as a girl. I have to be a dressy girl, and none of my clothes will be right. On any level.

Why this catastrophic breakdown during the season of light and joy? Because I have a new word, right? Dignity. I can't let us (Mylove and Me) down. I am horrified with looking like a dude in a dress. . . any girl's worst nightmare (okay, there are worse things, but I'm being dramatic to make a point). I am still afraid of what others might think. Where I'm going, I usually wear a coat and tie. Will I be able to pull off a woman's dressy look? I'm fine in big sweaters and tights, they hide more than they reveal... but where I'm going, professionalism is essential. What to do when testosterone has been building your body for four decades?

I don't want to be accused of merely "expressing myself" or just being "artistic"... I am a woman, and I'm not able to defend myself against judgment. I have no one to blame (once again) but MYSELF!!!! Now I'm judging myself for judging!

The truth is, I don't know how to step out of the desire to be me into the reality of being me. I've spent so long telling myself that this would never happen, that even as it is happening now, right in front of me, I still don't believe it. Holy shit! This, folks, is how the acid of denial can erode the foundation of your mental health.

This is why girls like me take refuge in dressing, make-up and hair; it gives us a distraction that feels like forward momentum without the self-introspection thingy that gets so messy. So what do I do? I have only three days before I leave. So, you guessed it – cook!

I am on fire: seven dozen Christmas Cookies, two batches each of Toasted Pinenut Toffee, Cranberry and Slivered Almond Bark, and Peppermint Candy Cane Bark. We're ready for "the goils," I'm speaking of Laurel & Elena, the angels in our life, the second most amazing couple on the planet. Mylove has wanted to tell them about me for weeks, but she waited so we could do it together. I'm walking up the stairs, I hope I look okay, nice blouse and slacks, hair up in barrette, and light make-up. Yes, they will love me, that's not in question, but will they take me seriously? Will they accept me as a woman? Do I accept me as a woman? We're about to find out, in just three-two-one... ta da!

They hug me, they hug Mylove. They hug me again. Their hugs are like swimming in warm chocolate chip cookie dough, sweet, nurturing, and home. They notice my clothes. Even wink at my make-up. They approve, but as I said, they are loving women, gracious and sweet.

They want to know everything. First, like everyone in our life, they want to make sure Mylove is all right, they take our love and marriage as seriously as we do. I serve maple glazed gingerbread cookies and toffee, and as I start all the way back at the beginning, they listen with rapt attention. As a newly married same-sex couple (ooh, so 2015, right?), they might know a thing or two about the journey we're suddenly on.

I exhale with the sheer relief of having cherished friends accept me. Mylove is better at telling my part than even I am, with keener insight into that which I have been unable or unwilling to see. And Laurel & Elena see it now, too, the deep cuts innocent children endure.

It becomes a rich and fruitful exploration of the paths we four have trodden to get here in each other's arms as adults. These two women are treasured, gentle and compassionate companions on this road called life, and I bask in the sisterhood that they openly share with such welcoming joy.

But the night is getting long and the ladies ask their last practical question. They know how important the project I'm about to leave to produce is to me. They know that even though I am the biggest and most exuberant fan, nay, "Queen of Christmas," I am still able to fly to another country to produce this broadcast.

They know that I "came-up" through live television; it's an addiction I just can't or won't shake – adrenaline and art is very powerful. Even though my career has veered off into adventure television, I still look forward to this once-a-year dose of "live." They know I can't be talked out of it. And they know that I will still make Christmas happen without missing a beat.

So when the goils ask, *"Well, what are you going to wear?"* you have an inkling of the weight of their question.

Mylove and I look to each other. If I have come to any conclusions since my packing tantrum this morning, she's all ears. I surprise her, as I actually have had some thoughts.

"This may sound strange… but I'm not planning on "coming out" at the production." Laurel & Elena sit back, slightly amused, letting me continue (more like watch me take enough rope to hang myself). But in fact, that's exactly what I DON'T want to do… "It isn't about me when I'm there. It's about the broadcast."

It's academic, it doesn't make sense on any planet to make a big deal of it. I won't be there that long, this crew only sees me once a year, *yada, yada* (I reason… okay, rationalize). And let's be real, girlfriend, formally informing anyone would require a quantum leap in my own acceptance of what and who I am, and right now, I'm just happy to be. . . okay, you got me there. . . whatever it is, I am.

Laurel & Elena smile when I confess, "Well, a turtle neck is a turtle neck and slacks are slacks, right? I can wear feminine clothes that are subtle and no one will really know the difference."

They challenge me, "And your earrings and hair?" I answer too fast,

"Everyone has already seen me like this, with long hair and earrings. I have become known for my barrettes, which lend a surprising air of formality to my hair." But I know what they are driving at, and they know what I am dodging.

So I make one last attempt, "I'll chalk it up to being "Hollywood Guy?""

They are so sweet as they shrug and smile and let me hang in the cold draft of denial. We laugh uncomfortably as we hug good night, "Well, we can't wait to hear how it goes…"

Me neither.

I get on the plane in two days, so it's a mad dash to slam all the kitchen prep I can, buy slacks and finish Christmas shopping (I'll have no time for that when I return), and I'm still catching up with friends I've neglected from a year on the road. They all know Christmas time is my catch-up time – no rest for the wicked! (My favorite musical. Color me green.)

We're going to see my "brother." There are only two men in my life who get this mantle, Ronny, my partner in my feature film, and Adam who's always on the road at Christmas time. I haven't seen Ronny and his lovely wife Val in months, since our anniversary party last spring. We agree to meet for Thai food. I'm sensibly dressed, my previously mentioned boat cut sailor tee and big hoop earrings.

But since we're meeting at a restaurant, I am not brave enough to wear make-up. I know I'm being weird! But I can't help it, not tonight. Of all people, it shouldn't matter with Ronny. I wore something similar when he hired me for a commercial we shot before I left for Alaska. But he didn't notice anything weird then, which figures. He really is "all boy" and even though he's the professional musician, I'm always the weird "experimental" one. He's rocking a dad's haircut and wardrobe. We're lucky if he wears shoes.

Val, on the other hand, is an actor and drop dead gorgeous, who can pull off leopard print tights and furry vest with no problem. I'm so jealous!

Dinner is great. I love these times with Ronny. Val, Mylove and I can "gang-up" on him and he just rolls over and takes it, as if we're tickling him. He is a very sweet man, quick to laugh, heart as huge as a Cadillac and supportive of just about everything I do. Val compliments my earrings and Ronny, whos never admits that he is surprised by anything, answers for me, "You had those for a while right?" I smile demurely and thank her for noticing my NEW earrings. Ronny challenges me, "No, I think you looked just like this when I saw you last." (Which is true. He saw me, but he didn't really get what he was seeing.) Mylove and I look to each other, and see Val register all of this, which is going to bite Ronny all the way home.

It does. In fact, my phone rings as we are walking in the door. Just as we predicted, Val has been interrogating Ronny all the way home, "What do you mean you don't know what's going on with Scottie? Are you blind?"

"Well, am I?" Ronny asks me with concern. So it's time for the chat. I sit down and I come out.

And, I learn another lesson for girls like us. Don't presuppose your best friend's (or anyone's for that matter) response. Ronny couldn't care less if I came out as purple; what upset him was that he felt that I didn't trust him with my news sooner. Never mind that I had come out to him even before I finished coming out to my own family; he still felt that by not telling him what I had endured in my life, I didn't trust him.

Now I didn't get to tell him at the time, nor would I, that I did have a good reason to check my swing. He seemed to forget that he had regaled me with tales of a doctor who was the father of a boy on Ronny's son's little league team. This doctor was smack in the middle of transitioning and was apparently not blessed with a very feminine physique. At over six feet tall, she drew more pity than respect in this white-bread enclave (my heart was breaking as he was telling me this!). She showed up at games to pick-up her son, and the whispers of a nasty divorce, surgeries and the "can you imagines?" would swirl around, despite the plastic smiles, as everyone talked behind her back, "how selfish is she? How could she put her own son through this?"

At the time, I tried to defend her saying that nobody had any idea what she was going through. Somehow, my Aegis defense system didn't kick in here. I guess it's because my Aegis crew knew Ronny would sooner see a leprechaun than he would my defense of the doctor as being my *own* issue. We would debate it till we were both blue in the face. (Like pretty much any subject for us – it's sorta how we talk.) He would always dismiss my opinion with, "you don't have kids." Apparently, according to my *bro* I would never understand why they were overlooking what she was going through, caring only about her son.

So, yes, I had a guess about how Ronny felt about the subject, but he showed me it's different when it happens to your brother (or in this case, as he now knows) his sister.

I love this man and he showed me that no matter what, he has my back. He pleaded his case: he was upset not because he was freaked out about me being his sister, but because he cared about me <u>as</u> his sister and he lost an opportunity to show his love. Taking notes out there? This is how it's done, folks.

We agreed that we needed to have coffee and talk this all the way through. And I owed him that. We would have to wait till after the new year, I still had to finish shopping and get on that plane.

12

HOLIDAY FLAIR

I'm here. The Great White North, just weeks before Christmas, a living Rockwell Christmas card – snow, frosted windowpanes and rosy cheeks. My head is always spinning when I return for this production. I love this crew – unlike my adventure crews, live production requires a crew that "plays nice" with others even when the red light says "on-air."

This production is always an adventure in adrenaline, with crew, equipment and logistics crashing headlong into the holidays that everyone is trying so hard to get to. I should note here that I use the word "production" as a noun here. And not just any noun; for me production is a state of mind and a sacred one at that. I have, since I studied this "avocation" in college, and later when I turned professional, regarded production to be the entire *experience* for both me and the audience. You cannot separate my molecular bonding with a mostly faceless entity known as "the audience" that I am in constant dialogue with in my head and heart before, during and after a production. It's an amazing experience that *is* my world.

One beautiful facet of this annual production is my being in the company of a loving, wise and sparkling crew that has come to love Mylove & me with incredible warmth. And unlike my reality work, I'm not the showrunner here – I can relax a little and "just produce." Okay, that's a bit factitious. There's no such thing as "just" an *anything* in production. But here I mean I've actually got a director who will be making the creative calls. I will focus on the technical execution – rather than my "usual." (Psst, there's no "usual" in production either). But, okay, when I'm a showrunner, my daily duties involve both directing and producing… whew, can I get back to what I was sayin'?) Every production creates its own family unit, but this family seems to hang together better than most. Maybe it's because it's always at the end of the year, and everyone is incredibly happy (filled with cheer?) as we work. It's here that I coined the term, "the Tarzan syndrome," because you literally swing from hug to hug trying to make your way down the corridors, every embrace the homecoming of a cherished friend. It is truly amazing.

I'm a bit of an enigma here. Just as with my blood family, to everyone here I'm the crazy Californian, the madman from Hollywood that just got back from some insane adventure in some remote part of the world.

I have some extra special friends that I can't wait to throw my arms around. Of course, every year I bring Christmas cookies and candy. I always take some time to make my rounds before I have to get serious; it's a tight schedule. I know that everyone is depending on me to bring this crew of over one hundred and fifty people together as a well-oiled machine in just three weeks. No pressure.

My first stop is Eva. This exquisite woman is in charge of hotel accommodations for the crew, and I use picking up my room key as an excuse to deliver her a hug and some cookies.

Eva is a brilliant, wickedly funny, stunning blonde. She uses her eyebrows like a Jedi light saber to cut the silliest notion to the quick, or probe your heart for the truth. I stand at the counter, waiting patiently for her to finish business with a woman until she sees me. She politely finishes then bursts through the swinging door to tackle me with a hug. She grabs my hands and drags me to a quiet place in the lobby, eyes thrusting into mine and without letting go of my hands, pulls me closer and whispers under her breath with a thick and sultry accent, "Girlfriend, what is this new look? You are gorgeous, darling, what is going on?" I'm speechless and her eyebrow goes in for the kill. It's too late to muster an excuse, she pins me to the moment.

Now, I'm not wearing anything special, just a black silk turtleneck, long rust sweater jacket and black flowing slacks. My hair is up in a silver barrette (semi-formal business attire) and I'm wearing sensible flats. I thought I was nondescript, but Eva, like most women, notices every little thing. So really, what did I expect?

I am caught off guard and Eva must feel bad for me, because she releases me from her steely gaze and instead hugs me again. I try to distract us both with cookies.

Okay, this is the part that nobody talks about with coming out: the awkwardness I feel as I try to share something with someone with whom I had a clean open line of understanding and communion. Suddenly, I'm questioning our years of working together; but they're only feeling a shift in the air that *is* my awkwardness, feeling me putting them on the other side of an invisible fence called "other."

But Eva is, as I've said, an amazing woman, and she senses my discomfort and makes me feel safe without words as we munch Christmas cookies. We hug goodbye with promises to have a lunch together, both of us knowing that very soon, I will "go dark," swallowed by the production; and that lunch might be just a nice thought.

After my time with Eva, I realize that I am not going about this properly. I have just gotten blindsided; I was obviously more obvious than I had thought. I need to get in front of this. I go straight to the director's office and sit down with the woman who is not only my dear friend, but technically my "boss" for this production.

Ruby and I have been working on this production for years. She is wife to my dear friend and fellow producer, Eli, and mother of an incredible girl, Emma.

Ruby and I are a great team. She is all mother energy. I am the petulant wild child. She's down to earth, I'm down to business.

So, it's not only responsible and professional to tell her what's going on with me as we prepare to launch the production, it's also smart. I know from running my own shows that communication is key. Plus, I could really use her counsel right now. I sit her down and tell all.

Of course, Ruby is wonderful, warm sweet and so delighted. Shouting "GOOD FOR YOU SISTER!" She's practically breathless as she tries to help me start running down this path to womanhood. She interrogates me for details. When did I know I was a girl? All my life? No way! How did I get through life this far? And how was Mylove with all of this? But bottom line, she's in my corner; actually, she's my biggest cheerleader. She jumps up to give me a huge hug, "This will be so much fun!"

Okay, a bigger reaction than I expected to be sure, but like I said, we're a great team and this (for her) explains so much. No wonder we've always seen eye-to-eye; no wonder we've always had each other's back without ever having to hear what back we were backing. We are sisters.

This is also a reaction that will be a trend among many of the women I respect the most. They all feel when they hear about me, that it seems so obvious, that they can't believe that they missed it. But now that they know, it explains so much.

Ruby has all of these ideas of what I should buy and what to do to solve my beauty challenges. What about my wardrobe, what am I going to wear? I should take a page from her play book. She's not a girlie-girl, she's a woman, and I listen to all of her opinions. She's like the woman I want to be, one that loves hanging with boys, but is a lady through and through.

Still, I need to pinch myself. I have surrounded myself with incredible, enlightened and loving people. Of course they will not only understand and support me, but they will also cheer me on.

Even if I am only taking baby steps at this point, I don't need to hurry, thank God, cuz I've got a production to run. I relate my experience with Eva, and Ruby has me stand in order to carefully scrutinize my attire. Yeah, she can see why Eva was able to "clock me" (she's so hip!).

She asks if I'm wearing make-up right now. I hesitate, "Yes, some brown mascara and a little brown eyeliner, but if you can't tell, then..."

She shakes her head, "that's sorta the point sister, you want to enhance your natural beauty." She digs into her purse and finds her Bobbi Brown lip gloss. "This is the stuff girl, elegant, but the perfect color for you. A gift."

Later that day, at dinner, I see an open space at a table with three men who always love to hear my adventure stories. As I approach, I recognize two other women sitting with them; one is a dear friend, that I know outside of this production; Jayne has her back to me, so she hasn't seen me yet.

I sneak up to give her a kiss hello on the cheek, and OOPS! I think I've scared her! She looks at me with confusion, then screams in surprise! I quickly try to diffuse the situation, but she's too embarrassed and goes into her own damage control, saying that she didn't recognize me in the MASCARA AND EYELINER AND HAIR BARRETTE AND NAIL POLISH!

It's as if she has Tourette's, and we both step back and try to collect ourselves. The men graciously change the subject back to the manly subject of survival television and Jayne finishes her dinner.

After some time, the men excuse themselves with hugs and bid goodnight. I wait until they are out of earshot, then look at Jayne with disbelief. She immediately apologizes, "I am sooo sorry, but you startled me, I didn't know what was going on, and, and, and... " We both break into uncontrollable laughter.

What can I say, really? I don't want to lie to anyone, don't want anyone to lie for me, and really, I have no idea what I am, in fact, doing. I am just slowly wresting control from my brain and letting my heart take a turn at the wheel.

The next day we're in Ruby's office. She's all business as she lays out the points we need to nail down before I head home for Christmas. Then she stops and looks at me, clearly disappointed, *"Hey, where's your flair?"*

I am dressed in pants and a black sweater, I've got my hair down today and I confess to "pulling back" a bit. I tell her all about dinner with Jayne the night before. It scared me. "Maybe," I say, "I should just chill out." Ruby busts me immediately, but I protest. I've got much more than my appearance to worry about; my reputation is on the line here, and I admit I'm losing control. Me, the Zen master, samurai production warrior, the dependable one in our crazy production tribe, is way off my game. Not good. I start to cry. *"Ruby, something is breaking loose."*

She hugs me, "Breaking loose or breaking free?" Change is never easy, even when it's right. I dry my tears. But I have to know: why did Jayne see what Ruby had not? Ruby grabs my shoulders and stares right into me.

"Do you want this or not? Cuz I don't really care how you look; I want you to be happy. That's it. Nothing more. If that comes because you're more authentic, then sister I'm here. And if it's not, then sister, I'm still here. I see a happy you. Do that, do more of that. Jayne saw a happy you too, but she hasn't had the benefit of hearing from your lips *why"* (you were happy).

I try to breathe. Authentic. That's everyone's favorite word about this subject. I only know what it's like to "act" authentically without allowing myself or anyone else to cross my fortress walls. This word needs some refinement, because it sounds like girls like me were in-authentic before; as if we have been trying to fool the world, masquerading as men. This makes us sound like treacherous people that can't be trusted and puts everything we say into question for the rest of our lives. It's difficult for non-trans people to get this, but we only know survival mode. Many of us are in real fear for our lives. Even with those we love, we've developed a skill to "ignore" our own feelings (to our spiritual demise) as we live up to the expectations of others. BUT only because we love you. We aren't trying to pull over anything on anyone, we just don't have schools for trans-integration.

So this "authentic" of which you speak... If it's the word that describes finally living the way that demonstrates who we are, then authentic it is.

With Ruby's pep talk, I get a wake-up call; people *are* noticing a change in me. And they want me to be happy. So happy it will be.

I realize I need to do the right thing for the same reasons (at least on the surface) that I tell Ruby. I will need to tell Cristina, the studio executive, and another dear friend. We agree that we should "read-in" Cristina, but the rest of the crew can remain on a need to know basis.

However, something switches. I realize now that I feel like I'm hiding by NOT wearing make-up. So bizarre! I decide to "freshen up" at the lunch break, just enough to add a little sparkle. And *voilà ... there's my flair.*

Soon the rest of the crew will be arriving and we have much to do, chiefly welcoming them!

We decide to go into town for lunch to pick-up Christmas trees! As the senior members of the production, we want to set a good example, and we all decide a little Christmas cheer is in order. Ruby and I whisper: is this the right time to read-in Cristina? We giggle, time will tell.

First some lunch. We sit in a restaurant looking at the menus, and we hear the waitress ask, "What can I get you ladies?" Ruby kicks me under the table, giddy that I've been recognized as who I truly am, but Cristina doesn't notice it (maybe she didn't hear the waitress?). Ruby and I can't stop giggling. But still, the time ain't right to tell Cristina.

We buy four trees, some decorations and head back to spread our Christmas cheer. Every moment is filled with laughter and joy as we set off our Christmas bomb! Everyone gets inspired, and suddenly the production office hall's have been decked, but still there's been no time that feels right for a chat with Cristina.

Cristina excuses herself to get some paperwork done. Ruby gives me the high sign: now's my chance. I bring cookies and bark to her office. I sit down, "Is now a good time for a personal conversation?"

She shuts off her computer and gives me her full attention. Cristina, as I've said, is a dear friend. She has the sophistication of a baroness, slim and stately, a liberated Latina, the kind who will rule the world one day. Having thrown off the constraints of her very Mexican up-bringing, she wears her hair very short in a boyish cut and rarely wears any make-up, but she doesn't have to – her classic, graceful features would make any painter cry for the opportunity to immortalize. She's married to Johnny, another one of my dear friends, an engineer.

And they, love, love, love my wife. We have had great times together in their home and ours.

They know me (or at least, they thought they did), well. And that's why my news is blowing Cristina's mind.

She is always the mask of cool. Unflappable, Cristina's the serene, unattached counterpoint to her intense husband, Johnny. She pledges (of course) to support and love me. But it's her hug that floors me – sweet, really sweet, sweeter than I've ever had from her before. She confesses that she always wondered why, since we were good friends, that there was a "thing," an invisible wall, between us. Now she knows it was a wall that I confessed to building.

It was time to turn-in, but I needed a walk in the cold December air. One thing that's hard when I'm on the road is my "goodnight kiss" call to Mylove. This has been a big day, and... yes, I'm excited!

I bring Mylove up to speed about Ruby and Cristina, but, she already knows! True to form, Cristina called Mylove as soon as I left her office. She loves us both and wanted to check in and make sure things were cool with her too.

This makes me feel really good. That our friends care for us that much is a beautiful gift. But Cristina and Mylove covered some ground that I didn't expect. My enthusiasm and joy for make-up and all things girlie (even though I've been subtle here) has Cristina wondering why she herself is so conservative. She had thought herself hip and sophisticated but admits that she has allowed herself to choose darker, less feminine pant suits and un-hip business attire for her executive wardrobe. Both Mylove and Cristina agree that I've inspired them to lighten up a little.

I'm speechless out here under the December night, starlight glistening off the snow, the spirit of Christmas singing in the pines.

The next day, again at lunch, my dear friend, Pam, who always gives me a hard time, stops me and says, "Are we allowed to ask what's going on

73

with you?"

Here we go again. Who do I think I'm fooling? Before you answer that, know that my hair is standing on end, I know I'm skating on borrowed ice. Pam is loved by both Mylove and me, having watched over our marriage like a great aunt. I never hesitate to tell her how I feel since she never hesitates to tell me what she thinks. I tell her to "step into my office," we take a seat in the dining room, and I come out to her.

She asks the question that everyone wants to know, "Where is this going?" My explanation (or rather deflection), sounds lamer in my own ears with each telling, and Pam merely shrugs. "I'm sure you'll figure it out," and she bids goodbye. I wish I had her confidence.

I find myself searching for one of the consulting producers for the production. Dee Dee and I share a special connection: stand-up comedy. We often make each other laugh by reciting only the punchlines from our favorite comedians. People think we're crazy. We have become close over these years, I can always depend on her for two things; a good hug and a light, clear heart, and right now, I could use a little of both.

I ask her if we can talk about something personal and we agree to meet for a cuppa' tea after rehearsal tonight.

It's great, sweet, and, as I hoped, *light* – the perfect setting for me to come out. I relate my encounter with Pam to Dee Dee. She asks, "Well? Have you? Have you figured it out?"

Now… You would think by now this should be almost academic for a girl like me. Except, I ain't a girl like me, yet. Or at least, I haven't really declared that I am, out loud, to anyone but my immediate family and no more than a mere handful of my closest friends. So… no, I haven't figured it out. I suppose, playing Philadelphia Lawyer here (thanks Pop) that the reason why I haven't figured out "where this is going" is because all I've ever thought about is the destination, never the journey. Yes, I've read countless accounts (is that even possible?) of girls before me who KNEW where they were going AND how to get there. And since I haven't ever really done that, I guess it's easy to hang-out in the relative safety of indecision and obscurity. No one will challenge me (not even God) if I just don't do or say anything, right? Sure, I *will* figure it out (where this is going), but right now, I've got only so many gray cells left to allocate, and besides, keeping it in the future tense gives me more time to *not* deal.

Right? Because that's been working so well for me.

She smiles as she stirs her tea and waits for me to catch up in the silence. Okay, I get it, that's the second time I've been asked if I know where this is going in less than twenty minutes. "Okay God. I'm… listening. I swear."

I start to plead my case to Dee Dee. I say I hadn't really given myself time to collect my thoughts; I've been crazy busy these last few years. "I'm not sure where this is all going or even where I want it to go…" But she stops me in my tracks.

"You can't know what you're doing or where you're going yet, so stop fooling yourself. I find that writing things down, makes it real, and somehow manageable. Why don't you write it all down, write what you're going through? That much you do know."

Write it down? What, like a grocery list? Okay, Dee Dee, my dear, I did mention that I've been going through this my entire life? Dee Dee must be able to hear my thoughts, (either that or I'm wearing my cellophane mask again) because she smiles reassuringly, "Like a letter, you know, doesn't have to be formal."

"Hmm, well," I say, trying to scrub any sarcasm from my tone, "and who am I writing to, God?"

She sips her tea, "If you like."

Of course. So simple. She's right. I'll write a letter to God.

We finish our tea and laugh a little more, and she offers her ear or shoulder anytime. I go straight to my office and start writing.

I feel only a little, I dunno, maybe, "Duh?" I often write letters to God. It's a good exercise. A grand and glorious, sometimes horrifying look into your own heart. You might be able to fool yourself some of the time, but you can't fool God any of the time, right?

But (God close your ears, please) this is a letter I have put off for years because I had no clue how to say in writing what I have said aloud in prayer and in my heart every day for close to forty-five years. My gender identity has been in my prayers since I first learned the words, "Now, I lay me..." I've prayed to wake up in my right body. When that didn't happen, I prayed to get "it" out of my life forever. When that didn't work, I prayed for strength. I don't pray for success, that's up to me. I don't pray for parking places, that's *not* up to me.

If you take out this one little detail (not being in the right body), I have had a very blessed life and so, sometimes, it didn't feel right to keep asking God for something that, apparently, wasn't going to happen. I have expressed gratitude for constant blessings, for Mylove, and appreciation for the Grace for every event in my life, from the passing of my parents to the birth of nieces and nephews. And general thanks for sunrises, my creativity and... life.

So it feels weird to be actually, finally, writing this letter.

I put aside misgivings and write from my heart, telling God everything. It is full disclosure. I need to settle this now and get back to the reason I'm here. I don't waste time with the obvious, like why, even though I have told many people about me, do I feel I need to write God in the first place? Why, if I have made the strides with Mylove, do I think there's more to do? Be? Or say? Why am I not standing fully in my heels? Why am I holding back? I don't spend time on any of these questions; I tell God only what

I've been going through. I take it very seriously. I am focused and clear for the first time in years. And I don't mince words, I don't pull punches and I lay it all out.

I finish and turn out the light at 2:00 a.m. and go to bed.

I am too tired to really realize what I have done. It feels great, liberating, and, frankly... I don't know what I expected, but I feel... I dunno, complete somehow. But I don't really have any time to process everything before I am asleep. At least, I think I slept, because when the alarm rings, all I know is that... I never changed into my pajamas!

I shower, almost forgetting that I spent the night writing and, within an hour, I'm back in the thick of preparations. Things are really heating up as we try to get the technical logistics worked out before the Christmas break.

More crew is arriving. Among these are my friend, Ray, and his beautiful wife, Roberta. Ray has been my "go-to guy" since our days on my children's show, that is, *when I can get him* (which is getting rarer and rarer these days). He's more than the skilled DP (director of photography), he's the steady ballast to my gale force creativity, and he's helped me navigate the rocky shoals between creativity and a ten-hour production day.

We each celebrate the marriages we have to the women we love with almost every breath. In fact, our names for each other are Roberta's Boy and Mylove's Boy – "Hey Roberta's Boy, when did you get in?" "Hey Mylove's Boy, late last night." So no, coming out isn't going to be easy. Of course, he's going to be lovely and supportive and, as with every guy friend that I come out to, I don't want our friendship to change, even as I'm asking it to grow. But this is more than a casual dude friendship; it's another place where the "me" I let him know is only the surface, and an armored one at that. Whereas Ray has let me know the whole him, surface and all. This is why people feel cheated when anyone comes out. They think they've been as open as they could be and expected the same from us. When we aren't, well, who wouldn't feel cheated? All I can say is life has layers.

I am right about Ray and Roberta, but as usual, my aim is a bit low. Roberta has her MA in social work, and of course she would know more about this subject than I, Duh! They are beautiful and warm as I tell them my story, and we celebrate a deepening of our friendship. Then it is time to get back to work.

I cannot underestimate the good fortune of having these people in my life. I am being received with love and it's making me stronger. I cannot imagine what life would be like without this. There are enough horror stories of what trans people face to make anyone seriously question their resolve to take that step out of the closet. (like we had a choice, HA!) But the lesson here is that love is the necessary power that will make life joyous for all involved. And the side effects are amazing.

As I float back to my room on the love and support of this great family,

I decide to call Mylove. The night is so gorgeous that I decide to walk the path behind the hotel that leads into the woods. Street lamps glow with Christmassy light and the crust on the snow is a sparkly diamond-like surface. Magic is in the air!

The path becomes a wide walking boulevard. The canopy of trees overhead opens up, and then it's only stars. I carry on for twenty minutes to Mylove like a teenage girl in love with everyone and the universe. She's far away, not in distance, but emotionally. And I finally catch the cold breeze in her voice. And then it hits me like a sudden winter wind when she says: "I just can't get over this feeling. Every time I ask you what you did when you were so-called exploring in New York and Denver, you never told me what you were actually doing, who you were doing it with, and did you…"

Did I what? I can feel the wonderful glow that I've been wallowing in like a vat of pure maple syrup suddenly drain away. I'm left cold and shivering. She's suddenly *not okay* with this, with me. With "it." With "she."

She is silent, then, "I'm sitting in the office furniture display at Staples." It's a picture that slams headlong into my Canadian Christmas Card fantasy. My wife, is so distraught and determined to stab her stake in the sand that she can't even wait another moment, even if one of the most searing questions in her mind has to be handled here and now, while she swivels feverously back and forth in her plastic wrapped executive chair with office supply shoppers milling about.

I know this because it was just spat through the phone at me, like a twisted play-by-play description – this is how we let each other know just how serious we are…

A switch trips in me and I go ballistic, as in ICBM ballistic, like nuclear warhead ballistic; how dare she bring me down! My Aegis system has been down for days and the crew is getting ready for holiday leave when the sirens wail to battle stations! They scramble up the steel rungs to the bridge of the war room.

But come on, girlfriend! Surely, you are better than this! I catch myself. I struggle to avoid an emotional nuclear war.

I hear myself ask in a very calm voice, "What are you actually wanting to hear from me right now?"

It dawns on me before she even answers. She wants to hear the unedited, unembellished, and un-sanitized account of my explorations for once.

For me, those early times "out" are not only a lifetime ago, they are embarrassing. I'm not far enough away from them to see my adventures as innocent or naïve or a misunderstanding of who I thought I was and what I thought I wanted. It still hurts to even think about. How could I have been so… silly, is the only word that fits.

I can hear that she cannot move on until she gets this. She's resentful that she has to ask, mad at herself for having to draw this line in the sand, mad at me for pushing her to this point. But there it is. Now that she's out on this limb, the only way around is through.

The Aegis battery crew is given the order to stand down; we will unconditionally surrender. I say, "Please don't make me repeat this ever again, because I'm only going to say this once, so listen carefully." And I tell her of going out overdressed as a woman to clubs and never feeling that it was fun, and seeing various versions, diversions and levels of girls like me *and* the rare times where I met someone inspiring, but mostly mundane and sometimes downright tragic and. . .

. . . and it isn't what she is asking to hear at all!

I stand there under the stars, suddenly alone – like I am drifting on a piece of ice that has just had been cut off from the land. Her silence is a roar in my ear. I struggle to get my bearings, "What do you want, then?" And she asks in a voice that is afraid of the answer:

"I have to know. . . did you... have... sex?"

This is her burning question? The one that threatens to engulf our whole marriage, our whole life, in a bonfire of chaos?

Suddenly my inner sky lights up, not by fire, but by brilliant light. That's it? All of the crap and confusion and hurt feelings that have crept in like a nest of maggots into our love can be washed away forever with the true answer to this question?

She isn't questioning whether I am a woman, but rather if I had stepped out of the sanctity of our vows!

I started to laugh with relief, "Oh god, no! Oh my god, if nothing else, it confirms even more how unbelievably blessed I am to have you! Not that I ever needed that, but. . . there."

I admit to her that I had been approached by men at these clubs, and engaged in that first level of "flirting" that is the good natured boy-girl sparring. But each time I was utterly blown away by the arrogance and (okay, without sounding like a stuck-up bitch) stupidity that passed for "pick-up lines." I was dismayed, not for me, but for all women. Is this really what it's like? Please tell me that guys don't really believe that any of those lines actually work.

To the guys who seemed redeemable, I turned those flirtations into dating seminars, coaching them on their approach. Some listened well, others, who clearly saw that I wasn't swinging their way, would cut their losses and move on. I wasn't sure who I was most sad for, the girls who had to endure these clods, or the clods who actually had no idea how bad they were. And of course, the worst would be the girl who went home with them.

But I wasn't looking to go home or anywhere with anyone. I am married and more than happy, I'm in love. After all our years together, I don't even care what else is out there. This was never what was going on. Finally, I could say that flat out, with no blur at all to Mylove. Why hadn't I thought to do this before? Do I blame it on the Aegis crew who shot it out of the sky? Or is it that it was never a threat because it was never a threat.

But it changes everything. The fog and storm on the distant horizon lifts. Mylove's last question answered, she too can stand down her own Aegis crew.

We both go to bed and sleep soundly, cuddling across time and space. We have just "one more sleep" before I will be in her arms for Christmas

13
(FINALLY) HOME FOR CHRISTMAS

Home, and what a blur! I'm celebrating love with more love. Oh, and cooking! It's a winter storm of pots and pans, sauces, dressings, sweets and savories. Christmas Eve is always a massive affair. But this year, Mylove's brothers and nieces, Sophie and Rosemary, will sit down with some of the usual suspects – Laurel & Elena, Don & Juanita, Duncan and Mark for our annual feast. A total of 12 for a formal five course extravaganza.

I've already spoken to Dáre (Mylove's baby brother) about the changes I'm going through. And he in turn, has prepared the girls to meet "me." He told his daughters straight up, then asked what they should do. His girls didn't miss a beat "Exchange the Christmas gifts you already got for something a woman wants?" Amazing!

Then began a round of "pre calls" with the rest of the guests, Don, Juanita, Duncan and Mark were all given a heads-up. I didn't want to blindside anyone; tonight is too important to me. I'm pulling out all the stops on a night where I have never held back except, of course, on me.

Tonight I will finally look like the me that only I have ever really seen. For this Christmas Eve, I will shine!

I've got a ton left to do and the guests will be here in two hours! I'm looking good (in more ways than one!). Been cooking since I got back three days ago: more cookies, more candy, and a gallon of marinara sauce that I've been nurturing along like a mother hen for days. I've got the feast on track.

It's a tradition that Mylove and I have honed over twenty years. What started as a night of revelry with friends and an eclectic menu has been refined to a now classic menu in a grand setting. A glorious Christmas gift from Mylove & me to our closest friends. But tonight I must confess, I'm giving this gift to us too.

For Mylove, every little thing will be in homage to Christmases past, just like she had as a child with her brothers in Massachusetts. And for me, even though my childhood was amazing, (except for that boy thingy) this will be the Christmas that never was.

Ever since I saw Stanley Tucci's film "The Big Night," my life (and

Christmas Eve) has forever changed. The center-piece of the seminal scene is a dish called Timpano. Legend has it that it's Stanley's mother's family recipe. A beautiful pasta dish baked inside a crust that looks like a timpani drum. Incredibly dramatic for an elegant affair, it's sliced into wedges, with each layer of pasta, cheese and sauce revealed. I have made this for over 20 years now, alternating different shapes and colors of fresh pasta with smoked cheeses, homemade marinara sauce, even a pesto for that bright green flair. It usually takes everyone's breath away (just like in the movie), and Christmas Eve veterans of our table look forward to it all year long.

It's not for the faint of heart to make and, like all big dinners, everything's on the line. It's the crown jewel in a feast that starts with homemade hors d'oeuvres, moves on to a Caesar salad made with homemade croutons and tossed with all the traditional ingredients (sans anchovies, we got some vegetarians in the crowd), then on to the antipasto platters (marinated and grilled Italian vegetables in Christmas spices). With the main attraction, I serve a four-story pyramid of chicken and pinenut meatballs that have been rolled in powdered chanterelle mushrooms, sausage and peppers, and a cedar planked salmon encrusted with whiskey, onion, caper and nutmeg.

Yes, it's food porn. And for dessert this year, I'll be serving homemade eggnog ice cream on top of warm figgy pudding.

So, yes, I've been working hard and, for once, my timing is impeccable. I even have time to change without sweating because tonight, I'm wearing a skirt. My family will see me the way I have always dreamed of looking for my favorite night of the year. I bought it last July, a birthday present to myself, imported from Scotland. But I have to pinch myself. I never dreamed at that time that I'd be able to wear it for this Christmas, or that I'd be, in any way, in a place where it's not just okay, it's almost expected!

Because ever since I finished my letter to God, I've felt stronger, more confident in showing the world (okay the world is easy, it's my family I'm worried about) that I am a woman. Still, tonight I am, as I've said, pulling out all the stops. I'm not even stopping to marvel at why (maybe I'm afraid that this wonder woman confidence will ebb away?). But whatever it is, it's working. I'm not holding back, and I even have some extra sparkle.

I look in the mirror. I look like a woman. Tonight I'm not critiquing my anything and, where I need a little more (of anything), I add it. I'm not garish in any way, I may actually be getting good at this.

OOPS! I've forgotten the croutons in the oven! I run upstairs, not quite ready to be seen by anyone, but I can't care as I open the oven. Whew! Saved just in the nick. OUCH!

Nick is right – I BREAK A NAIL! NOT TONIGHT!

I slam the oven in pain and frustration as Dáre and his daughters are coming through the front door. I hide my anguish and hug them hello.

Welcome, set your stuff down, don't look at me yet, and I excuse myself and run downstairs. What to do? It's that bad, worse than a Wes Craven horror movie. It looks like I broke my finger, the pain dies quickly, but the fingernail is a shattered, splintered mess. Seriously, this will not do tonight of all nights. I've been waiting a lifetime for tonight.

So, I throw on some jeans and a sweater and slip upstairs and pull Mylove into a quiet corner, "Please don't judge me," I say, lower lip trembling, "but I've got to go get this fixed." Something in my voice and eyes triggers all of her compassion. She's not a girlie-girl at all, I'm the "birthday cake" in the family. But she knows how much I have riding on tonight; and after asking if there's anything she can do (nothing, it's all on track), she says she'll cover for me, but hurry!

I'm back almost before they miss me. I slip back into the last stages of prep before show time, then disappear to get dressed <u>again</u> for dinner.

Remember, my skirt is not just any skirt but a genuine wool tartan mini kilt. And it's in my clan tartan. I'm an obnoxiously proud Scotswoman about my lineage, which is none other than the king who established Scotland's independence from England, Robert the Bruce. (Tonight, I will put aside that I'm one-third Irish, and a quarter Scottish, oh, and Finnish, Polish, and Swedish.) For those of you not hip to how crazy we Scots are about our sometimes garish plaids, just google "tartan" and you'll be lost for days. This is something I've wanted ever since I discovered that they can also be made for women; and the "mini" version is a super cute, very flattering way of showing off your legs, er, I mean your clan's colors. And it requires nice hose and high heels, what's not to love? To complete the picture, my hair is up in a sterling silver barrette. Hey, I look Christmassy! And damn if I don't look pretty.

Now is the moment of truth. I can hear that everyone has arrived while I've been downstairs primping, and though I hadn't planned on making an entrance – here we go.

I actually get hoots and hollers and "dayams." Mylove breaks through the hoopla and plants a huge kiss and hug on me. It marks this moment in time, forever.

Dinner is a huge success and I've blown the minds and palates of Mylove's family. Oh, and my kilt is a hit and everyone (including fellow Scotsman, Mr. Sinclair) welcomes this presentation of me with warm and loving arms. These dear friends, if they had an issue with my new outer wrappings, would have it surgically removed. Make no mistake, they are surprised; shocked even. But as I hope the rest of the world learns to do, they follow Mylove's lead and rewire our connections from *their* side. Love is love. How blessed am I?

Nobody wants to go to bed this night, least of all me. But Christmas is only beginning. After the last of our guests leave, it's a slumber party with

Mylove's brothers and nieces. I'm lighter and my face is frozen in a permanent smile. But, I've got apples to chop for our traditional Christmas Morning breakfast (Apple Chowder – see what I mean? This is the Super Bowl of food!)

Breakfast is on track and the last presents are just now wrapped. I am so happy, I'm buzzing! Exhausted as I should be, I don't want to miss a moment of the giddiness of being me! But it is Christmas Eve, and I know the rules. If I don't go to bed, Santa will just pass us by. I have to leave it to my brothers to put together a very special present that Santa got for Mylove: a vintage electric train set to go around the Christmas tree, just like she used to have as a little girl. That should keep the boys occupied until morning.

Which comes not soon enough, despite the exhaustion that has crept into my bones. Mylove and I have both been like this since childhood; sleep is what you do on days other than Christmas. It only comes once a year and through our entire marriage, we have always woken up just before sunrise, too excited to get the Christmas day started!

FINALLY – It's Christmas morning, and I give Mylove's brothers the agreed upon signal: start the train! I let Mylove climb the stairs to the living room first. The train's whistle greets her and tears form in her eyes. She turns to me, scorching me with her joyful smile – that's all the present I need!

We tear into stockings first, McVickar family rules! (The Maddens would never stand for that!) But in deference to Mylove and her family, we're going by their traditions; then coffee, and then, and only then, can we tear into presents! By this time anticipation is at a fever pitch!

It turns out that Mylove has been plotting for today as much as I have, and she's bought me two very feminine blouses and made me some fantastic earrings. I am overjoyed! She is celebrating my femininity with each gift, not holding back.

My nieces are amazing with me, treating me like a long lost aunt, and give me all kinds of advice, help me pick outfits for the day and curl up with me like girlfriends. We all bask in the warmth of a fire in the hearth, a beautiful tree, Christmas music and love. I am home. As a woman.

Dáre tries more than a few times to let me know how much he supports me. He, like Macky, "pre-apologizes" for messing up pronouns in the future, "It's going to take me a while to get it. It's just habit." But then he says something that utterly breaks my heart – in fact, it really pisses me off. He confesses that he always hated what I did for Mylove (his sister, mind you), not because it wasn't the most romantic stuff he's ever heard or seen (my Valentines I described were just the tip of the romantic iceberg), but because it made every other guy's life hell. How were they supposed to live up to the bar that I'd set? Their wives would always compare their acts to mine and frankly, they just stopping trying. But now they knew the truth – of course, I could out romance them, I was a chick! They could finally relax.

I am apoplectic! What the…? How could that be the result? I tell him I weep for the women in their lives – and I pray he isn't serious. I've shown that it's possible to show your affection in meaningful ways. That's the takeaway – at least for his own daughters, that someone should make them the center of their universe!

Luckily, that is the extent of our debates – the rest is just that wonderful, cinnamon and peppermint flavored creamy love. There's nothing better. And it's over way too soon.

If anyone had told me a year ago that I would be celebrating my favorite time of year as the woman I am, I'd have thought them nuts (wonderful, but crazy, all the same). But I did it. Comfortable enough around my family to be me for a short time. And it's having an odd effect. . . I won't even allow myself to think about the clock striking midnight when Cinderella has to lose the glass slipper.

Oh, and stop me if you've heard this one: I'm on a red-eye... again. Heading north, again! This was the Christmas that was, and I've got to hit the ground running. But for the next few hours, I'm just going to sit here and glow.

Yeah, girlfriend, you go ahead and close those baby blues. You have no idea how much life has changed while you were away.

14
THUNDERBOLT

And we're back! I've been flying through the night (oh, that's why they call it a red-eye), arriving back on location for breakfast. It's as if I never left. I am dressed a little more conservatively than my Christmas Eve wardrobe. (Ha!) My make-up is scaled way back to almost nothing but for some hastily applied mascara in the airplane bathroom and some neutral lip-gloss. It seems that all I journal about these days is make-up and food. Well, honey, what else is there? (Oh, yeah, life!)

I've been trying to document how my <u>mind</u> is changing (despite hanging on for dear life) while my life evolves. As much as I think I've opened up at this point, my appearance is the real indicator of my inner achievement. The more comfortable I am "presenting" myself to the world, the more I'm comfortable pushing the envelope.

I still have no idea how my crew (let alone the world) really feel about the newer packaging of me, and I'm not strong enough yet to not care what they think, especially as I stand in their presence. It's disheartening to realize that as much as I want this (being a woman), I still haven't grabbed the reins tightly.

This may be hard for anyone to understand. For many of us, (i.e. transgender) it's not cut and dried. That we are sure of *who we are* is not the question, but *how to be who we are*, has never been okay in our lives – with anyone. It's the reason we have such a huge trench to climb out of. We never had peer support, teaching or coaching. There wasn't a class in high school that teaches how to change the world's current perception of you to the one you are just now brave enough to declare. We watch those before us get cut down, shut down, and we think, "How can I endure that?" And, "There's got to be a better way." What the world (naively) says over and over again (just read any blog comments about high-profile transitions, from Renée Richards to Chaz Bono) is that this is a *choice* for us, and a bad one at that. Hello. It's not a choice. Not a choice. Who would ever choose derision, discrimination or any other negative word that starts with "d?"

At this point, I'm still keeping my mind from trying to take control, protecting my heart's shot at steering this ship. But that comes with a price; it makes the mind a hostage, again! (It's been doing a good job at holding itself hostage all its life – it doesn't need my help!) And though my mind is still zip-tied to the captain's chair, duct tape over its mouth, nothing can stop it from observing everything, judging everything and waiting until it gets its crack at the tiller once again.

Who's got time for a tug-of-war between the heart and mind? We've got just five days to complete our prep. The broadcast goes out LIVE (I love that adrenaline!) and things are looking good.

It's after breakfast, and I'm inspecting all the work that was done while I was away, walking the cable runs, making sure the miles of internet and cables are safe and secure... I actually use this time to let my mind settle into the environment. I am in the back of the production space. How many times have I been "here" – backstage, "hanging back" behind the scenes to produce an experience for the audience "out" at the other end of all my cables.

As I check the work done in my absence, I am absorbed in my own thoughts. It's only slightly amazing that I am capable of maintaining a handle on the massive amount of technical tasks yet to be completed while simultaneously being consumed with the nuances of creating the best experience for the audience. I and my brethren are genetic mutants that are capable of both science <u>and</u> magic of live production. It's the same skill, I realize, that has helped me live a relatively happy life while simultaneously being trapped in the dungeon of my own creation.

And like a pilot using peripheral vision to see objects that are invisible when stared directly at, I catch something out at the corner of my consciousness… and that's when it hits me…

A thunderbolt of clarity.

A white flash of confidence and understanding vaporizes the walls of my self-imposed fortress. Sunlight of reality floods my inner vision.

As long as I hang back in my life, the rest of the world will follow my lead. If I am "upfront" with everyone, they will also follow my lead. They will accept me when I accept me.

I have no idea in this moment that this thunderbolt has shattered forever my enslavement to being something, someone, I am not. I realize I have no idea how long I've been standing here. I catch my breath.

What to do next? What any self-respecting girl would do. I call Mylove. I am so excited I can't even make sense and have to explain it three times. Finally, she is able to glean what has happened. We bid each "ciao" (we never say goodbye it hurts too much) and I make my way back to the set.

And as I try to remember how to operate these things called feet, I realize… God must have gotten my letter.

Things are humming along nicely – and so is my head! I need to get myself together. I go and sit with Ruby to get my feet back on the ground and she can see and feel how the earth has shifted beneath my feet. She hugs me to calm me down. Okay sister, get it together; we've got a broadcast to produce.

The remainder of the set-up seems to flow effortlessly, everything finished smoothly and on time.

I take my epiphany to heart in all aspects of my life and start by getting "upfront" with my crew. I had crafted a loud and glorious Scott, one that many people were in love with. Even when he was getting on their nerves, his devotion, passion and skill would shine brighter than his brash ways. He was, apparently, fun for my friends to hang around and was well liked. I assure them that none of that will be lost, even though I may tone down the brashness if that's okay.

I should point out, however, that it isn't all peaches and posies. Not everyone is cool with me. Some are understandably taken aback, some so surprised when they realize that the woman they just held the door open for or smiled at them from across the buffet line was, in fact, me.

This is, I confess, a little weird for me. Not as dramatic as Jayne's Tourette's, but still, I've surprised some very old friends, mostly men, with my new me.

I am coming down a hallway when I surprise one of the production managers. He looks up at the last moment (lost in thought), and realizes he's about to plow into me like a linebacker! He ducks his shoulder just in time and is about to mumble an apology for knocking me into next week when his mind's recognition software must've finished booting up. He interrupts his own apology and, suddenly going silent, puts his head down and continues to charge past. I can only imagine that his operating system crashed, and he had no idea what to say.

This isn't the first time, but a situation I will face many times I'm not sure if it's because some people don't recognize me at first, then suddenly do, or that I get "read" or "clocked" as a guy who's suddenly dressed in women's clothing.

But the prize for the best double is actually a tie between Travis and Mick. Both have known me for years. Neither recognized me, which is a bit disorienting. I'm still on the fence whether it's a good sign or not. At least, my make-up is on straight, or is it? (Some people ignore you when you've got spinach in your teeth.)

That neither recognized me starts to get to me the further I got from either incident. We have stayed in touch outside production; this is not just a casual relationship. We're practically family.

Both men are "guys' guys," and neither is ready for the girlie-girl that they just met. With Travis, it starts with a wink and smile as I look up from the buffet line and notice that he's there. I switch sides of the line, thinking nothing of the way I'm dressed. I'm just "doing what I always do" – giving and receiving a hug hello. But it catches him off guard, embarrassing him (he knows he should recognize this person that is showing so much genuine and familiar affection, but he just doesn't). It so unsettles him that he still doesn't realize it's me even after we finish filling our plates. And that says, well, something? Maybe I am getting good at this mascara thing.

With Mick, I stop by to handle some additional business with Eva at her office, when he also stops to get a question answered by her. I forget that I look different from the last time we saw each other, and step in for the hug that is naturally mine to take. He, of course, embraces me back (he's not a monster, he's a genuinely nice man, who's not afraid to hug first and ask questions later). But he steps back, clearly flustered, and introduces himself to me. I feel bad and don't want him to feel embarrassed when recognition does kick-in. But before I can diffuse the situation, Eva, acting the gracious host, dives in to save me, and asks Mick if we have met yet.

It is the classic simultaneous "Yes" from me and "No" from him, which only further confuses him. He is warm and welcoming (his factory default settings), shaking my hand and asking me if I've ever worked on this production before and if I'm an American. Eva answers for me (she is wonderful and, this way, he won't be embarrassed). She and I wink at each other.

And speaking of guy's guys… I got my first taste of, well, I don't know what, because I tried to spit it out immediately. Okay all that's a bit harsh, but it is a lesson in boys being boys and not knowing that since girls are girls, words matter. You can guess that I'm easing into this because I don't want to hurt anyone, and I'm sure that my friend John had no idea at the time what he was saying… that is, I hope he didn't…

I had to meet with John, part of my IT crew. (I can hear you now, and yes it's ironic.) Some boys have relationships based on playful verbal sparring, and John is a blackbelt. In fact, it seems that my appearance just gives him more ammunition. He suggested that I consider getting a haircut, and he was still not sure about my earrings. Now I admit, I took the bait. In my defense, I'm on such a high at this point that I think he's good naturedly (like a dude) teasing me, to let me know he's okay with my being a she, and that our relationship will continue as it always has with our natural "running gun battle" intact. Wrong. It's a through and through. His next shot grazes my heart as he says, "You look like an ugly old woman."

"OUCH," I said, trying to make light of it. But he persisted, "It's true. Looked in the mirror, lately?" That last one hit bone I think. I mumbled, "Wow, sorry 'bout that." Or something equally witty, patted his arm, "Thank you" and left.

Again, it was Ruby to the rescue. "Yes, guys can be so dense. He probably doesn't know that you are a woman. Techies never get out much, and news probably hasn't traveled out to their trailer. If it doesn't come as an email, to them it didn't happen. I'm sure he meant no harm."

I have to take refuge in her words. She's right, this is how guys spar with each other. He would never say that to his wife, or any women friends. He just doesn't get it. He is still relating to me as if I am a boy.

I'm a little torn, is it up to me to *not* take offense? (ANSWER: YES) this is one of the basic tenets of self preservation, regardless of gender. It doesn't excuse anyone's actions, but NEWSFLASH! I'm not in charge of their actions, only mine. I need to lighten-up cuz if my skin is this thin, I'm in trouble... But I never get the opportunity to finish the thought before the clock strikes midnight and suddenly...

3-2-1, AND WE'RE LIVE... The broadcast goes off smoothly, and finishes successfully. While everyone else goes off to celebrate a job well-done (and sleep), a producer's work is never done. "Live," in the professional ranks, in 2015 means it was live at the time you put it out, and now it's available "on-demand." I used to love that live meant "done;" now it means another week in post. BUT I'm not complaining, because I get to hang-out with one of my most favorite men in the world for what will be another week of laughing and intense round-the-clock editing. Neither of us would miss this for the world.

"DC" is not only a gifted professional, but one of the coolest people in the world.

He's also at once a total practicing curmudgeon and the biggest mush-pot ever. We share a love for the hometown team, the Canadian Power trio, *Rush* (not the pill popping talk radio guy), chocolate and great coffee. DC and I have spent countless hours laughing when we're both too sleep deprived to make any sense and we both know so much about each other that I know I'm about to deliver a huge wallop.

I pour us each a cup of fresh coffee (we make our own here in the edit bay) and sit down beside him at my perch at the console. He never takes his eyes off the monitors in front of him but this is where most of our deepest talks have been, while we're inflight on a show and aiming for an elegant landing. I cross my legs in the chair and spin to face him (he hates this). "So, DC, um you, no doubt, have noticed that I'm a little, shall we say, 'better dressed' than the last time we worked together?"

He smiles, eyes still glued to the monitors and tells me that yeah, he noticed and he's also noticed that I'm much more calm these days. He hasn't missed a trick, just waiting respectfully for me to bring it up. Not only has he been studying me, he's honored that I'm taking this time to bring him up to speed with something so personal. He turns to face me, as serious as a heart attack, and says, "I don't understand it, nor the pain you've had to endure, but I've seen it before. You're gonna need your friends and I'm here. Always. But, this does not buy you a pass on teasing, and oh brother – sorry, sister – there's going to be some teasing!"

I choke the tears back, saying, "I feel like we should hug or something to seal this," and he looks down his nose at me with that withering DC stare, "Don't get crazy, girl." And we laugh until I cry.

Things are a little quieter during the five minute breaks when I do come up for air, and women friends keep sidling up to me, discreetly slipping presents into my hands – mostly make-up. "This is the stuff, sister, I never go anywhere without it." Each little gift, a tube of acceptance and love. It's a good thing that the hottest tip (and at least two of the gifts) is waterproof mascara!

One day, as I'm grabbing some snacks for DC and me from the craft-service truck (called "crafty" in the vernacular), I get a playful tickle on my neck. It's Michela, Travis' wife. She is the hippest lady around and checks out my wardrobe. I pass the test. Not bad she says. We hug and sit and I confess that I think I scared Travis on the buffet line and she rolls her eyes. "Don't take it personally, it's because you are now as you are supposed to be, that he didn't recognize you. It's a good thing, darling." I stare at this woman and realize I am surrounded by so many great women who will gently and lovingly help me mature as a woman, that I have nothing to fear. I will be better than okay.

After a week of hard work and laughter, it's time to head back home. I spend a morning hugging old friends, being upfront with the people I've missed, and wrapping things up.

At my last lunch the dining room buzzes – the crew is wrapped and we're all heading back home. The laughter and relief of a job well-done are palpable. I find an open seat at a table and sit.

This is the first time I'm eating without a to-do list spooling off in my head. I can relax… And as I bask in this glow, I feel a head come gently to rest on my shoulder. It's Cristina. She nuzzles in to kiss me on the cheek and whispers, "I like this version of you so much better than that guy thing you were doing. You're so, I don't know… just better, that's all." I freeze, not wanting even my breath to chase this moment away.

A brand new year has started with a thunderbolt and an answer to my letter. God does know where to find me – knee deep in cameras, lights and a good story. It's not lost on me that this momentous shift in my life occurred during production; that's where I'm at my best. It's where I am already looking at the world in 360 degrees, and things just always seem so much clearer at warp speed.

Like now. I've got business back in the states before heading home once again. . . and oh, a life to start. . . finally!

15
A LOT LESS UGLY THAN EXPECTED

I'm waiting at the cancer treatment center at Sloan-Kettering Hospital in New York. True, I've had more than my share of hospitals, but for my cousin Tommy's wife Maureen, I'd do almost anything, including facing New York City! This is very important to Tommy. He's been strangely insistent that I meet them here for Mo's chemo session and, knowing how hard cancer is on everyone, I agree. I can help Tommy with what the spouse goes through, and heck, I love him dearly. So who cares how I feel about hospitals?

Even so, it's a very weird place to "come out," which isn't really accurate anymore. 'Being upfront' is.

And, rather than surprise him, I thought it would be a good idea to put my Thunderbolt to work and be upfront with my cousin, so I called him.

"Tommy, I want you to be prepared when we hook up. I look a lot more feminine than when you last saw me."

"What? Do you have boobs?"

"Really? That's what you're leading with? Well then, actually yes, but…"

"You had boobs the last time I saw you."

"Okay then. So I guess it won't be a surprise."

As vulgar as his question was (he is a retired detective), I thought, "can't get more upfront than that, we're good."

Turns out, no. Tommy's been in the hell of his own imagination. He's had no clue what is really going on and called me several times after that, always dancing around, never asking me straight up. I, of course, can be evil (we are constantly sparring) and have intentionally given him enough rope to hang himself several times over. Is that bitchy?

But after days of calls, I finally let him off the hook, telling him in plain English that I am, in fact, a woman. That was two days ago. And now, here I am, standing in the lobby of an insanely busy cancer clinic in one of the biggest cities in the world, dressed like any fiftyish-year-old woman would be in January in Manhattan. Things have made a quantum leap.

I remind myself this is Mo's time. I'm here for her. And as they walk in the front door, I see them first and surprise them, sneaking up to stroll casually beside them as they scan the crowded lobby for "me." Mo notices me first (she is a retired NYPD Captain) and smiles as we both wait to see how long Detective Tommy takes to catch on. It finally dawns who this smiling woman standing next to him is, but, no surprise, he tries to play it off as knowing all the time. But we girls know.

I can see it in his face when we settle in upstairs, waiting for Mo's chemo room to be prepared. He stares at me, and with a Cheshire Cat grin confesses, "You're not as ugly as I imagined you to be." As much as I know and expect this, I sigh. "You smooth talking devil, you. No wonder Maureen married you." Maureen rolls her eyes, "Welcome to my world."

The exchange begins a line of interrogation of all the things you can imagine, starting with the three most asked questions: 1. "How long have you known?" 2. "How's your wife and how is she with all this?" 3. "Are you into guys?"

But it's not until the ninth or tenth question (somewhere between, "What should we refer to you as," and "Are you going to get surgery?") when we get to:

"So can I ask you another question?"

"Sure," I say, "what's one more between kissin' cousins?"

But he's waited until Mo excuses herself to go to the ladies' room. With furtive side glances and a conspiratorial whisper, he asks, "Remember when I came by and surprised you at my Mom's house?"

"Yes," I reply, feeling the adrenaline cascading from my head to the pit of my stomach (who could forget hiding in the bathroom, curls drooping), "I was in the shower."

"You *ran* for the shower." Like I said, he never misses a trick. "Well, I saw a purse by the door and thought shit, he's got a girl in the shower so, am I right? Were you stepping out on your wife?"

I think my cough of laughter catches him by surprise. "Uh I can't believe I going to say this out loud (all part of being upfront, I suppose) but no. That purse was mine."

He wipes beads of sweat from his brow. "Well, I can't believe I'm going to say this out loud either, but that's a relief!"

That we both are so relieved that it was my purse demands some attention here, because neither of us would've thought this before. It is a new day!

After some more whispering and giggling (we always laugh a lot together) about how strange all of this is, we watch as the chemo drugs take their effect on Mo and she slips off to sleep. I ask Tommy to keep this to himself only until I've had a chance to "be upfront" with the rest of our cousins. He grins, "You better get started - that could take months!"

He's right, Tommy is only one of ten Donohues, and that doesn't even count the Jevonses (three of them).

Tommy hugs me goodbye with the requisite assurances that he still reserves the right to tease me like a guy. (Why do boys think that's cool?) I reply, "As long as you're cool if I cry." Two can play at the cliché game.

I left the hospital, walking into the January night to meet my boss from the last Alaska show, Sarah, the woman who has been on the other end of all those phone calls and emails when I was freezing in Alaska. Time to meet face-to-face. Finally.

What's weird is that I have no idea what the production company thought of me back then. I know I did a good job, but as for my "presentation?" - how can you ask that sort of thing when commerce is involved? A whole set of legal issues governs what can and can't be said aloud.

But I have an inside man, Marc, a dear friend who I mentored in production, oh so many years ago. Marc has gone on to make a name for himself, in Reality TV - so much so, that I was able to get them to hire him without reservation. Sarah would be bringing her assistant Roberta and my counterpart, Sam. Again, no pressure. The meeting goes really well, all of us a little surprised to put faces on the voices we'd been talking to for the last three months. They are grateful for the job I've done for them, and I in turn for the job they'd entrusted to me.

After they leave (everyone has kids these days!), Marc and I are able to get some dinner and compare notes. Marc is one of the founders of the Pink Mafia Network, a Gay coalition of television and film professionals who watch over each other in NYC. He says he is proud of me and thinks I look fantastic and reminds me of the trials he had as a young gay man growing up without role models. It wasn't until he grew up and went to college that he found the answers to his own identity.

I am proud of this man and we have a great time. He shares that the president of the company (whom I met in LA) had relayed her acceptance of me to the New York HQ, so everyone knows that their showrunner is a "me."

I still have a ton of practical questions, and I grill Marc. What did they call me? Refer to me as? Marc realizes that they only talked about me without specific pronouns. Hmm. But he notes they never said anything with so much as a raised eyebrow or "air quotes." They have to be cool with me or they wouldn't have shown up tonight.

We both agree that it is a different time than when Marc grew up, and only getting better. Kids today hopefully will have no idea how much people have struggled, and that is a good thing, for all the right reasons. I hug him goodnight and head back to Staten Island and a hot bath.

As the soothing water takes the icy chill from my body, I dial Katrina, who I call my "big sis." Katrina is an incredible friend who has known the boy version of me for many years, and we spent a good part of last year working together on a consulting gig for a large corporation.

I just received a card of thanks for our work (together) and am using this as an excuse to give her a phone hug. She is an amazing woman with whom I share a passion for cooking and for my Dude show. She's a big fan of me and my work. But tonight, I'm taking advantage of passing on the gratitude we both received and as I'm telling her this news, I hear "be upfront" in my head. And though I hadn't planned on this being a coming out chat, suddenly, here it is.

My big Sis is a consummate corporate professional; the most polished person I've ever known. She always knows what to say and when to send that thank you note. She has a black belt in corporate diplomacy and a Ph.D. in corporate speak.

But tonight, even though she can tell I'm saying something earth shattering, she can't quite understand (between the static and echo of the tiled bathroom) if I just said what she thought I just said. And when I repeat it for the third time, and it still hasn't landed on all four wheels, I get really basic:

"Sis. I am a woman."

"I think you just said you're a woman."

"Yes."

"Yes?"

"Yes."

"Oh? Oh. Oh, uh. . . and are you happy?"

"Yes."

"Well then. I'm happy too."

And we sign off. I know there will be a part two of this scene, down the road, but it will do for now. What's on my mind now is that the next day I'm having one of the biggest lunches of my life.

I have been trying to get Ellen on the phone all week. She's my mostest favorite network exec (suit) ever, and I always swear that I'm going to take her with me to every network for the rest of my career. She's smart and fun and really knows what we in the field are going through. We've worked side by side on DYS for the past three years and I love the heck out of her.

I'm also scared to death of what she will say with my being upfront with her. This is where the rubber will meet the road, so to speak, because this is my livelihood we're talking about. It's the network suit that has the final say on whether I'll be hired or not. My ability to work with them as I'm working for them is my stock in trade. I am known for my passion (which in network speak means "royal pain in the ass"), but Ellen not only loves this about me, she has defended me – and my right to be that way – countless times. To her, it's one of my assets.

Like I said, she's smart and she's got good taste in showrunners. We've made some good TV together and it was her recommendation that also got me hired for the Alaska show even though it wasn't for her network. She has that much respect in the biz.

So I have that much riding on a simple lunch.

But also, as a woman, I want her acceptance. I want her sisterhood, and even if our paths never cross again, I would like to be friends. She's that cool.

This is my first chance to put my faith in being upfront. If it doesn't go well, it could seriously hurt my career. (How's that for a clichéd end of act recap? Sorry, but I'm that freaked out.)

I look over my wardrobe figuring I should pull back: no make-up, hair in a ponytail and a black turtleneck. It's cold outside so I better go with jeans, (girl jeans look just like boy jeans if you ignore the blingy pockets). I should ease into this slowly, no need to freak anyone out. This is corporate America after all. What if they're not ready?

But I immediately feel bad, like I've kicked myself in the gut. I've just had a monumental epiphany *and* have seen it work like magic, so am I really going to quail at the first opportunity to use it for my life? Was I "shoulding" on myself?

If I am going to start living my life for real, I better start now. If I don't use this opportunity to be upfront with Ellen, then I'll just have an even harder time down the road, and the trench will be even deeper. I suddenly see myself riding a rollercoaster. I *am* going to go down that hill, I can ride in the front car or the back car. I can see where I'm going in the front, I am merely following everyone else in the back. The front car is way better. And P.S. I really, really like rollercoasters.

So no. I won't sell myself short; I'm sittin' up front.

I put on tights and my most feminine boots. I curl my hair and put on my make-up, and Ellen will see me as I really am.

SHIT! But I can't reach Ellen by phone! I need to give her what will become known as "the five-minute heads-up" – the newest strategy that Ronny and Jayne taught me is a must. And Tommy taught me that too much time between hearing and seeing and their imagination begins to eat its own tail. Frantic, I email Ellen that I need to run something by her before we sit down for lunch and she immediately calls me back. Whew!

I explain that I want to warn her I look a lot more feminine than when last we met. She pushes for more info and I want to say, I don't want to do this over the phone, But instead, what I hear my mouth saying is, "I'm a woman. Always have been, but now I'm starting to live that way." I hear her take a breath and say, "I can't wait to see you."

I'm sitting in the cafe, alone but for the waiter and the busboy. It's early for the usual midtown lunch crowd at a cute little fish restaurant where Ellen and I first met three years ago when Dude was a mere pilot and finally got its "go." The door opens and Ellen takes off her scarf and scans the room. She sees me and SCREAMS: "Oh my god! You're gorgeous!"

She practically runs across the room to hug me like a big sister embracing her little sister, home from her first year of college. She breaks the hug to hold me at arms length, long enough to study my look, then hugs me again in approval.

We sit for lunch and she has a million questions, but I love telling her everything. She breaks my stream every once in a while to shake her head. "I can't believe how good you look." When I challenge her, she answers, "Girl, really, last time I saw you, you were quite the Dude! You always looked like *the* dude! The outdoor survival dude!"

When you put it that way, I'm astonished, too.

I'm able to ask her my burning question: what she thinks about my future. She throws it off without a second thought. "This is a different world we live in," she says, "we don't care if you're polka dotted, as long as you bring home the show."

Like I said, I'm taking this woman with me everywhere.

Too soon, our heady, giddy, wonderful time together winds down. She gives me a huge hug goodbye and I head to the airport with hope in my heart. This "being upfront" with people is some powerful stuff!

I was only beginning to scratch the surface.

16
THE THRESHOLD OF TOMORROWS

I'm home and I'm still pinching myself. Today's Sunday and we've moved our normal, lazy lie in bed cuddle time to the living room. We both want just a little more of our Christmas tree. I build a fire and wink to the Angel that has sat atop our trees since the second year of our marriage. She has always gracefully presided over the room with real dove feathers for wings, a Victorian red velvet coat and bonnet, and her benevolent smile; a beautiful ray of reassurance, like the rising sun glinting on snow crystals.

This is the Christmas spirit that Mylove and I traded for the "full house" of mirth and cheer of this Christmas Past. This is that special flavor of our sacred bubble that we look forward to all year, a relaxed and quiet sphere of "just us." Here everything is possible, nothing is ever bad. And, holy moly! I can't believe I am about to test that right here and now…

My mind is struggling in protest against the duct tape and zip ties; it can't believe we're going to do this now! What about the tree, the fire, the ANGEL! How could you take advantage of YourLove like this! We want no part of this!

It seems the heart has been very busy, and while we all were looking the other way, it jibed downwind and we're sailing into waters I have never even dared to hope possible.

As the fire crackles, I look to my beloved wife, hold her soft cheek tenderly and say, "I want to start hormones."

Hold that thought, while I press rewind.

Mylove went through menopause almost ten years ago, and when the doctors mentioned HRT (Hormone Replacement Therapy) to ease the symptoms, well, let's just say they're still looking for the bodies. Mylove is the poster child for "Hell no, I won't put horse urine in my body!"

And when it came up in the context of anything transgender, it was dismissed with even more derision. (As in what kind of an idiot takes hormones willingly?) I, of course, always took the chicken exit each time and kept quiet. Until now.

You should know that Mylove has a very learned and grounded opinion and philosophy about health. She is the perfect balance of common sense and *common sense*. Not so arrogant or militant as to shun the surgery and chemotherapy (and all of their ancillary tests, drugs, and regimen) of a cancer regimen, while not afraid to consider cannabis, acupuncture and cutting-edge alternatives.

She has always scrutinized everything she puts on, in, or around her body. She stopped drinking thirty years ago, never did recreational drugs, and indulges in chocolate only. In short, she's all about the health.

So, for me to even consider elective hormone therapy is to swan dive into a rattlesnake nest. Here's the thing. After our many years of marriage, there is no "my life" and "her life," there is only "our life." I know I can't just go on hormones without her blessing. And "going rogue" is not an option, it would put us right back where we were. I may be crazy, but I'm not stupid.

I have <u>always</u> wanted to take them. I did enough research to be dangerous but had to stop. The longing for them and what they promised became too painful. And the loss of not having them naturally was a constant slashing of my heart; a crime that made me angry and ferociously sad.

How could I miss something that I had never had? Glad you asked. The explanation of the "estrogen wash" (while in utero) makes the most sense to my experience of how a "me" could be a "me" in the first place. I had it once and I want it back!

Heck yes, hormones were a big step. They would change the outside of me, no doubt, but it was the effect on my mind and heart that I was really desperately seeking.

I had had brief flashes of intense femininity; lighting bolts of bliss that made me feel, well, there's just no other word than "womanly," unless we go with "right." These were so brief that I almost didn't want them because the crash afterward was too painful to willingly seek out. If hormones could give me that feeling all the time (without the crash) I was "all in."

So, going back to the crazy part and the Christmas tree, I dive in, arms spread wide, and say to the woman I love, that, I cannot, will not pretend to be a man anymore. Her man anymore.

Thank God we're on such a high as a couple. She is able to unclench her teeth as fast as they set and interview me with valid double checks, which I would do for her.

*If you're being accepted by everyone else, isn't that enough?

*Have you considered the real health risks?

*Is having a woman's body that important to you?

I take all of her questions in. This is not a debate. She can feel that I am giving her the space to say it all. I know that once down this road, there's no turning back.

Which is really what we're talking about here.

No turning back. It's our moment of truth.

Because, as hard as it would be right now, it would only take a few weeks of excruciating embarrassment and spin control to hit the "reset" button and everything would return to "Normal" (whatever that is – I can't remember, but Mylove has a vague wistful notion).

If we head down the hormone highway, any U-turn back would never get us back to zero without permanent change and emotional damage. But let's be real. I can't even intelligently engage in this as a choice. As hard as it might be to go forward, going backward is suicide.

Because as crazy and as life altering as this is, the "normal" that is wistfully remembered, was a "me" who was imprisoned in despair, wearing a mask of stern masculinity, dancing on the strings of the world's expectations.

Yeah, normal, baby. How 'bout some o' dat? Huh?

The next day, I'm in my doctor's office coming out again. My doc is a beautiful person, her face always a wry smile. She nods and shrugs. *Oh, my god, I'm her first one.*

However, she does know the drill for girls like me. She has to consult with the endocrinologist; they'll look at my blood and history and I'll hear back in a few days.

I begin my transformation from "was" to "should have been" (ignoring the icky part in between). Mylove is not happy, she's scared. I probably should be, but I can't even pretend to be fair and partial – I'M ECSTATIC!

I got my prescription for HRT from my "healthcare provider!" No more ignoring the "it gets better" campaign… it does, or will, soon!

This is not only a new day for me, but for our society. Take my HMO. The girls in the trans community have been all a'twitter about Kaiser Permanente taking a leading role in trans health (lucky for me), even going so far with our president's health care initiative to approve SRS (Sexual Reaffirming Surgery), now referred to as GAS (Gender Affirmation Surgery). Or in the vernacular as just "*the* surgery" or just plain old surgery as in, "oh, you're trans? Are you going to have "surgery?" (Yes, *that* surgery.)

And there it is in black & white – my prescription: Estradiol for estrogen and Spironolactone as the anti-androgen. That's the scary one, the one that turns off the boy valve. It's not easy to describe the dichotomy of feelings; on one hand, it's what I always wanted, I never asked to be a boy, never wanted the boy's body, never liked the exile, but…

It is the only way to be completely intimate with the one person I love most in the world. I've never been a rock star sexually, but the moments of complete union with Mylove are the times when the earth stops, the deepest most fulfilling spiritual moment of life ever.

Did I have to sacrifice that in order to get me?

I hoped not. Was I being naïve? Probably. Maybe if the changes were gradual would we grow into a new life together naturally? Maybe? Kinda? Sorta? Is my being cutsie with it another layer of denial?

I admit my heart does pretty well with her hand on the tiller, but even she is torn in separate directions with this one, the mind smirking behind the duct tape, "You're on your own with this one sweetie." So my heart throws up her hands and prays – a great example of how denial can cut both ways. By narrating this inner discussion, even I get to remain "just a spectator" of the turmoil, instead of responsible for myself. Not the bravest way to run one's life, and I admit that my trust in the perfection of life is leaning heavily on Grace. I have to be She.

So, without allowing time to second-guess myself, I opened the bottle and started hormones right there in the parking lot.

Within weeks there's change. My body responds instantly and the sex is still good.

Since then, there have been times when I haven't been able to "answer the call," but I wasn't so much frustrated as I was sad that I hadn't been able to satisfy Mylove. However, even when I or we "missed," our intimacy is deepening and Mylove is patient.

Sex is changing for me, even coming close is an insane joy ride in my body; an all-over electrified bath in joy and bliss. The times when I don't go "over the falls," doesn't matter; I feel way better for a lot longer than I ever did as a "boy," even without the moment of clouds and rain. (Thank you Mariko and Mr. Clavell – And I think if I try hard enough, I can actually fit-in one more metaphor involving water.)

But this was still a duet and I want Mylove to be fulfilled or what's the point? I've never been a selfish partner. This moment of intimacy has always been the oasis for me, the one place (and this might be counterintuitive) where gender identity never mattered, because as we were going over the falls together, we became one. But if that goes away, what happens to our "oneness?"

As I think this through more and speak the unspoken, I realize that once I truly fell in love, sex and making love became two completely different acts. The former, I never had any interest in, the latter was all there was. I guess this explains why I scared the living shit out of every girlfriend I ever had before Mylove. I was too intense in the love department and not at all in the sex department. Too much pressure? Whatever happened to just getting laid?

Not for me. What's also odd to admit is that, as much as one might think I need to focus on my male parts to make love, I never give it a second thought, because I'm consumed with Mylove, and her body, and her parts. And even when the concentration of sensation "down there" happens, it is only a tiny part of the fusion that explodes into a bliss as bright as a thousand suns.

You can probably guess by even my description of the above how I can/did/need/will relate to my male biology. (Amateur psychologists are rubbing their hands with glee.) But I keep one last teaspoon of denial to get past physical realities – what choice do I have?

It's strange to see my fumbling with this fundamental aspect of being human in print. As for intimacy with Mylove, it's beyond cosmic, the frequency is less than the beginning of our marriage (where weeks were measured by how many times during, rather than the times between) but isn't that life anyway?

But I'm getting ahead of myself (how unusual).

My wife is ever vigilant with my medical care and she's not sure I have done enough thorough research (department of redundancy department), taking only Kaiser's word.

Guilty as charged. I was just happy to be taking hormones and feeling change.

Mylove wouldn't just let me off that easy. (Whereas you were just going to let me prattle on). She has relationships with a legion of doctors, everything from neuroscientists to veterinarians. (I'm not joking, everyone knows that if you really want to know what's going on with your body, ask a vet.)

Mylove confided in her naturopath that her husband was transitioning to be a woman (a reply every doctor expects on the intake questionnaire). Instead of "professional restraint" the Naturopath replied that she had been in practice with a doctor who had gone through the change and was now an OB-Gyn in Northern Cali, and would she like to have me speak with her?

Nah . . .

OF COURSE! Dr. Richards was wonderful and generous with her time and expertise. (Which she did not owe me, I was not her patient.) She could speak as one of us.

She was passionate and insightful about the differences of the goals between the trans world and the Medical Establishment. The Establishment, as evolved or enlightened as they currently were, treated trans women with the same protocol as a post-menopausal cisgender woman.

In other words, they use HRT (i.e. putting back what was lost), which may work on a body that has had estrogen (and progesterone) all it's life, but may not be quite enough for girls like us. We have lived a large part of our lifespan with only trace amounts of estrogen (each biology has the opposite hormone in smaller quantities).

She suggested progesterone. If I didn't get any, I would never have mature breast development. I would only get "tuberal" growth (whatever that was, I didn't want any!).

So I did some more research, and the more I read, the more sense Dr. Richards made. Genetic women get estrogen all their lives (well technically, most of it, until the "pause") and progesterone during the menstrual process. Going further, Dr. Richards was getting good results mimicking the natural menstrual cycle with oral progesterone (micronized, if you care). Perfect sense! The standard protocol is daily doses of progesterone, but by mimicking "the cycle," Dr. Richards was getting great results; the body has times of influence from progesterone and times of rest/integration, like normal female physiology. (NOTE: though I've pledged to not misuse the "normal" word to describe human psychology, it is accurate enough here.)

I couldn't wait to take progesterone. I stated my case to my doc. The endo would need to weigh-in (again).

And she made me wait. And wait. I bugged her. And bugged her some more. Finally, my doctor got back to me with the answer from Dr. Harris:

She would not recommend progesterone for me or anyone.

Wrong answer lady, I had my teeth in this bone. But she was toeing the Kaiser line, and as evolved as they were, they were not willing to go the extra mile. Boobs you could have, but peace and well-being? Hmmm… why would you want that?

So I took it back to my doc. I told her that a "no" was unacceptable. She could see my point and invited me to plead my case to the endo myself.

Within a week, I was sitting in the waiting room of Dr. Harris, endocrinologist. Armed with Dr. Richards's arguments, regimen, and philosophy, I met this lovely woman. It's too bad, she had so much to live for…

Dr. Harris looked at the results of my blood tests and announced that I was very healthy, in good shape, and as far as she was concerned, would benefit from the adding of progesterone to my regimen.

Wait? What?

Hey, Lady, I'm ready for a fight! You're no match for me!

But you'd be proud of me, I took yes for an answer. (A girl can learn!) Dr. Harris wished me health. I left in a daze.

I can say this now. My body is loving its most important nutrient. I have always been an athlete, always been healthy. But I had no idea how deprived I must've been because the before and after picture of my body, my mind, and my life is so dramatic.

What I'm taking way too long to describe is how my "default" sense of being has changed. First, glimmers of feminine energy ripple through my body – 10 to fifteen minutes of overwhelming bliss, sometimes lasting longer. Everything feels more than right, more than perfect, and echoes of that ripple continue long after. The beauty of the world is one hundred times brighter and vibrant. The wash of gratitude that accompanies this is a knee-buckling, head swirling, emotional vertigo. It's like coming home and flying to the moon at the same time, a familiarity and a longing satisfied, with an exhilaration each time it dawns that a lifelong dream has come true.

And it came true in this lifetime while I am young enough to enjoy the journey and mature enough to hold on.

Powerful stuff.

Another unexpected effect of hormones is that I am getting further and further from being able to even find the emotional pain that had peaked before my breakdown, or any of the pain, for that matter. I can find my thoughts, labels and inner conversations about the pain, but not the actual pain itself. I even hesitate to label any of the above things as scars. Everything is just right. It happened as it was to be.

However, I confess that I do keep looking over my shoulder for them thar clinically documented "mood swings," we hear so much about; like the feared white whale, I wonder if they are actually waiting out there at all.

Because control freak that you can guess I am, one of the biggest signs my therapist used to recommend hormones for little ol' me in the first place was my admission that, "I had a cry stuck in my throat for over forty years."

Okay, so this is where my sainted father's halo dims a bit. In his world (which I had been a proud citizen of for roughly 18 years) not only was there no crying in baseball (or football, or basketball, for that matter), but tears were only for girls. Boys <u>didn't</u> cry, period, ever, end of story. I know this because it was shouted at me almost weekly right through my high school years. Yes, I shed a bunch of them, which, based on the above laws, should have been empirical proof that I was definitely not a boy.

As I got older, I guess (though I don't remember making any conscious decision to do this) I stopped crying, capping the leak with cement and barbed wire.

Since hormones, tears happen all the time, but it's not the snotty-nosed sobbing that I was afraid of, that loss of control that every woman fears will happen at the worst time possible. Instead, I cry a lot at the smallest kindness extended to me. I cry when I see a breathtaking sunset. I cry when I allow myself to recognize that my beloved Yellow Labrador, Zuzie (Zuzubird, Babybird, Zuzubean, the Labrador Queen) who we raised from a puppy is probably not going to be around to see the completion of this… I can't even complete this sentence.

IN FACT, I just now had to take a break. I still have to master the art of crying without destroying my morning's work. But I'm back now. Ah yes, hormones? Well, read all you want about them (and trust me, there's an ocean of info on the web) but it doesn't mean a hill o' beans until you catch yourself in the mirror. And *that*, dear ones, is getting exciting and better every day.

Okay, I like the physical changes too. What girl wouldn't? I love having a waist and small wrists and slender fingers and softer face. I love looking into a mirror and seeing a woman stare back.

But wait, what's that smudge? Darn it, I thought I had fixed that.

17
"...FI FIE FO-FOTTY..."

I hate having to ignore the raised eyebrow stare of TSA agents whenever I hand them my passport – <u>I am not that guy!</u> That picture! Ugh! Scruffy, surly, oh, and it's a dude! But to get a new picture, you have to get a new passport, and to get a new passport, you need to get a new driver's license, and to get a new driver's license, you need a correct social security card. And to get a correct social security card, you need a correct birth certificate. And to get a correct birth certificate you need to get a court order.

And if I'm gonna play this version of "I know an old lady who swallowed a fly," that means... Gosh! I'll also be able to change my name.

Wait, what? My name? For real. For real? For real.

What would it be? Stephanie? Susan? Sara? Keira promised to hold a contest, but she hasn't followed through. I want something Celtic, something with an S, and something feminine.

A girl's (or boy's) name is not supposed to be a choice; it's called a "given" name, right? The name given should have family history to it. It has to have thought and love and good (or bad) blood in it. It does seem that people become their names or they define that name by their character. Any way you slice it, it's got to have an emotional origin.

I feel I should indulge myself here (beside the fact that I'll be living with it for the rest of my life). Because my parents put tremendous thought into my given name, I won't take this lightly. I was Scott because my father wanted me to have my own name; he was James Henry Madden III and my mother lobbied hard for a IV, but Dad knew what it was like to wear another man's mantle. He countered with Michael, which obviously didn't make the cut. Incidentally, I did try on Michelle in his honor, with good intentions, and even began preparing the necessary extenuating circumstance arguments, but it died in committee (in my head).

Okay, true confessions? When I first ventured out into the world, presenting as a woman, I <u>gave</u> myself the name: "Kendra," which was a woman I knew in college who was everything I hoped I would one day be. Fiery, redheaded, gorgeous and cool. But now, I don't relate to it at all. And please excuse me, I'd just as soon forget the girl I was then. But I digress.

Growing up, when I cried, my dad would deride me by calling me "Mary

Jane." I considered MJ (also in his memory. That almost won, because MJ was, after all, Peter Parker's love. Who wouldn't wanna be Spiderman's girl?) but no.

As a child I referred to myself as "Katie" (no idea why – there's a buncha Katherines on the Irish side of our tree?). It was the only way to soothe my feminine self when things got hard.

But before we get to the lighting round, let's remind our contestants of the rules:

*It has to start with an "S." In my family, we're proud that we've got 2 J's, 2 K's, and 2 S's. We've got my mom Judy and Dad, Jim (the J's), Kimm and Keira (the K's). Shane and I are the 2 S's. So, I can't betray the family symmetry; I have to stick with S. I love my family and my place in it.

*It has to be feminine. I already have enough hurdles in life. I don't want to confuse anyone, and so, if my name is feminine in print, then my documents just may be the tipping point for anyone staring at me wondering, "Oh, but she's got a girl's name." (I told you this trans thingy is a mindbender, you try living with our minds for just 10 minutes.)

*Mylove has to like it. Let's be real, if it doesn't pass muster with her, it will die a lonely death.

*It has to have dignity.

*It should be Celtic or, at least, Irish.

My signature is my initials, S.J.C.M., so if I did this name change thingy right, my signature could stay the same.

This name game is a huge deal for most girls like me. There's gobs of opinions and conventions; some say to make your given *first* name your new *last* name and then pick a girl's name that you always wanted for your new first name. Still with me? Wendy Carlos did this (Oscar-winning composer of the score for "A Clockwork Orange," among others). Christine Daniels did this (the former reporter for the LA Times who sadly took her own life).

But this technique won't work – Kendra Scott could be pretty, and might be a weather girl in San Diego – but sadly not me. I'm a Madden through and through and darn proud of it!

Some play porn star roulette and use the name of their first pet and the name of the first street they lived on as the last name (try it). However, Snoopy Marin is just not gonna happen.

Some play stripper and choose a name that makes it obvious that you are NOT a boy: here's where you get your Sugars, your Gigis, your Chloes, your Trishs or anything with a gem, fruit, or wine. Nothing against this technique, but it rarely produces a name that's more than a passing fad. Although I will never agree to "act my age," I also don't think anyone wants to be a footnote when they could be a novel. It's really about a place in time, when you were born in this family of humans.

Met any sixty-year old Megans, Briannes, or Brittneys? No? Of course, you haven't – they're named, Maureen, Carol, or Susan. Met any fifty year old Rihannons, Lenas, or Arianas? No, we're all named, Denise, Monica, Sheila or Tracy.

And yes, I did consider Sheila for a day, but I was getting desperate and it didn't pass the Celtic test.

And one last rule? Sorry to have left it out of the first set of rules, but this is a biggie, it has to sound good with all of the other names that go with it.

My full name was Scott James Christofer Madden. Not bad, eh? So, what girl's name (that meets all of the above criteria) sounds good with a J middle name? Christine is a no-brainer for Christofer and yes, I did toy with Catherine for about fifteen minutes. (But tossed it, too much like the past.)

But first names first. Mylove confided that a character on her favorite show ("Suits" if you must know) was named. . . wait for it. . . Scottie.

I've been Scotty all my life. Even my sisters refer to me that way. Thanks for playing, but no.

The search continued. We had the "Scarlett incident." Our niece, Acey, was here to meet "the new me." (We worship the ground she walks on – if Ace wanted to go to the moon, we would learn to fly for her.) She mentioned our dilemma (finding a name, not the transgender thing, silly) to a friend, who blurted out, "Oh, she needs a strong name. She should be Scarlett!"

The name rips through my body like a mid-summer set wave – strong and powerful. Scarlett is one of those names that you've had to have your whole life to completely own. I try, I really do – it meets all of the other notes perfectly (even found some baby naming websites that claimed it as Celtic). Scarlett is aspirational, yes, but ultimately, not *me*.

We continue to circle through the dim fog of nothing, that misty purgatory that envelopes you when you forget a favorite movie title or your cousin's name. While I am looking for the way out of this dead zone, Mylove comes back to Scottie. Only, this time, she has had time to formulate her pitch. Beginning with the I-E:

"... that will make it feminine; it's really cute, without sounding cutsie." (I love girlspeak.)

I don't shoot it down, this time, deciding to give her a chance (and by "her" right now, I'm not sure if I'm referring to Mylove or me.) I start coupling it together with J names:

Scottie Janine – A dear friend of mine and role model. Not bad.

Scottie Jean – Would Keira feel honored or robbed? Jean is her middle name. I can't risk the latter and I need my own name anyway.

Scottie Jeanette – Lots going for it in the Irish lane, very feminine, the frontrunner, for sure.

Scottie James – Mylove keeps reminding me that girl middle names are rarely feminine on her side of the family. (Her middle name is Kane, in case you're asking.)

Scottie Jane? June? Jamison? Jo? Nah. Not really. Never. And no.

Jeanette? Now I'm liking the Jeanette. Lots of great women carry that name and it hasn't been used by the immediate family in a generation. And you can dance to it.

But Scottie Jeanette? Scottie-jeanette? Scottiejeanette?

Mylove was falling in love with her idea (might as well surrender Scottie, it'll just be easier). "Come on, it's Celtic, Feminine, unique (TV characters don't count?) And it's an "S."

Scottie Jeannette Christine Madden.

And then, it settles around me, not caring whether I like it or not. It just is. As if it has always been my name. Of course it's perfect because I'm not trying to become something or someone else, I am trying to get back to me – the me I always was and was supposed to be. I'm finally allowing myself to be me; which is more than I had been. Scott-ie.

But most of all, it just feels right. We're good. Done and done. Except that it's not done, it's just starting!

Now the real work begins. Paperwork.

Still with me? Remember, I started this dogleg to change my passport picture – this is how denial works, my heart (so smart, that one) knows I would probably chicken out if I knew what I was really doing – which was sneaking up on a full gender change through the side door of convenience – fooling myself that it was just a way to avoid those uncomfortable stares at airports. But seriously, girlfriend?

Birth certificate? Really? Change the past? Could it be that easy? Go back and make it all better? Turn back time.

All it takes is a doctor's letter. (What, no DeLorean?)

Three days later, here they are. Six original copies of my doctor's opinion on company letterhead. I am, in her professional opinion a woman, and I have completed the appropriate clinical treatment for gender transition.

Even through this entire effort as we're working to change my gender *marker* on all of my identity documents, every time I see the term gender change, it hits me like a ton of bricks. I'm doing this. This is real.

I am really, really, really changing my gender. Not just the papers that proclaim my gender, but my whole life, my whole identity in the world, my whole me. For real.

Mylove keeps reminding me this is huge. Whenever we talk to friends and family, we hear them say the same thing, "This is huge." Whenever I get overwhelmed, she calms me down saying, "Of course it's scary, this is huge."

I've tried to get through it by making it a small, no-biggie, ain't justa thang thing, never admitting that it's fucking huge.

Okay? I said it, can I go now? I've got work to do.

After a week, I have forms from the website[2], a name and some letters, and head for the Superior Court.

Something that comes from being first born, artistic, stubborn (and maybe even as a woman born with different biology?) is that I've never needed, nor looked for, outside validation for anything in my life. Could it be that I didn't trust that I would get it so I never sought it? Hmmm, maybe?

But this exercise has consumed me and yes, I do care what the government thinks I am. I want their validation on all of my paperwork. But first, I have to take steps to correct its wrong impression that I ever was a boy.

The clerk is very helpful and stamps all of my forms gives me a set and files the others. I pay the filing fee (close to five hundred bucks) and leave to wait the six weeks they take to dig into my past.

It seems too smooth to be true and that's because it is. Two weeks later, I receive a call: I need another form. This makes no sense – it didn't appear on any requirements either of us (me and my new BFF, the clerk) have ever seen. I need "An order to show cause for name and gender change."

I'm not superstitious, but it sounds presumptuous as if I am filing the judge's decision before she (at least I hope it's a she) has ruled. I don't want to jinx it, plus this makes it look like I didn't file properly in the first place, and I don't want to give them any reason to dismiss. I swallow my fear and confusion, download and fill out the mystery form and run down to the clerk's office. The clerk can sense my fear (could it be the sweat?). What are we going to do? Will this set us back? But he takes the form, raises his mighty date stamper (have you seen these? They're like Hermione's time turner) and with the flick of his fingers takes us back two weeks in time to my original filing date, and stamps that puppy right.

"See?" He smiles, "just like magic, no problem."

I want to hug him, but there's this window thingy in my way. So I settle for a smile and a wink and leave again. And just like that, I'm back in the waiting game.

Funny how a little vanity goes a long way. A looooong way.

---

2 Transgender Law Center - http://transgenderlawcenter.org

18
GETTING SORTED

It's been a week since I emailed my sister Keira for the fifth time and I finally called to see if she is okay. I got a vague apology, asking if we can talk later. I wait. Later doesn't come. Meanwhile, I'm getting love and support from strangers on the street, but my own sister can't even respond to my emails. So yes, I'm starting to stew.

I want to catch Keira up on all things me. Most especially, I want to prepare her for my new name which I haven't started using yet (I don't want to jinx the judge's decision). It was Keira who wanted to hold a naming contest in the first place, so she deserves to know we have a winner.

I try again. I'm not getting her, again. No response to my inquiries until finally, I get this cryptic response:

"I've been meaning to email you, I need to sort through my feelings first. I'll be in touch."

Sort through your feelings? Be in touch?

I can feel the crush on my heart.

I relay Keira's message to Mylove and she is livid, "Can you imagine what she would've done if you had said the same to her when she came out? She would've gone postal!"

I can't argue with that. I am very hurt. Is the love and support she pledged at Thanksgiving gone already? I have no idea what "feelings need to be sorted through." They could be good feelings, right? She was great when I came out to her, I have no rational reason to think it's any different now, right? Right?

This is how vulnerable I am. I can say with reasonable conjecture that all girls in my heels go through the same thing. There are well-documented, heartbreaking stories of both girls and boys whose families out-and-out reject them. Kristin Beck's own mother couldn't graciously accept her own daughter. Could my gay sister be rejecting me?

But instead of calling me back, Keira fires off an incendiary email that contains many shots across my bow:

"I didn't have an issue with your decision, but when you signed-off saying that you had originally planned on dropping this bomb when we had come for our only vacation in ten years, I was livid."

"Dropped the bomb" and "livid." Huh. Girlfriend, I'll show you livid. Leave it to my dear sister to engage in emotional jujitsu, and make my coming out suddenly about her. It is not lost on me that she, as a lesbian, considers "coming out" the dropping of a bomb. Something strange is going on.

I know in the pit of my stomach that whatever it is, it isn't good.

I call my sister Kimm for insight. "How's it goin'? Ya know, with me?" (meaning my she-ness) and before she can answer (because, last time I checked, we were not only good but amazing), I say, "Have you talked with Keira about it, about me, she?"

"Uh huh."

"And?"

"Oh, you don't get to know what we say about you behind your back."

Hmmm just like a real girl. I guess I should be flattered.

"Well, is everything all right?"

"Oh, you know Keira – everything is drama."

"Hmm, well are we okay?"

"You have to understand, you rocked my world. I have to reconstruct how the world works. You were the example that I used for how a man should be."

I am speechless, both flattered (shouldn't I be?) and gobsmacked. Apparently, Kimm also has had to sort through her feelings, but she took it upon herself to do the work. So what's Keira's problem?

Kimm tries to distract me with shiny objects, "Have you talked to Shane, yet?"

It works. I confess I've been putting it off. Shane's the baby of our family and we're all scared of her. Seems every family has one: the southern Republican, back-to-Mass, conservative-Catholic, and so opinionated that any political discussion turns into a surreal fight with fly paper.

I call her – She is absolutely beautiful with my news (of course!). Her only question: are you happy?

But what a question it is. Everyone else has assumed I am or should be, but Shane checks in genuinely invested in me and the real answer. "Yes, I am. Shane, I'm giddy, I'm so happy."

"Well, that's good enough for me."

I hang up and wonder aloud why the baby of our family has always been the most adult of the four of us. (But never tell her that, she'd be impossible!)

Why can't Keira be like Shane, of all people? My *gay* sister should know how freakin' vulnerable I am at this time. That she willingly puts herself before me is infuriating.

And it's not lost on me. I was the big brother. I was the protector. I was their emotional security, there when even their own father was not. There in the background, ever vigilant, always just a phone call away.

And now, here "she" (me) is admitting that I'm a little brittle, and needing just a gosh darned shoulder. Could that really be too much to ask, or are they genuinely clueless? I've never needed any support before. I've always been rock steady, cool under fire, the one who was in control of any crisis – the world traveling, survival show expert who swims with anacondas in jungle rivers, climbs glaciers, and is probably calling from the Arctic Circle by satellite phone to apologize for missing another family function.

I've never needed their support, just their hug every few years or so.

It's a grave I've dug for myself. I'm doing it right before my eyes, letting them off the hook, holding myself responsible for their foibles. They can be vulnerable, unsure or even wrong. It's cool with me, I'll always make it okay.

My becoming their sister is scary for them but mostly scary for me. Is this how it's going to be? My family merely *tolerating* a new big sister, but things never really being the same?

That's not what I'm hoping. I want things to be better than before, not worse. Why does the feeling that it "could be bad" even come up?

But hold on girl! You just got an atta girl from your baby sister, so what's with the Debbie Downer act?

She's right (whoever she is). And so cheered by my great chat with my baby sister, I dial Aunt Phyl.

Aunt Phyl is my mother's baby sister and the only one living of her generation on either my mother or my father's sides. My mother left us first (age 42), followed by their big brother Uncle Rob (age 70). Aunt Phyl takes her role as aunt and elder of the family very seriously and she moves heaven and earth to stay active in the lives of her nieces and former nephew/godson with great joy.

It helps that she has more than her share of brash Bronx gumption; she was an elementary principal and teacher there for a zillion years and spent her childhood in Brooklyn. Aunt Phyl is a hurricane of energy, love, opinion and more love.

She is also my Godmother.

She has, for over 40 years, lived with my Aunt Mish (no blood relation but connected by love). Aunt Mish is still one of the foremost experts on education in the country. A Ph.D. and a great soul, she adopted us as if we were her own blood. And she has been there for all of the special moments of all of our and the next generation's baptisms, confirmations, and graduations. Birthdays are never forgotten, and at Christmas, there's always special something in the mail.

They are the best example of "cool Aunts" around. They travel the world, stay connected with life and family, and always brighten our lives with special little reminders and long distance tickles.

As the only grandson of the Owen clan (my mother's side). I had the distinction of being the little prince. Gram (my mom's and Aunt Phyl's mother) was old school, and I was "Master Scott" until my 18th birthday. Aunt Phyl & Aunt Mish kept up that respect, grooming me to be the patriarch. And though they loved my father, Aunt Phyl felt that it was I who had kept the family together when Mom passed, including keeping Dad from dissolving into his own grief.

I always appreciated that Aunt Phyl recognized that. She told me this many times and depended on me to keep the family tight, even after the girls married.

But as for being a Godmother, Aunt Phyl, as staunch a Catholic as she still is, never responded anytime I tried to play the Godchild card. She was my *Aunt*, no question. If I referenced my position, like "Since you are my Godmother…" she would never pick up that ball. And though she was always attentive and remembered every holiday and anniversary, it was *Aunt* Phyl, not *Godmother* Phyl, who did the loving, and I was never sure why. Any direct question about it from me was met by a, "Really? I never noticed. Of course, I am." This, by the way, is still not an admission!

But with that as the picture, imagine her hearing, "Aunt Phyl, It's me. I'm a woman."

Silence.

Then, "Good for you."

She is astutely aware of what I am saying and measures her words carefully, sensing with great love how vulnerable I am. We talk for an hour, and during that time, she grasps fully what I am saying as she drops into her default mode of *the educator*.

First, she asks about the girls (my sisters) and I have to confess that as of this chat, only Shane is really cool with it. Keira is being her usual dramatic self, and Kimm is supportive but still wrestling with it.

Aunt Phyl knows exactly what to say. "You always seemed superhuman for a guy. You protected everyone's feelings and put everyone before yourself, their needs before yours. You are the rock and now we know why!"

We both laugh. What man is capable of doing that! No offense to the men in the audience, it's just a joke (not really) and I need the laugh.

Okay, so this day was improving. First Shane and now my Godmother, I am ahead of the game. Aunt Phyl recovered from the shock and awe quickly and lovingly asked more questions and apologized for the pain I suffered growing up trying to keep it secret for so long. But before I moved too far away from my past, she wanted to make sure that I know how grateful she was that, despite pain and hardship, I completed my mission before coming out.

Aunt Phyl has one last reminder: "You are (now) still the matriarch. Don't think this changes your responsibilities one bit. The girls will still look to you to keep the family on track. Promise me you'll still fulfill that position?"

As we sign off, I ask if she can stand having a Goddaughter. She says it will take some time, but she admits that what I had always felt was true. She confesses that she could never say the word "Godson" before and now realizes it's because her heart must've known that I wasn't. She chuckles warmly, "I have no problem calling you my "God Child."

I'll take it.

19
GERHARD

I'm driving along the 210 freeway, skirting the foothills of the southern Cali mountain ranges that define our northern borders. I'm alone but my thoughts fill the car. Of all the people that I want to come out to, Gerhard is where I've truly got the most on the line. That Gerry is important to me is an understatement. He's been the foundation of all things that make me the me I want or aspire to be. And I cannot, will not, mess that up.

Gerhard is many things to me, and to many others: mentor, friend, guardian, and example. He's what many call a "second father." Not me. My dad was doing a helluva job, I didn't need a second one (besides, my godfather "Uncle Jerry," lived with or around us my entire childhood; my father's navy mate and partner in crime, literally, helped raise me. So, no, I didn't need a third).

But I did need a Gerhard. Even my dad and Uncle Jerry would agree. And though he would (and has) frowned on that title, "second father" (he loved my pop), he still gets all the respect and responsibilities that come with it.

To me, and the men who are my brothers in an illustrious gang known as Gerhard's Sons (Casey, Jeff, Willie, Mark, Chris, and Troy), Gerry was a force of nature. In his strong, stern, always no bullshit manner, he was the love, caring, and commitment that everyone is supposed to get from the man from whose loins they've sprung.

Thankfully, I never needed that from any man – my father, as I've already mentioned, was the best even though he had his faults (I even have a problem saying that he has faults). Gerry and my Pop often conferred about me and the various ways to keep a constant boot to my ass for my own good.

Which is what Gerhard did. As my mentor, a true one in the Michelangelo, "So you wanna be an artist kid" way, Gerry made me work to earn the right to work under his wing. And when I did, I would never leave, except, as the apprentice must eventually do as a matter of course, to honor the master. Even so, I still sit at his feet with all things artistic, even in my own medium of film and storytelling, because that's how amazing he is. He's been there my entire life, starting as the legend that I'd only heard whispers of when I was a middle-schooler, then getting into his ceramics class as a freshman in high school, and on to the present.

Gerry won my heart and forged our relationship from the word go. I had done not only my first sculpture for his class but all three of my best friends' assignments as well. I loved ceramic sculpture and the chance to do four pieces instead of just the one was. . . four opportunities to make art! And they call this school?

I never saw it coming. Gerry went on and on about how great each of my friends' projects were, and how great they as students was, and how creative they were while I got a "C for Charity." He pointed me out as a lesson to all – that if you at least "try," no matter how "mediocre" your work is, he would always give you a "passing grade." I was shocked (I didn't know that word until then). Charity? Mediocre!!! I went after that hook, line, and swallowed the sinker down to the pit of my gut!

I was furious! Of course, he knew I did their work for them. Of course, he knew how to "get my goat." It was as if my father had given him not only the owner's manual to my soul but the keys and pink slip!

When I challenged him, he merely smiled a smile that I would come to hate, the one you see when you hear the word "checkmate." He said, "For them, it was "A" work – pretty smart of them to hook up with a freak – but for you? That's just C work, you are way better than that. If you choose to cruise, then get the hell out of my class. I only have time for a freak."

I was dumbfounded. "But if you only have time for freaks, why give the others A's?"

He shook his head. "They're harmless, and they don't take any of my time. They do as they're told and nobody gets hurt. And freaks like us need "normals" around to remind us who we're talking to. If you just make art for other freaks, then what's the point? Freaks don't buy art, only the normals do. And if these normals develop an appreciation for art and show up for my class, then we all win down the road in life, yes?"

Oh great, I'm studying art with "Yoda the Barbarian."

For the next four years, it would only get better. Gerhard kicked my ass up one side and down the other to be better, better at being a freak, better at the craft, better at life, better as a person. And he stole my heart forever.

Why? Because he saw an artist in me. Saw an artist worth developing. Saw a hunger to be more than a mere student of art, more than a skilled craftsman, hungry to be worthy of art itself. And I proved myself a freak again and again. He taught me ceramic sculpture, and pottery, gold and silver jewelry casting, and life. The only thing I wanted more than being a freak was to make sense of my identity. A freak was not an artist, let's get that straight. Gerry rarely used that word. But he did use it as a reference point for freakdom.

A freak is someone who can't not make art, double negative intended. It doesn't matter the medium, from food and beer (Gerry was an award-winning brewer) to even your weekly grocery list: if there is a way to tell a story with your hands, eyes, and sensibilities, a freak won't be able to walk past. Every stroke of a pencil on even a mundane form, every knot in your shoelace, is an opportunity to make art that a freak can't pass up. I still have notes from Gerry that were nothing more than a simple "to-do" list, but it looks like a Da Vinci doodle. Gerry is why my signature is like a Japanese calligraphic "chop." He's why I can't even pour myself a bowl of cereal without adding a little sumpin' sumpin' to take it in a different direction.

There weren't even rules (rules are for the normals) for being a freak, and here's where we frequently crossed swords. Even Gerry tried to adhere to the laws of physics, but if rules were for the normals then why wouldn't I test those too? Okay, sometimes the results were disastrous, like the time my sculpture exploded and took out everyone else's piece in the kiln as collateral damage. "Puppy, I told you that at 2345 degrees Fahrenheit, air pockets will find a way out – like through everyone else's pots."

I joked at his retirement party five years ago (I had been asked to say a few words as a former student), that I set the indoor record for most periods of ceramics in one daily schedule. As a graduating senior, I finagled four out of six possible periods to stay in his studio. One period as TA (teaching assistant), one period as an ST (student tutor), my own period of study and a period of "independent study" for the fourth period. My only regret was that I couldn't get them as one long uninterrupted block, having to take a break for AP chemistry and AP English. But I would often work through lunch as well as before or after whatever sports practice I had at that time of year.

And like the men who became Gerhard's sons, I found a way to get out of my other classes when it was time to help load the kiln (or unload even better). Or make clay, mix glazes or whatever else the "crackpots" (yes, we were even an official club on campus – The psycho-ceramics gang) were called on to do.

First and foremost, Gerry made us appreciate our own art. And we were relentless. The ones who stood the test of time, far after our graduations, staying active members of Gerhard's family and making art, were bestowed the hallowed name "Gerhard's Sons" when we made our rite of passage: marriage. And each one of us had the job of explaining to the loves of our lives that, *"Gerhard makes the rings."*

I dropped my bomb hours after I proposed to Mylove, unsure how to explain this law of the universe (side note: in actual fact I had proposed spontaneously three times previously and took each one back, not because I had second thoughts, but because I had such an elaborate plan for the real proposal, that I just could not allow anyone, least of all myself, to spoil).

Okay, I should back up a bit. We'll get back to "Gerhard makes the rings" in a sec because this is important: I knew I would marry Mylove after the first date. I was not only sure, it was as if it had already happened, and we were just catching up like the hubris of an astronomer thinking he had discovered a star. The star was always there, the astronomer just finally saw it.

But my star had been preordained, and so was the location of her proposal, which was not the front seat of my Ford pickup while we waited for light to change (number 1); or the produce aisle in farmer's market (number 2); or the lobby of the church at the reception of a wedding of people we barely knew (number 3). Heck yes, I meant each one, and believe me, taking them back was not easy but this has a script written when I was a child.

You see, I had discovered a tree that grew into a forked trunk on the edge of a forest while hiking in my home mountains. At sunset, the ball of fire would set, not only between the edge peaks of the range but right down into that fork. I swore that this would be where I proposed to my true love. Never mind that I was twelve years old when I made this vow.

Praying that it was still there, I egged Mylove on through the ferns and bramble as the golden hour glow was seconds away from its most perfect light. And then, excitedly, I made her turn and see the magic alignment, her own face lit with that golden light plating her face with molten gold. I got down on one knee and her tears were like diamonds, "Only this time," I stammer, "it's real. Mylove will you marry me?"

That night we slept under the stars in the back of my pickup, with our dog Mukti at our feet. And as we snuggled, I whispered, "Gerhard makes the rings."

"What does that mean?"

It means Gerhard makes the rings and you really have no say in what he's going to make – believe me, you can try, but the two who tried before only got what *they* wanted when what they could've gotten was *Gerhard in a ring*. Something truly amazing!

No girl in this state has ever really understood what she is being told. And really, it's not fair. She is in no mind to get the ramifications, still clinging to the delicious moment that she, too, has waited for and dreamed of her entire life.

Each would be aware of how important Gerry is to each son's life, but they wouldn't understand, that takes years, and not everyone will ever get it or him. We don't expect that (pretty clannish, we know, so sue us).

I knew Mylove would get him, but it would take time, so the sooner we started, the better. I rolled up the bedroll and we drove straight to Gerhard's house.

He looked her up and down. Now he's five foot four, both tall and wide. Like the dwarf kings of Middle Earth, he's a force of nature, the god of fire, and a total man's man; more at home with the sweat, fire and intensity of a crucible, kiln or blowtorch, and as strong as men hope to be, he's as sensitive to the heart's subtlest murmurs as artists have to be. I proudly introduced Mylove and Gerry hugged her, then held her out in his powerful arms to examine her like the diamond that she is.

"Oh, son you got your hands full with this one."

Like an eagle worried as it kicks the chick out of the nest and then relieved that it will fly, Gerhard saw immediately that Mylove would be more woman than I could ever handle. He told her so but followed it with a hearty laugh because he knew that this was the only way I would be happy. I always did best, he told her, when playing over my head.

And though Gerhard makes the rings, each soon-to-be-wife gets to choose her diamond. Which meant that we had an appointment with Harut at the LA diamond mart. So after dinner with Gerry, we hugged and left. I was glowing, a day I'd dreamed of for years. Mylove was shell shocked, but even to this day, he has that effect on her.

Gerry had been many things in his career, leading up to being the premiere art teacher. Having his own custom jewelry shop was one of them. The broker that supplied all of his diamonds and precious gems was a man by the name of Harut Yepremian. If you know anything about diamonds, you know a major portion of the diamond trade is run by the Armenian community. Harut was "the man" both inside the Armenian community and the diamond trade. Gerry and Harut would deal with no other than each other. Harut had been through this drill three times already, and I was told by Gerhard (and this was the first time I heard this phrase), "Tell them you are my son." I couldn't be prouder.

The buzzer sounded and a heavy accented voice squawked from the speaker. I gave my secret passphrase (just like a Tom Clancy novel!), the iron bars opened and Mylove and I were in. Harut offered tea while he took out a special selection for "Gerhard's sons" only. Mylove was shown by Harut what to look for and how to choose a diamond. This was part of the plan: it made the fact that she had no say in the ring's design a little easier to swallow and Mylove will admit, only now, that she was happy that she got this experience better than any dumb ol' wedding ring factory.

And our wedding day was the first time either of us laid eyes on it. With music starting up and the last guests being seated, Gerhard arrived and handed it to me as he himself took his seat. I had to look at it and opened the box. A beautiful diamond flanked on either side with two channel-set sapphires. Incredible. And my ring, just as I had asked, was not a male version of Mylove's, but an echo of the design. I had been clear that I wanted hers to be the center of attention.

Mylove didn't see it until I placed it on her finger during the ceremony. I fumbled, nervous that I would hurt her finger by forcing it, but she whispered "just push" and it slid into place of course, a perfect fit.

Gerry's solution for my ring was explained to me at our reception. He admitted that this had stumped him at first. So he used the design that was his master's thesis, incorporating as many aesthetic principles in one three by six rectangle as possible. The idea that I, as his apprentice, would warrant Gerhard's master's thesis, was humbling and mind blowing.

So, yes, needless to say, Gerhard is that important to me. All of this is raging through my mind as the Santa Ana winds buffet the car and I race toward the mountain. Of course, Gerhard will love me, even if I am a woman. Of course, he will support me in making any change in my life. And of course, he will protect me. But what I'm most worried about is will we, he and I, master and apprentice, be able to grow with this. What if we grow apart? Would we change away from each other? What would I do? A huge cry of fear stuck in my throat.

I had been in Gerry's studio under his eye and wing as recently as the previous year, as I sculpted a ceramic crucifix for my sister Shane. (She was reconnecting to the Catholicism of our childhood.) So my regard for what Gerry and I have is not the misty-eyed memories of a childhood long ago, but the active dance between master and apprentice that is supposed to last forever.

Mylove has called me three times as I drive to my hometown, and each time, I have to confess to my procrastination. I'm speaking of course, of the heads-up call that has become part of the formal coming out ceremony, giving everyone a few minutes before seeing me in person to get prepared for the woman that greets them.

Yes, I'm procrastinating. this man has read my mind since I was a child; he knows when I'm fooling myself even before I do, and what I don't want to do is upstage my entrance. My demeanor and appearance are far better at demonstrating the obviousness of my true identity then anything I could say. But I've learned that every heads up call immediately turns into an interrogation, and I never know how to deftly say, "Wait until we see each other."

So, I put off calling until I make the last stop before I "drive the hill," as we call the mountain. The last leg of the trip climbs the 5000 vertical feet up to Rim of the World Highway, from the valley floor to the San Bernardino Mountains. This is a customary stop for all mountain folk, a potty break, before the half hour white-knuckle drive up the Panorama highway. But once again, I chicken out and put it off and instead call Mylove. "No, not yet, but I'll do it when I'm on the mountain."

She understands. She and Gerhard have grown to love each other (it worked!). She knows the stakes for me, especially now. As I reconcile who I am, it's stone cold evident: without Gerry challenging me, nurturing me, and loving me, this Gender Dysphoria would've crushed me during the years where I was the most fragile and confused. I do owe him my life, and so do my parents, and by extension, Mylove.

She gently reminds me: I'm running out of time, If I don't call now, I'll T-bone Gerry! When I'm less than five minutes out, I take a deep breath and I call…

"Hey, Gerr… yeah, almost, almost, I'm at the cutoff, hey listen… "

And I give the standard line that I look more feminine than when last we met. And he laughs, "What? Are you wearing a bra & high heels?"

"Bra yes, heels? Well, they're boots so yeah, I guess they qualify as a hint of a heel."

"Well get your butt over here. You know I love you, no matter how you're dressed."

Now, that's what I mean about upstaging my entrance. Did that sound to you like he had no idea what was going on? He jumped right to reassurance and enlightenment, knowing how vulnerable I am – I told you, he knows what I'm thinking before I've even thought it.

In two minutes I'm pulling into his driveway and I'm praying, "Don't come out, don't come out." Usually, Gerry's so happy to see me, he's opening my door for me before I've got the key out of the ignition, pulling me into a bear hug. But today I'm a bit disheveled (after a two-hour car ride through the Santa Ana winds), and I want – no, I need – to look my best. Everything is on the line here. Thank you God (he must've heard my plee) because the driveway is surprisingly, almost spooky… quiet.

So I take advantage of it and get my self sorted. I'm looking good, sexy tunic, silver belt, sleek black tights and my hair up. Make-up survived. Whew, he's gonna be all over my color choices: this is art, after all. And I'm walking up the front step and can see in the glass doors of the front door that he's still not coming out to greet me. Oh no, is everything okay? I let myself in, and there he stands with his wife, Mary. I'm feeling a little faint, I realize I've holding my breath, and so are they.

In this frozen moment, I can squeeze in a word about Gerry's wife Mary. She's a beautiful woman and, like Mylove is for me, she's more woman than Gerry could ever handle (he does his best playing over his head, too). Mary's British and has been here for over forty years, raised two kids and coaches figure skating. She's the perfect English lady, so much so that she never goes out in public or lets anyone see her unless she's completely together: hair, make-up, nails and attire. She always wears the most appropriate thing for the most appropriate time. Classy and striking, Mary doesn't know it, but for years, she has been one of my role models (it's a big club). But I'm suddenly worried that we're not cool. I haven't ever talked to her about trans anything, so I have no idea if she could even be not cool about me. . .

"FAR OUT!"

Blessedly Gerry breaks the silence, the words cradled by his hearty laugh. His smile gives me a flash burn and within seconds, he grabs me into his arms like there's no tomorrow. I can still feel his hug to this day. This paves the way for Mary, and she steps in between us and takes me by both hands to the dining room and sits knee to knee with me. She doesn't let go of my hands for the hour it takes to pour out my story.

As soon as I'm done with the first stage and Gerry's got it all figured out, Mylove calls – I knew she would. Gerry confesses that no, he didn't see this coming ever, but that he was always struck by my artistic "solutions." The ways I solved creative challenges was never the way a normal boy would, he tells her, and though he didn't see it as a gender thing at the time, now it makes sense.

He did know I was struggling internally with something growing up and was always a little concerned with my drinking and drug use (come on, weed and every once in a blue moon, some 'shrooms, coke only for a short time, who had that kind of money?). But that's one of the reasons why he loved Mylove's spirituality, crediting it and her with saving me.

He always was struck by the devotion and intensity I had for my family. And he also was proud when I stepped up (and not surprised, which is nice) when my dad checked out. I was a ball of nuclear energy that seemed to always be directed toward love, but even he was never sure why there seemed to be something huge looming just under the surface. And now, today, he could see that it was all gone. The seething roiling molten core was calm and settled.

We go to lunch and Gerry makes sure to open every door for me, and hold my hand as we walk across the street. It is so sweet. As Mary continues to interview me (as everyone does) Gerry watches and as usual, finishes my sentences for me, but he is always right. He interrupts Mary at one point and shrugs in utter amazement.

"It's so weird, but it's as if you've always looked like this. You are quite pretty, girl."

As we toast with jasmine tea, he says with a cry caught in his throat, "This is one of the greatest days of my life!"

How could it get any better? – a sincere compliment that goes right to slaying a girl's deepest fear. It's one of the greatest days of my life, too!

Mary has a turn at amazement, herself. Knowing now (having been around Gerhard's sons) what a premium we have put on artistic output, she says she is baffled how I could've possibly gotten anything done as I struggled and endured (and I'm the only professional artist in our clan though we've got one art teacher). Gerry laughs, as he bores into my apprentice heart with his master stare: "Just think of your output now."

Pressure's on.

We finish lunch and drive back to the house where I've done so much growing up, and it's time to hug goodbye. I ask Gerry if he's cool that one of Gerhard's sons is now his daughter. He wells up. "I didn't think it could be possible but I love you even more."

I drive home through a shower of tears.

20
CAT'S CRADLE

Sometimes it's a wonder how I'm still standing. I drive the long way home from Gerhard's, re-visiting the many places my family lived on the mountain. The car biz was very volatile in those days and Dad got "blown out" a number of times; sometimes the last paycheck didn't stretch to the next month's rent. And well, only the children of a car salesman will understand this, but "it's cheaper to move than pay the rent."

As I travel these darkened streets, I realize that this era of my upbringing was when I first clued in as to what Dad went through to keep us clothed and fed. He was a gladiator who entered the arena every day and won his commissions by bare-knuckle charm. Good performance and high sales were never a shield against the treachery of the fragile egos he did battle with and alongside. A job could be here today and gone tomorrow.

Driving past our houses on these lonely streets makes me miss my parents even more. My dad loved this mountain and my mom loved him, so we were raised under the trees.

But, cruising past like a ghost floating through its life, is too poetic a metaphor – bringing me back to the pain of adolescence and its wistful confusion, and I suddenly get fed up with myself. "Oh, boohoo girlfriend! You're throwing that pain word around like you're the only one who ever suffered through your teens. When the truth was, you wouldn't let yourself feel pain; you were already a master at ignoring the dragon in your psyche that kept your girl in the dungeon."

It's weird that I should be introspective as I am becoming aware that life is taking on a monumental momentum like today. Geezus, girl! Gerhard was amazing! You can still feel his hug! He embraced you AS A WOMAN! Take yes for an answer and MOVE ON!

And as I talk myself down from a pity-party of one, I have to admit: I did a good job of navigating the rapids of messed-up, confusing messages and signals I received as a child. I have to hold on to a simple handrail as I scale the mountain. "God doesn't make mistakes."

That means that all of God's creation is exactly as intended, even if it doesn't fit someone's fantasy of reality. Because that's all it is; despite what anyone tells us. Nobody has the patent on reality. Any view/opinion (other than your own) is just someone else's vision of "should."

No matter what I tried, I was not a boy. No matter what my body told me, I was not a boy, never ever going to be one. After 52 years of watching and waiting, it only got harder, until my beautiful brain, my precious mind, was able to finally get its bearings and realize that the stupid games could be over, life could be as wonderful as life is supposed to be. I now was beginning to understand what embracing "acceptance" actually meant.

Sure, at this point you'd think I wouldn't be fighting with something as basic as acceptance, but as you start to inspect ever corner of the fortress you've built, there's a lot of nooks and crannies, and every single one of them needs to be scrubbed.

Getting at the big pieces of identity is relatively easy (once you start), but it requires a daily re-wiring of your perception and your mental orienteering. For example, every mirror for most people may be just a tool to make sure that nasty spinach is gone from their smile; but for girls like me, the mirror is a spiritual gymnasium, where we confront reality, desire, our shortcomings, fears – and, yes, even spinach.

Checking my make-up each morning, I catalog the changes happening and the changes not happening. I get to stop myself from beating myself up for both wanting and not wanting fixes, or changes, things not done right, things done over right, and ugh! Even as hormones soften my features, just seeing a hint of that boyish dimple in the chin, or a jawline that's a little too strong is enough to stick a tiny splinter of doubt into my mind that will fester all day. Doubts can escalate from, "Will I ever be able to draw a straight eyebrow," to "Will I be able to change the orbit of my planet? Will I be strong enough to be a woman?"

And so you dig through that box in the attic of your head and sometimes you have to drag out a voodoo doll that still has the pins stuck in it from countless conversations and arguments with God. Why did you make this so hard? Why do other girls get to yada, yada? Why don't other girls have to yada, yada?

And if it's a good day, you realize how far you've come from walking these darkened forests of "never going to happen" to finally stepping into the sunshine of your mentor's embrace. And it works to talk you down from the emotional ledge. You breathe deep and you realize, of course, you're strong enough. The women in the family smile upon you, and they are proud of you, proud that you finally know who you are – one of them.

And as lovely as it is to be walking on my home turf, I've been back in my car for ten minutes racing down the mountain, before I "come to" in my body (I've heard of sleep-walking but this could get dangerous). I'm zigging and zagging across the two lanes of, legend has it, the only highway in California actually designed to be a scenic highway. I bank a hairpin turn that creates a switchback that gives almost a 270-degree view of the "Inland Empire" as it meets LA and the Pacific Ocean. Yes, it is scenic but it's also an incredible race track and those who know the road use every bit of it like me: the freedom I feel as I rocket down the mountain matches the vertigo I still feel from Gerhard's hug. I call Mylove, "two hours out."

Because Cat is waiting. Our dear friend Cat couldn't take my news over the phone. She's begged to come up and wrap her arms around me so she can wrap her head around what we're going through. They're already at our favorite sushi bar. At this rate, I'll be there before dessert.

Cat is one of my mostest favoritest people in the world. She's… where to start? A biologist, massage therapist (the best) yoga instructor, legal mediator, grandmother, mother, and friend. One of them thar underachievers, if ever there was one.

She's also got a laugh, rather a cackle, that can break glass. And it comes at the drop of a hat, just like her. When Mylove went through chemo the first time, there was only a handful of women I would allow to "support" her; including Cat, Sko, and Deb, three angels who would come and stay with us after each chemo session and deliver what she needed: healing and sisterhood. Not "well intentioned" giving. I needed the women Mylove loved most who would know how she wanted to be cared for. There were many who gave lovingly, don't get me wrong, but some people do healing better than others and I wanted the archangels.

Of the three angels, Cat came most often. She has always treated our marriage with as much reverence as Mylove and me, and credits us and our marriage with restoring her faith in love.

So you can see why Cat is having the hardest time. And I guess, if I squint, I can see why. Just like my sisters, she put me up on a very high pedestal; and like my sisters, Cat held out for her perfect love because she saw it work for Mylove and me – and if I was a woman, well really, what did it mean to our marriage?

I'm walking into the darkened sushi bar and as I emerge from the shadows, I think to myself could it be more dramatic? I'm led to the table. Mylove has her back to me, but Cat sees me instantly and her cackle shatters the air. She squeals, "Oh Sweetie! You're gorgeous!"

This is good. We're gonna be okay. I'm a little breathless from playing speed racer – I got there even before the second round has hit the table. Mylove raises an eyebrow (she knows how long it should've taken), but she's happy to have me and dives into a thorough interrogation of Gerhard's visit.

Cat listens with rapt attention, and I know she's observing my every move. She has met Gerhard and knows how important he is to us. Finally, I'm done and so is the sushi, and we head back to the house for dessert. Cat's staying the night with us, so it's gonna be my first girlie slumber party. She won't let go of my arm all night, and for now, is letting me drive the conversation, which is a little unnerving. Cat's not saying anything – she's studying me, making sure I'm as good as I claim. Okay this is huge (I have to keep reminding myself) for both of us, and if Cat's got her tongue, then I should be cool with that.

And that lasts until the sun rises. As we sit round late morning and sip coffee in our bathrobes and slippers, she's had time (and a night's sleep) to collect her thoughts and I suddenly realize I haven't had quite enough coffee for this.

Because I do care what she thinks – for all of the above reasons. But mostly, like Mylove, her opinion as a woman is how I'm remapping my world. Cat is a role model of how women should be, are supposed to be, aspire to be; wickedly intelligent, brilliantly funny and light, wise and so compassionate that her hugs can heal bleeding wounds (well you get the picture).

She asks, respectfully, if she can take my picture and send it to her husband. He wants to see what I look like. But I frown and she immediately backs off. After some mulling, I can see the innocence of what she's trying to do (she wants to let her family know she's okay with me and they need to get on board too). And really, this is a rite of passage.

I have never liked my picture taken, nor my voice recorded. I told myself that this was because I am a director, not an actor, and I always look and feel so painfully awkward that it embarrasses me to death. But the truth is even worse. It hurts to see what the camera captures.

I'd rather she wait until I have a chance to take care of my "bed head" and put on some make-up. "Hey you're lucky Scottie's sitting here in robe and slippers," chimes in Mylove, "usually she would be downstairs for another hour putting on her face."

Which is true, I did consider it. But I felt like it was more appropriate, since it was just us girls, to go bare naked (meaning face and hair). Cat says she completely understands and her compassion makes me feel superficial and silly – what am I so afraid of? Heck, let's do it. "Snap away," I say.

And she does, receiving a warm response from her husband almost instantly. ("Beautiful," he says.) That wasn't so bad now, was it? Actually, it was, but I'm workin' on it. Feeling lighter, we all get our coffee klatch on, with joy and love.

Cat admits that she's feeling better now that she's been able to touch me. Then her questions turn to Mylove and her seemingly superhuman ability to have rolled with my/our change without so much as a second thought. But Mylove is able to trot out the nasty little creature called fear (he's on a leash, but he's actually a little better fed than even I would've guessed) as testament that it wasn't easy at all. She explains that it takes a constant re-wiring of her psyche that's on par with what I go through every day.

And I want to make this clear it's not that Mylove is superhuman, it's that she's putting forth superhuman effort. She chooses to make her side of our marriage right. That's why it's called love.

Mylove confesses that I have more faith in her then she has in herself. Every time she feels a pang of doubt, she reminds herself that she fell in love with me. And she likened it to Christopher Reeve's wife, who married Superman, but spent much of their marriage caring for a man whose body completely failed. She could never have known what the future held when they fell in love (who saw Christopher's accident coming?) and, though outward circumstances changed, love hadn't.

In Mylove's case, she was in love and loved the soul of me. That this soul had wrapped itself in the wrong paper when we first met did not change the soul's essence. And despite telling herself that if she "cut and ran" not a jury in the world would convict her, she knew she'd be losing the love we have and the love that we are.

This experience revealed what her soul's purpose was for taking birth: to truly know love. To love and be loved. By me.

Cat reveals that several of our closest friends back in San Diego (where Mylove and I were first married) are having the same issue she's had – needing to wrap their arms around me – and if it worked for her, it would work for them. She would host a party for Mylove and me in San Diego to meet "Scottie."

A real coming out party, a debutante ball, if you will. Oh boy, I always wanted one of those.

Whatever will I wear?

21
COURTIN' FAVOR

I can't believe this day is finally here! I'm nervous! My appointment at superior court is 8:30 am and Mylove has taken the morning off to accompany me. I have a wardrobe that will be taken seriously: red knit skirt and ivory lace top with a black shrug and peep toe pumps. I look very business-like and feminine. But if this were any later in the year, I'd be overdressed for our So Cal climes.

I admit, getting dressed is a distraction from a day I never thought would get here. I'm so excited, I can barely focus. What could possibly go wrong?

Apparently a lot, if I'm to believe the Transgender Law Center's website, which hasn't failed me yet. But last night, as I took one last look before bed to make sure all was in readiness, I discovered a section labeled, "What to do if:"

Like what to do if I encounter an uncooperative judge who…

WAIT, WHAT? UNCOOPERATIVE WHAT? JUDGE?"

Judge as in weighs-in, as in judges me. I haven't taken it that way until now. Apparently, a judge can decide to go back to the judge part. And judge me not worthy, and not grant my petition to grant a legal name and gender marker change.

Hold on. I thought the doctor was the one who judged me?

I don't have time for this, I need my beauty sleep. But that doesn't stop me from reading that I should "prepare a script" in case I meet with an ornery judge. A script? I'll be lucky if I can remember my name as I stand before his bench.

Do I stop reading, shut off my computer for the night? You've been reading my account so far, right? You guessed it. I read on.

There is what to say if the clerk decides to make it tough for me even after the judge rules in my favor. I am still trying to fathom the ruling part – this is just a formality, right?? Apparently not.

But that's what they had 4-8 weeks to do, right? Shoot holes in my right to have my name changed? Am I running from a crime, shirking financial obligations, hiding from legal (or illegal?) responsibilities?

If the answer is no, then call me Ms. Right.

I don't sleep. But now it's morning and I'm up, dressed and looking quite cute.

Because if this isn't enough, I've got a job interview right after we get out of court and this will be my first "in-person" interview as full metal Scottie.

That is, If I'm judged worthy.

Mylove and I walk up the steps and both of us have to put our purses in the metal detector. The Officer stops us, "Ladies?" We both stop and look to her (oh God, what did we do wrong?). "You know where you're going? All courtrooms up the elevator, clerk's office to the right. Please have a nice day."

I exhale and Mylove grins, "Relax you're doing fine."

The click of my heels on the marble floors echoes like gunshots and Mylove rolls her eyes, "I still can't believe you like to wear those." She's right, I'm wearing my big girl shoes, with about as much grace as a fifteen-year-old, and I'm scared to death I'll fling one across the halls with each step.

Finally, we're at the third floor with a bunch of men wearing ill-fitting suits. I can't tell if they're plaintiffs or litigators. This court sees those changing their name and gender marker, and also those who've been injured slipping on someone else's floor. I'm afraid that I can see connections, but everything I picture is, well, not worth repeating.

The clerk opens the door from within and welcomes us with a grunt into the courtroom. Two flags (guess which ones) flank a huge cliff of a desk for the judge (as tall as a poster for a bad Pink Floyd cover band) beneath the seal of the State of California in mosaic tile. Classy.

The clerk is not ready to affect his clerkship mantle just yet and waves us to seats as he busies himself with shuffling papers at his desk, which is subservient to the judge's lofty promontory. Besides Mylove and me, there are two sets of litigants/plaintiffs and accompanying attorneys, and we take seats in the theater-type wooden seats.

The clerk ignores us for fifteen minutes until we're almost at our appointed time of 8:30 and then suddenly, his clerkiness stands and clears his throat, "His honor has called to say that he's running 5-10 minutes late, and apologizes for any inconvenience."

Now there's the clerk I expected: a polished tenor that cracks off the back walls with authority and confidence. He calls roll by case type, and though there are two legal name changers, only moi has deigned to show up. Next, he calls the other types, which are "slip and falls": one at a fast food joint that sells tacos, and the other, *another* fast food joint that sells tacos. The first is here to say that their floor was clean and therefore, they are not responsible for the plaintiff's injury; the other that the damages asked for by the plaintiff are too high for someone who slipped on guacamole.

Gosh, and all I want to do is change my gender identity.

The judge arrives and decides to hear first the cases for the name changers (miscreants that we are). I guess so he can get on to some real business. He calls the other name changer case first, "Michael Myers" (wasn't he in Halloween?) but as the judge scans the room (all six of us) and receives only blank stares, the clerk says, "Your Honor, Mr. Meyers is a no-show."

So the judge tosses the file down from on high to the clerk.

"Tough room," whispers Mylove, but I barely hear as my breath catches in my throat. I'm next, and I try to remember the right order for uncrossing my legs, standing, and straightening my skirt without falling off my heels when I hear the judge call the next name, "Michael Meyers."

I consider sitting back down but it's a process, so I pause, looking to Mylove.

The clerk couldn't have poured more disdain into his voice if he tried, "As I said, your honor, Mr. Meyers is a no-show." I don't think it was just my imagination that he sounds a little like the long-suffering wife who has to remind her husband that his glasses are on his forehead every time he loses them.

Which may have been why the judge replies with no patience either, as he stares at the file still on his desk, "But you said we had two name changers."

"I did your honor. You threw the wrong file at me."

Guys! Not now. Not with my file, please. Everyone just calm down. I look to Mylove as if to say, "See my fears were grounded!" She pats my hand and smiles. It is (in any other universe) sorta, maybe, kinda, funny.

The clerk stands with a huff and begins to dig among his files for the file the Judge had unceremoniously thrown at him just seconds before... and finds MY FILE!!!

Yes, he had discarded that which I had stewed over for months with no more care than the junk mail that no doubt clutters his kitchen counter.

I hear him call, "Scott James Madden" to the bench. And the woman who pushed through the swinging low door (the infamous "bar" that lawyers have to study to pass) to stand before his court now clears her throat and says in a much lower alto than any woman should have, "Here your honor."

But he doesn't even look up. I am prepared for him, as the arbiter of the state of California, to ask a question and as he clears his voice, my mind races ahead, hearing Mylove's coaching: be clear, respectful, and save any engagement about anything that could possibly screw this up for after his gavel hit. Instead, I hear him say:

"The state of California grants your petition. Please see the clerk. And good luck to you."

I nod, and I think I say thank you (at least I hope I did) and turn around to leave. The clerk hands me a slip of paper with instructions and bids me good day, and then Mylove and I are hugging in the halls. I am too shocked that it is over that fast, just like that.

We have six stamped, original copies made, needed for all the various governmental agencies, so I can complete the process of he to She.

We get home and I feel like celebrating and can't understand why there isn't a surprise party waiting for us! Instead, Mylove makes us each a celebratory cup of fawkey and we sit together on the couch to read aloud what has just changed my life forever:

DECREE CHANGING NAME AND GENDER

The court orders that:

The (present name): Scott James Madden

Is changed to: Scottie Jeanette Christine Madden

The court further orders that:

The gender of (new name) is changed from male to female.

The court further orders that a new birth certificate be issued reflecting the changes in name and gender.

This date March 24, 2015, by superior court judge: James A. Kaddo.

And then I'm running out the door, back to real life and my first interview as an "official woman." Invoking my new BFF (none other than my very own thunderbolt) I won't hesitate to be upfront with these guys from the word go. Am I excited? Come on! I am interviewing for the showrunner spot for a show that will follow OneRepublic on a middle-eastern tour and it feels like more than divine providence. Look out world, here comes Ms. Scottie!

I am different in this interview. I usually close the deal as the cocky gunslinger with world traveler swaggah, who usually does all the question asking to decide if this company is worthy of my time. Not the other way round.

But I have grown weary of being the slinger of guns, dealing with all the same old answers and challenges of practicality that production companies feel make them sound experienced. The road is the road, and it's unforgiving of television's adolescent behavior. Only the smart or rich make it out alive and I am tired of being smart. And I am really tired of having to "outsmart" the production company to keep a crew alive and safe.

I am also sick of my swaggah; hard won or not, it is still bullshit boy bravado. The best women showrunners in the biz aren't gunslingers, but savvy, creative and cool! My friend Monica doesn't need to act with bravado and she is respected for bringing the story home. I should be able to do that, too. She would expect that of me.

So I meet the panel (yes there are three): the Executive at the company, his assistant and the publicist for the band. I'm not sure if I'm just high from the court order, or that these are just high-energy people (I didn't get that this was a normal state from any of them) but something is clicking and I blow the roof off the room.

I do it by pure, unadulterated enthusiasm for their music and the opportunity to capture a new chapter in my career. Theirs is a project that seems too good to be true.

So I say, "Guys, I usually would sit here and ask if you have all of your I's dotted and T's crossed, which I'm sure you do, but I'll be upfront with you. I want this. You might find someone as good as me, but you won't find anyone better, and certainly no one with my *passion*, to care for your show.

So I just have to ask, what do I need to say to you to get you to hire me?"

I'm pretty sure that my being upfront catches them off guard.

They try to get back control of their interview, asking how I would shoot their show. I reply that I would need the hard details on how their days would actually play out to make an intelligent guess; but I've seen others stall here when, in fact, the interviewers are just trying to get a read on your creativity and grace-under-pressure quotient. So I paint a possible day for them to use as an example, then proceed to formulate an approach to spending their money efficiently to cover their story with the most dynamic process possible. This is what I do best, it's a no-brainer, cuz I shoot from the heart, not the hip, and they are impressed.

I leave feeling really good that Scottie Jeanette was even better at this than Scott had ever been.

And the follow-up letter's response from the exec says much of the same. He writes that he's never in his career ever encountered someone with as much enthusiasm or passion for one of his projects as me, and to please hang in there.

But one thing is certain, if and when we go into production, I will need that passport! I can't have them pass up one of the best-traveling showrunners in the game cause she doesn't have her papers, and there is no way I will use my drug mule likeness of before.

I get busy filling in the passport forms and arm-wrestling an appointment to get an expedited renewal for the following Monday. I admit, in Hollywood, they are used to having frantic crew members calling them everyday with, "I need it yesterday before I fly to bumfuk Egypt tomorrow at o'dark thirty." I say "they" meaning the feds – those guys who are supposed to have even less compassion or efficiency than a DMV clerk, yeah those guys. But guess what? They squeeze me in because if I do get this gig, we leave the following Wednesday.

This really is *hurry up and wait*, but only for four days. My head is spinning. Did this really all happen in just one day? It's going so fast, I don't know what to savor.

22
TOO LATE TO GO BACK TO SLEEP

Now that the court says I'm me, I can go public and I've been gearing up for the big announcement. In today's social media world, you really can "go wide" about anything from a baby's cold, to your opinion about the next president. I have never been much of a facebooker, preferring email or (gasp) to actually talk to my family and friends. But since I can't sit down and have "the chat" with everyone, I'll get through the concentric circles that define my life by phone or in person, and then take to cyberspace for my far and wider universe. Instead of making a formal announcement, I'm just gonna post my new profile picture and name, pictures being a thousand words and all, oh, and change that M to an F. (Does it come in bright red?)

That was the plan anyway, and I had almost completed my circles. Those concentric rings of family and friends that emanate outward from your sphere of influence to those who fall in the upper stratosphere labeled "might find it of interest."

Mine were:

Mylove, heart of the center.

My sisters (and their families), the center.

My family (brother-in-law and families, aunts cousins and children), the other side of the center.

Close friends, around the center.

Tight friends, guarding the center.

College friends, concerned about the center.

Childhood friends, like to hear about the center.

Business associates, outside the center.

The world, as labeled.

I still had a few that would be considered tight friends and one or two business associates before I would handle the rest by print.

The tightest, and probably the most critical of the tight friends circle, were the guys that I studied TV & film with. In college, we referred to ourselves as the "Tag Team." Like the knucklehead wrestlers on Saturday afternoon TV, we would all dog-pile on everything from an instructor's challenge to a keg of beer. And we've remained very close for the last thirty years (thirty???? Yikes!) despite living now in more than four different states.

We stay in touch with each other through an email chain called "ski or don't ski," which determines, among other things, where we'll meet each year for a long weekend to ski and pretend we're all thirty years younger. "Ski or don't ski" reflects our philosophy of life: put up or shut-up we won't judge one way or the other, either you're on the bus or you're not, we'll catch up when we return, and still love you if you don't.

Fair disclosure: though these guys are some of my closest friends, I haven't been on the "ski trip" in years (funny how verb and adjectives get fused together to form nouns of incredible power to small groups of humans, isn't it?). They will admit, only if pressed, that I am not just one of, but the founding member. Being the only mountain kid at a beach town university (SDSU), I talked everyone into pooling our money and heading to Mammoth one year and the annual event was born.

Now, I also NEVER AGREED that this is, and should ever be, a boys only trip, having brought my girlfriend more than once but somehow along the way, these guys decided that that was always the way it had been. So it would stay that way. Funny that they always tried to remember the past to their advantage, forgetting that some of us were actually there and paid attention.

This didn't become an issue until I got married (I never knew I was breaking a rule, nor would I have cared), but when Mylove and I were queuing up to have her come, the fit hit the shan and I saw a side of my "bros" that made me queasy. I was welcome, but the girl was not. What is this? When did we become the "he-men woman-hater's club?"

I admit, I didn't take their decree seriously I mean, how could I?

First off, these trips ain't cheap, and as we all got older we wanted more, bigger, better and cooler, which made the cost of the weekend the same as if Mylove and I both spent a week together skiing at Mammoth. It didn't make sense. If I was going to blow that much powder (pun intended) on seeing them, Mylove would, should come too.

But here's where my tendency to see how everything could work slammed broadside into the group mentality and I admit, I was caught up short.

This started world war three, which resulted in each one of them taking turns trying to convince me of the folly of my feelings. It wasn't as simple as me "not skiing," they wanted to make me change my mind and come. This was completely against our stated philosophy (see above). WTF?

I couldn't do it. How was I supposed to kiss Mylove goodbye and have fun when she was at home wanting to be with us? This is the conundrum that these guys could never understand because they were looking at me as a guy.

So I opted out quietly, but missed them terribly, and after a while, it festered into a full-blown "hurt" that my "protest" never yielded the change. I did stay in touch with them on, "the ski or don't ski email chain," and tried to see them separately as the opportunities presented themselves through the years.

We remained close, despite not seeing me in winter clothing, and when my schedule in these recent years made it possible, I'd call in from some remote part of the world by satellite phone, which added to my legend.

But the email chain gets… well, as everything boys do when they think they're alone; *raunchy* (and that's putting it mildly). If it didn't include several homophobic jabs and, at least, two references to farting, then it would be a gross description of each other's mother. (As a side note, most men allow one "your mother is…" joke per man per day. But that's it.) In other words, normal boy stuff.

But these are the men I love, and I needed to have "the chat" with each one individually before they read about me on Facebook. So I began a week of calls.

The first one was to my ol' buddy CL or "Stay puff" (as he's called in the Tag Team, a reference to a certain thrift store parka he once rocked on the slopes). Puffer is a father of three college students, he's one of the Angelinos (there's three of us) who produces movies for Lifetime, and we see each other all the time. I owe Puff a lot, he bought the first show I ever created and, since then, we've made some great TV together. I finished with my "news." He was quiet for an eternity (a master of the pregnant pause). Finally, he spoke, "Wow, well, I have two questions. The first may cancel out the second so, here goes… "Are you punking me?"

"No. Puffy. I am not."

"Okay. So… secondly, are you okay? Happy? How can I help?"

This is why I love this man.

Our conversation dug deeper into my past and pain and whatever… but he started what would becomes a common thread: each member of the Tag Team would bet that the other guys would be the ones to have a problem with my coming out.

Boys can be so weird!

P-Daddy pledged support and love and I signed off by asking that he keep this to himself until I had had a chance to have this same chat with everyone else. He would know that it was all clear when I "came out" on the ski or don't ski email chain.

He said he looked forward to it, and I said I looked forward to reading about something other than who was going to sodomize who, or whose farts stink more.

I went down the list, each man beautiful and loving, reminding me why were all such dear friends and I surprised myself most of all. I settled into this new role as their little sister, like a duck to water.

And then it was time. In each ski or don't ski email chain, the first dude to get his deposit into that year's "producer" to secure the condo, gets first pick of the best bed, and so on, until usually only the couch is left for the last man. So, I sent out the following blast:

"Guys, I'm writing that I'm officially 'don't ski' for this year… since girls aren't allowed, count me out. Brendo, earlier in this string you asked if you could have the closet, I say take it, it's not comfortable, it reeks of old dead things, oh, and it's just now available; I'm not using it anymore. The tease light is on, Boys. Let the games begin!

Scottie Jeanette Madden"

But nothing happened. By nothing, I mean nothing gross or nasty, or misogynistic, happened. These guys were treating me with wait, was it… respect?

It was sweet and reassuring, maybe there was hope for us? Being husbands and fathers had made them grow up! The closest thing I got to the razzing I expected was Puffy's response:

'Scottie,

Just to really break the ice on the subject, will you now be riding snowmobiles sidesaddle? (Too Soon?)

How about this, you are now subject to the glass ceiling which means that you will be paid only 70% of what men are paid. Thank God. Now I might be able to hire you on a production.

I'm sure that I speak for the group when I say that, though much has changed, nothing has changed. We would like you there if at all possible.

Ciao Bella! Oh, I mean see you soon Scottie!!

Stay Puff."

The rest of their responses were even more benign, falling into the "though everything's changed, we will always love you, sister" category. And pledged support and admiration of my courage.

What had I been afraid of for forty-five years? I was beginning to forget. But okay, lest I act like I'm not paying attention (1,700 trans people murdered in the last ten years), these are some close friends whose only stake in the game was losing a drinking buddy.

But the next group had a dog in this fight, "me." It was on to my old boss who might be a boss again in the future.

Oh, and a little circle all its own, known as _The Dudes_. I've been putting off "the chat" with these guys and with good reason. This circle wasn't just the cast of DYS[3], they had become my family.

---

[3] "Dude, You're Screwed" which aired on Discovery Channel and Animal Planet 2013 – 2014, and Internationally as "Survive That!" through 2015.

I haven't fallen in love with a show this hard since I had done "The Contender." This was my baby, and I poured everything I had into it, and I was really close with three of the guys. On paper, Tezzer should be the toughest case, so he's my canary in the coalmine. Tezzer is an active duty Master Sargent in the legendary Green Berets. We share a love for Rush, teamwork, being Irish, and old cartoons. Tezzer is the manliest man I know, and the biggest, biggest heart ever. He will, and has, laid down his life for his soldiers through tours of duty in Kosovo and Afghanistan. In his words, if something doesn't increase his lethality, it's not worth his time. I knew in my heart he would be OK, but like my other very guy friends, I was most worried that our friendship would change. After I told him, he was not only supportive but he said, "If anyone ever gives you any trouble, just let me know."

So be warned: my big brother is a Green Beret. I thought I was going to get away clean, but as were about to hang up, he said, "I will always love you. I've got your back, sister."

This was getting hard. Yes, I was being showered with love and support, but it was heavy stuff. I've never cashed in my chips, preferring to know I was rich without having to test it. This experience was giving everyone a place to come out with their true feelings about me. No one could fully understand what it meant to be "me," but everyone was willing to at least try. They wouldn't let themselves off the hook with a shrug and throwing up of the hands – they now knew someone who was transgender.

I was flopping into bed each night like a dishrag drained by the tsunami of love that was pouring from the phone with each call.

I wasn't able to reach the other Dudes; each was off doing real manly stuff. So I left messages.

Next I turned my efforts to my cousins. Not a small task. There's seventeen of them, and though we don't talk every day, everyone stays connected. My cousins all know I'm the California freak (land of fruits and nuts, yeah, I get it), and, as with too many working class Irish in the Northeast these days, some are swinging Republican red. But, I soon discovered that ideology wasn't thicker than blood (I know, but sometimes, I get scared…) and they still loves them their Scottie, and each can't wait to see me in person. The nurses of the family, Peggy, Joanie, and Dorothy, had more experience with transgender than I did, and I spent most of their calls learning from them.

It was time. I couldn't hold off anymore. I love the song Defying Gravity from Wicked, "Too late for second guesses, too late to go back to sleep, it's time to trust my instincts, close my eyes, and leap."

I got dressed in a soft blouse and did my hair and make-up. Mylove took my picture. Well, thirty-five takes later (with hat and without) I got a photo worthy of a new profile picture on Facebook. Oh, and a seriously peeved wife. Really? Thirty-five takes? Really?! Sorry, Mylove.

Unlike my misfire with Google Plus over a year ago, I took deadly aim at Facebook. Ms. Scottie Madden quietly, with no explanation whatsoever, smiled at the world from under a red hat like she's always been here.

And the responses started coming instantly. Of these, my favorites are my sister Kimm's reaction, "I look more like Scott, than you do." And my friend Val, "No fair, you look 35!" But the one that crushed me, was the one from my sister, Keira, that read, "That is a Judy Madden smile." Thanks, Mom.

The responses led to many more conversations (via email, text, and phone) and reconnections with friends I hadn't talked to in years. It seemed that I have inspired something in those connected to me. I guess that this is how we change things for the better, be the best example of who we are, and people will notice and be inspired to be their best example of who they are.

I was staring at the responses to my new "face" blowing-up my FB page when I saw one that stopped time. It was from "the Grenade." This is the nickname for my dear friend and member of the cast of DYS. Jake's a former navy SEAL who's lust (and I do mean lust!) for life is equal to his lack of social convention. In fact, the unofficial leader of our cast (Tezzer the veteran Green Beret) calls him "the social claymore," a land mine that will go off at the most inappropriate time. Which, of course, Jake wears with pride.

The Grenade had just posted "I love it, Lady." For those of you who don't speak "Jake-ese," this, loosely translated, means:

A. The cat was so far out of the bag, that she's forgotten what a bag is.
B. (But more importantly) He was <u>more</u> than cool with it.

Now word was going to ricochet amongst the cast. I knew it was only a matter of time before everyone would be "read-in."

I hadn't even finished reading his response when my phone rang. "What's up Scott?" This was always a loaded question, and with Jake, it's usually both barrels. Backing up a sec, Jake's the kinda guy who loved loved

LOVED knowing things and loved letting me know that he could find out anything (still has ties to Naval Intelligence, I suppose). After working with him for over two years, I have to say that I always suspected that he suspected that I was a woman.

Case in point: last year Kristin Beck, the Warrior Princess, came out. This former navy SEAL made one of the most powerful statements ever, "I laid down my life several times for America and the promise of life, liberty, and the pursuit of happiness. I'd like a little happiness for myself now."

The documentary about her first year of transition, "Lady Valor," premiered at the SxSW film festival. I know this because, on that night, my phone rang also, and the Grenade was on it, "Guess where I am?" When I heard where my hair stood on end, and I went to Defcon 2, feeling the noose tighten. Why is he telling *me* this? He must know! But how could he?

Because he's the Grenade.

With my pulse pounding in my ears, he laughed his patented Jake laugh, "I told Kristin she had to stop working out if she wanted to look like a chick – hugging her was like hugging a strong dude."

Back to present, when I remind the Grenade about that call, he exploded with laughter all over again.

Over a three year period, my friendship with these guys had been forged by the fire of exhaustion, creativity, danger and brotherhood. They accepted me as the longhaired Hollywood leftist freak, which is not something Special Forces Ops like to do, whether soldier or sailor. Neither Tezz or Jake cared, nor were surprised when it turned out that I was their sister-in-arms all along.

Jake went all big brother on me too, giving me advice about dudes (sweet, he's changed me in his mind already!). "Guys are weird about shit like this (true) so don't worry about it. Don't waste your time on the idiots. Be careful out there, there's a lot of haters. I'm with Tezz; anyone even looks at you funny, just let me know."

How could one girl have so much love? Any fear about how I would be received by the people that mattered to me most was evaporating as fast as frost before the rising sun. I wish for everyone to know this love.

23
BROUGHT TO YOU BY THE LETTER "F"

Court order? Check. Birth certificate? In progress. Today I take on the mighty icon of Bureaucracy DMV, V, V, V . . . But I'm not scared one bit, I've got this government documentation thingy down to a science. As long as my "senior-itis" (the same antsy-in-the-pantsie feeling that tortured me in the waning days, hours, minutes, seconds, before graduation) doesn't take me down, we're golden. All I have to do is keep my eye on the prize, which is. . .

. . . to live as I should be. Free to be "you and me" – thank you, Marlo (and for those under the age of fifty, look it up). Even so, this is the very un-glamorous part of coming out. It's easy to get lost in the fabled sea of red tape.

It's been 2 hours already, DMV is nearing closing time and I'm praying I make it. FINALLY, my number is called. The clerk has never seen a gender change form before, and it hits her, this is HUGE! Her eyes go wide and she starts to say everything in a respectful whisper. She pledges to help me push this rope uphill.

But her supervisor changes the hill and, while she's at it, the rope! Yes, I do have the required letter from my physician, BUT it's not on THEIR form and of course, "She's sorry but there's nothing she can do." Sigh.

Maybe it's the hormones. Maybe I can smell the finish line. Either way, I'm not the legendary hot-head of my youth. I'm not going to start throwing my toys out of the wagon. I'm going to smile sweetly, thank them for their time, and then go into the parking lot – and SCREAM!

I call Mylove and give her the bad news and she takes it in stride for me. She, too, recognizes this very un-Scott-like behavior. Her Scott would've been in the back of a squad car by now (yay Estradiol!).

In these times, Mylove is a lemons to lemonade kinda gal – she suggests I try to get my biz at the Social Security office done so today won't be a total loss. What would I do without her but curl up and die?

The empty parking lot isn't enough to stop me, nor the "closed" sign on the door. But the locked front door finally does the trick. Better luck tomorrow. Sigh.

So the next day, I make myself pretty, AGAIN, for a photo that will have to stand up for more than 10 years, and I head out. AGAIN. On my radio NPR is celebrating, wait for it. . . Caesar Chavez Day! And that means all state offices are closed today. Frankly, I love national holidays as much as the next gal, and if we're celebrating Washington and Lincoln (on the same day? Did anyone ask them?) and Martin Luther King Jr. gets his day, then Señior Chavez certainly did some things that should make us stop and take notice. (We'll get into the "where's the women" debate later.)

Because I want to finish this! Wait! Social Security is a federal building, isn't it? (Apparently, Don Chavez's contributions stopped at the California border.) So I make a U-turn and retrace yesterday's route.

Within two hours, my court order has changed my social security number and Scottie Jeanette Madden now has some number previously assigned to some dude named Scott.

Now, all I can do is live to fight another day. Which is tomorrow.

But while I've been doing battle with bureaucracy, I realize a huge fumble. I never had "the chat" with my Godson, Sam (nor his parents for that matter). Oops!

Sam is 21, still climbing out of the trench called autism. Through the relentless diligence of his parents and years of both alternative and conventional therapies, that trench has been renamed several times, and now, Sam is thought to merely have learning disabilities.

I'm so proud of Sam and inspired and blown away by his parents, Sally Joy and Ed, two of the most important people in my world.

Yes, this is a big fumble. I need immediate action. I defer to Sam's parents to know the best way to handle and inform Sam. He has always looked up to me, and I'm not sure how to get him to understand what I'm going through. Which means, of course, that first, I have to come out to Sal and Ed.

They are shocked. Though they live in the epicenter of liberalism, Berzerkley, they never saw this one coming. Sam even has a few friends who are gay, transgender <u>and</u> queer (he's big into theatre) and still, they never saw this coming. I know, I know, I was a good dude, had many fans, it's a dungeon of my own creation, and believe me, I've learned my lesson; next time I won't try to like living so much.

It is strange. If I had just given up (like so many do) and became suicidal, homicidal or both, no one would've cared when I came out as a woman. But since I did *dude* so well, tried hard to contribute to the world, and lived up to everyone's expectations – protected my family and friends, provided for my wife and tried my best to play the hand I was dealt – everyone is *that* much more shocked by my admission.

Sal and Ed (after CPR), agree to think about the best way to inform Sam and with love and support, sign-off.

Ten minutes later the phone rings, and I hear, "Aunt Scottie? It's Sam."

143

Freakin' kid! It's like getting struck by lightning again. He doesn't skip a beat, using the right pronouns effortlessly like we've always spoken to each other this way. And until this moment, I hadn't thought about my prefix. Aunt? Oh hell yes! I'm an Aunt! Did ya hear? An aunt, and I love it!

Aunt Scottie? This is She. I love you, Sam.

It's a new day, literally. Revised forms in hand, I'm running the DMV's gauntlet for the second time. It's raining and I'm worried that the hair I've worked so hard on this morning won't hang in there to make a decent picture. It will be my face for the next ten years!

The clerk makes me surrender my stinky old boy license and punches a huge hole in it, rendering it VOID. Damn girl, this is really happening! He hands my temporary license to me to check spelling, but my eyes immediately find the worst mistake possible!

The sex reads "M."

SERIOUSLY? Somebody up there is really making me work for this. I take a breath and smile sweetly, "Um it's all good except," and I point to the offending letter. He bites his lip, apologizes profusely, but when he tries to correct it, the computer won't print another temp. Only one to a customer, I suppose. This is feeling like a Woody Allen script.

He excuses himself to retrieve his supervisor. I am ignoring my inner software that's programmed to see everything as a sign of the Universe's grand plans. I'm looking the other way as the prompt proclaims, "If it's supposed to be right, then it should be easy!" When it starts to shout, I put my fingers in my metaphysical ears. Not listening! la la la la la.

The supervisor types in her override code and I thank her, apologizing for causing the trouble, saying, "I've never had to work so hard to get an 'F' in my life."

She stops and looks at me and then bursts into laughter, joined by the clerk. I hear her repeat the line, walking back to her station, as I'm handed the new print-out. It's gloriously flawless this time.

The clerk is still laughing as he directs me to the next line – the one for getting that darn picture snapped.

Here's the thing, they're on to us. They won't let you see the photo once it's taken. After snapping over thirty-five takes for my Facebook profile shot, Mylove would agree with this practice.

But this clerk takes two, coaching me to smile on the second take. I thought I had smiled on the first one, so I'm not sure what to change for take two but she says, "That's pretty." How pretty, I won't know for another three weeks, when I receive my new correct license (and my F) in the mail. I can check off another "to do" on the list.

I make it through the week. This old lady swallowed a court order to catch a birth certificate that swallowed a social security card that chased a license that wriggled and giggled inside her. But it was her passport that started off this crazy dance. And tomorrow morning, I take on the federal government and homeland security!

My appointment with the passport office is 8:30 am, which seemed like a good idea when I booked it last week. I wake up early and get serious – a red knit dress and big girl heels. I want them to know that this professional woman is all business.

Even though I haven't been hired for the OneRepublic gig yet (which means I don't have the required "proof of itinerary" I swore I had to qualify for expedited processing), I gambled, forgetting one key element. . .

In my defense, our very dear friend, Lisa, visited over the weekend, and I did my usual: cook something no one, including me, has ever had before. Which also means, forget everything else that matters right now, we're cooking! Needless to say, I spent all of Saturday and part of Sunday letting Lisa get to know my softer side.

Then last night, Mylove and I and Lisa joined the goils (also great friends of Lisa) and I was too busy basking in the sisterhood of women to keep my eye on the ball. I honestly can say, everything slipped my mind. . .

Lisa was just "welcoming me to the gender" when dinner was suddenly cut short! Mylove was feeling warning signs that her medication was about to mutiny. Mylove never cries wolf, so for her to cry "uncle," was red lights and sirens time. I scooped her up (I still have a little white knight in me) and excused us with quick hugs.

As we drove home, Mylove asked (between waves of nausea) if I had everything I need for tomorrow. (That's her in a nutshell, even when she's on the verge of vomiting, she's thinking of me. Wait, what?)

A dim light bulb flashed on my inner warning panel. THE PANIC BUTTON WAS ACTIVATED BY HER SIMPLE QUESTION – TOMORROW IS MY PASSPORT APPOINTMENT. I need 2 passport photos and it's 8:00 p.m. on a <u>Sunday</u> night. Gotta be someone who can do this, right? Mylove just shook her head.

I got her comfy on the couch then raced to the nearest Walgreens. As Grace would have it, I am still all dressed-up from our night out, so I looked as good as if I planned it.

The picture, as you can well imagine, completely sucked. Hey fella, NEVER SHOOT A WOMAN BELOW HER EYE LINE! Anyone who's taken a selfie should know this. The camera's already a cruel witness; can't a sister get a break?

When I returned, pictures in hand, Mylove was feeling much better, thanks for asking. It's easy for us to fold in all kinds of "new normals" as we deal with cancer and it's related effects. And we're just as nimble to let them go when it's their time.

In this case, an hour of quiet and being prone hit her reset button, and she was good to go. That's Mylove. And She takes the credit (and deserves it) if she hadn't cut the evening short, I'd have stayed at the restaurant all night, and then I'd be sunk with the passport office. She just saved the show, again!

And with that, we jump forward to the next day, where I'm driving down PCH with everyone else (and it feels like everyone who's ever lived!) hoping I gave myself enough time.

Changing one's name on these sacred documents is, oddly, more serious than a silly old gender marker change. I'm not kidding, change your gender, whatever, but change your name and it's a federal case! They want a letter from your doctor (I have a stack) stating you've completed your transition. Back in the dark ages of five years ago, they demanded proof: you had to produce medical records that showed you had sexual reassignment surgery.

But today, the doctor who knows you best is the last word. Completed gender transition according to accepted medical practices? Why yes, yes I have and thank you for asking. Medical is a piece of cake – it's identity document updating (and oh yeah, only re-meeting all of your family and friends face-to-face) that takes everything you have and then some.

The man behind the glass is all about clerical precision, thanking me as he finds all of the papers *he* needs to do *his* job. I hold my breath, as he asks the fateful question, "And you have <u>proof</u> that you travel in two days?"

"No. Sir. I. Don't."

And before the silence crushes my hopes and dreams I add, "The network and the production company are still haggling over details."

He nods with bored resignation. "Hmm. Shocker."

Yes, this is LA, and this guy probably has heard it all. In LA LA Land, even those "not in the biz," are "of the biz."

He doesn't miss a beat, stapling my hideous, below the eye line photos to my paperwork, sliding them all into my surrendered "old passport" and handing me a golden ticket that says I can pick up my new one tomorrow.

Okay, it wasn't really golden, for you Willy Wonka fans out there, a pale pink, actually, but it was gold to me.

And it's tomorrow, finally. And I'm back. My appointment today is a sane 2:00 p.m. I'm actually early.

I skip across the parking lot to the five-story concrete canopy that shades the walkway that is easily a thousand yards long.

I'm in heels again, and a dignified pencil skirt that, I'm learning, is definitely not designed to be walked in. I make a note for the future, as I gingerly take the steps up to the plaza while *also* trying to demurely keep my skirt from hiking up to "showtime."

And then I stand in the line that forms outside the building (we're post 911 here. It's all about crowd control and flow). We all wait outside until we're invited in, one at a time, to go through the metal detector.

The INS officer, who I must say, is looking smart in his crisp white shirt and gray pants sporting a blue and yellow stripe down the leg, looks at me from under his officer's brim and says, "Ma'am? Can I help you?"

I don't know if I'll ever get over being called ma'am. The joy of that is equal to the hell I feel when called sir, and as I stammer to answer his question, still clinging to the waft of his acknowledgment, I show him my golden ticket and say, "Yes, Sir, I have a 2:00 pick-up."

"Well, ma'am, that would be the will call windows over there." He points to two windows that are just like every rock concert "will call" window I've ever seen. "Two windows, one line, ma'am."

Three Ma'ams in row. I know, right?

The sheer enormity of the walkways here has me walking another 100 yards to "over there." (I played football for 12 years, I know what 100 yards is.)

It's a gorgeous day. The escalating Santa Ana winds are beginning to dry and chill the air and scour the skies of any clouds. It's just glorious April sunshine! As I take my place in the line of other "passport holders" (we're an elite group doncha know?), I notice the flags are at half-staff. I'd been listening to NPR on the way here and though there was the usual heaping of bad news (and death) none would warrant this Federal show of respect and mourning. And then it hits me.

Scott James had passed on.

Scottie Jeanette would be taking it from here.

And even as I type this, I'm choking up. I'm not sorry to see him go. But he deserves a respectful farewell. He was a caring, warm, dedicated, gentleman, leader and artist. Loving Husband, Big Brother, Oldest Son and Best Bud.

BUT through God's Grace, all of his best qualities will live on. His memory is more than a beautiful chapter. (Almost half of the book that is still being written.) Joyful and curious, he had done well, seen us through to the threshold, then stepped aside graciously with a courteous bow and a great big smile.

"NEXT IN LINE?"

I'm fumbling in my purse, snapped from my reverie by the need to produce I.D. to pick up my I.D. I still have to use the even worse picture (and now with a huge hole rendering it void) driver's license and the temporary printout receipt. But this clerk doesn't care as I shove the paperwork under the glass slot; she can tell from my exuberance that I'm definitely who I say I am. She double-checks the light blue envelope for its contents, then hands it to me.

I thank her and step to the side to call Mylove. We will open this together. She is touched that I have waited for her, even though we're miles apart. I open the passport: crisp and shiny, not hammered by three years of international travel to the world's most funky, humid, and extreme locations and. . .

It's a GIRL! Staring back at me, her nose is a bit, uh hello, wide! But that's me! Hair is nice, make-up perfect, but the most beautiful thing (besides seeing my new name in print and all official-like with it's US Government's seal of approval and certification), is a simple letter: underneath the three languages stating Sex/Sexe/Sexto, the U.S. Government's official opinion of the gender of one U.S. Citizen, Scottie Jeanette Christine Madden:

the capital F. F for Female. F for me! One magic letter, and it's decided.

Now both my home state and my country agree.

*The paper chase is almost over. I'm calling it a divine gift – like a piece of bazooka bubble gum for my brain, so it has something to do while the world catches up with me. I've done it. I've actually done it. I've crossed a **Finish** line. Now, all I've got to do is grow-up.*

Oh, and I never did find out who the half-staff flags were for.

24
AGENTS OF CHANGE

Lots going on today. I'm typing my fingers to the bone (oh poor thing). I'm going to walk down to get the mail and enjoy the fresh air and sunshine. Hmm, the mailbox is slightly ajar, and there is a huge envelope . . . from the DMV! My new license is here!

I run up to the house, but Mylove is on the phone, so I'll wait for her (which is a total act of love). I AM JUMPING OUT OF MY SKIN!!!!!!!!!!!!!!!

And breathing. Trying to calm down. After all, it's only my identity. (Scuse me? Suddenly more important than the holy passport that was so hang fire important days ago?)

She finally hangs up! And don't say she's not enjoying teasing me. I'm pulling out the letter and, okay, picture's not so bad. Will I ever like photos of me? But it's got an F right where it should be! Okay, I need to process this. Excuse me.

Okay, I'm back and it's out with the old (from my wallet, that is) and IN with the you! (And by you, I mean me! She! With an F!) Uh well, like I said, big week for Ms. Scottie.

OK, now it's time for my agents to meet their client for real.

Agents are a necessary fact of life in LA LA Land. I've had several since I made the big move to Hollyweird, and most have been out-and-out train wrecks; complete knuckleheads with egos way bigger than the 800-pound gorillas they are supposed to represent. But for the last five years, I've been blessed with the best in the biz for Adventure Reality. In fact in their "shop," it's the whole department that is technically my agent, as opposed to just one person. And I've been on fire since I signed on, having jumped steadily from gig to gig, even before my shows are dry.

The two leads are Jason and Andrew. And they keep me busy and I keep making them money. It's a match made in Hollywood. And though I've come out to them by phone already (I didn't want them blindsided by any news), it's time for them to take me to lunch.

So I put on my best slacks and white leather jacket and silk blouse. Hair up and tasteful, though still rocking some flair. We're ready to "be upfront." I'm the first to the restaurant, but the hostess knows where Jason and Andrew like to sit and leads me there. I have time to make sure my look survived the Hollywood lunchtime traffic and then study the menu. And I look up to see both men smiling at me – they could be ninja! I smile and extend my hand (I've been told a lady doesn't stand to greet men) and say "So, that's how you get me into all those jobs."

And I don't realize it when I say it, but it sets the tone for the lunch: happy, light and cards on the table frank. We're not fooling anyone, nor do I want to. I want to work as a woman. I want to be regarded as a woman (and I still haven't thought about a pay cut - will that really happen? What will I do?)

But this isn't about that, at least not right now. These guys have steadily guided my career to the top of the reality food chain as showrunner. I'm the lead creative voice and head adult for all things business; in other words, the buck (literally) stops with me. And that's an important distinction to make clear. I am the link between the Network who has bought the show, and the Production Company who has sold it. I protect the Network's investment and the Company's liability. But for all my logistical and fiduciary responsibility, it's my role as the lead creative voice that is both my right and position, and is why I do it in the first place.

My experience and track record as a cool-headed field general, marshaling my troops through a production, makes me attractive. And it's my creative voice that so far has produced a successful audience experience. In essence, we are really meeting today to test our success and whether I have put enough into the credibility bank to cash in a few chips to be me.

That I might encounter some discrimination doesn't feel likely. Our biz is one of the most open minded – heck, we make stars out of criminals – so we're good at forgiving. That's not what I worry about. What creeps into my happy place every now and then is the understanding of human nature (my stock in trade as a reality show producer, remember?). Many may actually be excited to say to their friends and colleagues that they know "one of me," but will they hire me? Or will it be NIMBS (Not-In-My-Broadcast-Show), and will I even know that this is happening? I suppose not. It's how the dirty little secret will remain a secret.

My agents both listen and reassure me that "nobody even cares if you're purple, why would they care that you're a woman?"

And then, despite the fear that I've just confessed, Andrew says, "Wow, it's odd, but you have a calm, quiet confidence that you've never shown before."

"Amazing," adds Jason, "obviously this was a good move for you." Which, I admit, is a mind blower. I've always thought of myself as confident. No, that's not accurate, more like, I'm just *right*. It's the granite foundation underneath confidence. I'm usually so sure of my actions, or the need for whatever strategy I'm currently implementing, that I find it a little hard to back up to explain it to anyone. I usually blow past them and pick them up later.

So to hear that I'm calm and quietly confident is, well, reassuring. That it would be expressed with a certain "ladylike" decorum is better. As I've said, I hate my own brashness in my own ears.

And it's great to hear it coming from the guys who are selling me.

Jason is the thinker of the two and he strokes his chin before declaring, "It's time to broaden your base. We need to get you out to more companies, not just the outdoor survival-based shows. This will be a challenge, your resume screams those right now. But we'll get you in front of other companies, if for nothing other than to get you visible. Are you okay with that?"

We laugh as I wink a mascara'd eye at him and say with a sultry voice, "Do I look okay?" then I switch to nervous Nellie's voice, "No, I'm serious, do I look okay?"

Jason almost spits his espresso at me.

Then, I'm able to pick up my favorite subject. My writing career. I've got a script that Jason and I agreed would be the perfect one to start putting me out there. I've been writing it since I returned from the holidays. I'm almost done and they promise to jump right on it when it comes in. We've got a lot to do.

We finish lunch and hug, they're both glowing, and Andrew, who's the taller of the two, gives me a hug like I've never had from him. It's warm and loving. And supportive. And then I turn to hug Jason. In my heels, I'm towering over him, and our hug is warm, but a bit awkward which makes us both laugh.

Leave 'em laughing, I guess. I head for my car on cloud nine.

I'm looking back over the week's events. I've got almost everything done to start life. I always hate it when people refer to this as a "new life." Yes, it is new-ish, but I've seen it before, in dreams. And yet, here I stand for real, on a street in Hollywood, looking quite smart and pretty. Someone pinch me!

It's my time. A time of healing. A time of more beginnings. A time for reconciliation. A time for living, darn it.

It only took fifty years to get here. What will it take to leave here? To leave this place called "the beginning?"

A gig would be a good start. . .

25
THE CIRCLE

How many people do you know look forward to doing their taxes? Well, Mylove and I do. We have turned it into an annual celebration that includes a trip down the 405 to San Diego, where we've been seeing the same accountant, Steve, since before our marriage. In fact, Mylove has been seeing Steve longer than me. Usually, after we sit with him for two hours to relive our past year's success, we have lunch with our dear friends Maura and Jeff, then head back to LA. But this year, after lunch, Cat is making good on her promise (I told you she was incredible) to host my "Debutante Ball." It's turned into a weekend holiday.

Steve has always been a big fan of Mylove and me. Nobody knows better how my career has grown than Steve, and he's religiously watched (sometimes on the set) my work. I love hearing what he has liked in each show, and each tax session is filled with laughter, love, reviews, stories, and more laughter.

But he's always had a special relationship with Mylove and dotes on her like a cherished uncle. He's seen her through an audit and a divorce and couldn't be happier that she found me.

He's a deeply religious (Christian) and conservative man, and our philosophical discussions have always been rich, so you can imagine that we're both a little timid as we prepare to find out how Steve will react to "Scottie."

And I'm about to concede a special honor. Steve has always had a three-year jump on me, and since I am officially bowing out of the running, we can tell him he's now the man who has been with Mylove the longest.

We give him the five-minute heads up call (or Mylove does; she's more succinct) and she says he sounds curious and anxious.

But as we come through the door into his suite, he rushes out of his office to lead us back to his office, and as we all blow past his receptionist, I am wondering if he has a problem. He closes the door. He hugs Mylove first, then looks at me and says:

"Cool!"

We all breathe a sigh of relief. He shakes his head and says to Mylove, "If you hadn't warned me, I would've wondered who the woman with you was."

So we're cool, in fact, we're better than cool. Mylove and I agree, Steve has the second best reaction (Gerhard is still first), and we are both relieved. True to form, Steve has a zillion questions, but first wants to hear whether "Dude" is going into a third season. "I love that show, I can see you all over it." Which is lovely to hear, but really, it's the Dudes. I'm just along for the ride. I break his heart, "No."

Steve is all ears, and this is another time where I let Mylove do most of the talking. I like her responses better, and I'm getting tired of hearing my answers.

I have to say, one of the reasons we drive all the way down here each year, other than it makes good business sense, is Steve himself. He is not only an excellent accountant, and really has our backs, but he's an excellent teacher, helping us understand complex financial issues. Even more than that, he is a very spiritual man and looks at providence and wealth and Grace as we do. I never feel that the amount of taxes I have to pay is a burden. In our household, we regard the taxes we pay as a reflection of the monies earned, which has come through Grace and hard work. The more you owe, the more you made, and not the other way around.

It makes the session a time of gratitude and thanksgiving, a ritual that makes us sky high every time we see Steve. And it doesn't hurt that we usually get a refund. (I learned a long time ago to overpay my taxes as I go along. Nobody likes coughing up a big check at the end of the year.)

Soon, we're done. We're getting back a chunk from three states and the feds (this international adventure thingy is working) and we're hugging Steve goodbye until next time. His eyes are glowing as he wishes us well and he shakes his head "You never fail to amaze me, girl."

Whatta guy.

And then it's lunch with Maura and Jeff. Mylove and I cannot for the life of us believe that Steve took it so well, In fact, he should be training people how to react when I come out!

And it's the first question out of Maura's mouth, "What did Steve think about Scottie?" (Maura already had "the chat" about me, via the phone.) She is dumbfounded when we related Steve's "Cool!" Maura and Jeff are a very special couple – another pair who, back in the day, gave love a second shot after seeing that Mylove and I had found our perfect love. They've been together one year less than we have. Maura, one of Mylove's dearest friends, is Mylove's age and used to be a corporate firecracker. I've always supported their friendship because I can tell that they share a spark found nowhere else. A Marketing director for Fujitsu Systems of America, Maura is the buttoned down, crisp lady to Jeff's "total surfer dude," who never wears socks. He teaches the starched and staid Maura to lighten up. But something must be said for Maura, that she fell in love with Jeff in the first place, and their love is nothing short of amazing.

Maura is also in a very tough place, as she suffers from a rare neurological disorder that has all but trashed her eyesight. And Jeff has been taking care of her. But nothing has dampened her spirits, and I know when she says I look amazing that she's repeating what Jeff has whispered to her, which is a good sign on both levels. She wouldn't have repeated it if she felt he was making it up, so he must think I look amazing, too!

Maura conspires with both Mylove and me like high school besties, which I have a strange reaction to. Heck yes, I want sisterhood. I want the friendship with these amazing people that I have watched from the sidelines for years, which is crazy to admit. We've been friends all along. But I know that the areas of sisterhood have been closed off to the boy they thought I was. And I have not pushed past those doors until now.

But as I said, it is Mylove and Maura that have a special friendship. Not me. And I don't want to intrude on that. As they laugh and catch up, I can feel myself shrinking back a little, watching as a spectator, not a participant.

Jeff and I usually have a parallel conversation going while our girls catch up. But today, I'm only half there. He's a great guy and he's going easy on me, asking me how the guys are doing with my news and wondering how my work world will do. He relates some well wishes from some of his friends whom we have met. And he gets his pronouns right. Like I said, Jeff is a great guy.

But not just for these reasons. Mainly, it's because he's tuned into the frequency that is our friendship and sees that I'm a little pensive, and rather than running roughshod, he gently allows me to be as quiet as I need to be. This is what a thirty-year-old friendship looks like.

As we hug goodbye, Maura squeezes my shoulders and I remind her that now we're Madden girls together (her maiden name is Madden), which makes her laugh. She says, "You can be the pretty one."

I promise to uphold the family name.

And then we're heading to the next moment of truth. I realize that my life right now is one continuous coming out party. I want to title my book, "The Night of 300 Coming Out Parties."

But this is a biggie and I've actually got plans. I text ahead to Cat, "Do you have a blow dryer?" I'm going to need to freshen up for a party of this magnitude.

And without getting crazy, there is a lot happening tonight. Cat is the only one of the San Diego clan to have seen me. Mylove's matron of honor, Deb (one of the aforementioned Angels) and her husband David, and one of our most cherished couples Norm and Nan, and of course, our original cheerleader in our marriage, Kali – all will be there.

All friends for over thirty years. All attended our wedding and all have supported our union as sacred, as we do theirs. They will, of course, support us, but they will be checking us out with a microscope to make sure we really are okay.

So I need to rock this party and I've got the perfect dress for it.

When we arrive, the backyard garden has been decorated as if for a wedding. And Mylove beelines to the hugs and kisses waiting for her. But I hook a quick left and head for the front door. Too late, they see me but I shout, "Sorry, I have to go to the potty" and dodge their disappointment. Cat is blessedly waiting with the hairdryer as she directs me to the bathroom. (I told you, Pure Angel.) She'll run interference with the guests while I get pretty.

And then – ta da. I get applause as I try to make my way out into the garden, but it takes a half-hour to get through the kitchen wall of hugs. This is going to be a good night.

Between tacos and more hugs, I'm asked to tell my story and here's where Mylove turns the floor over to me. They genuinely need to hear the whole story, so blown away are they by the revelation. I give it all up, and through tears and more hugs they see many events in our lives suddenly coming clear. They are dear, dear family and we've been through a ton together. Kali confesses that she felt a scary intensity in me that was always confusing: how could this wild, happy person have such a dark shadow?

This prompts everyone (even the guys) to confess they, too, had felt this. Who did I think I'd been fooling? Apparently, not these folks, either. But they also all notice that that shadow has not come to this party. It is gone, replaced by a sweetness that they always thought could be me.

And all of them admitted to being shocked by the news, but that now, in my physical presence, feel that I have always been this way (hmmm, just like Gerhard).

And then Cat is standing before me with a cake with candles and says, "Well, Ms. Scottie Jeanette Christine Madden, welcome to the world!"

And I feel each of my names shake my heart with a powerful yet gentle force like I am being christened. As I am about to blow out the candles, she stops me and says to make a wish. I close my eyes and feel a gigantic, happy galaxy open up before me, an infinite universe that I try to wrap my arms around. And as it expands, my arms grow bigger and I suddenly feel I will never be able to keep up with this. And that's when it dawns on me that this is the love that is *already mine* and waiting for me, as I've made the absolute right move and stepped over the threshold of reality as a woman.

When I open my eyes, everyone has their eyes closed, too. Something amazing and significant has happened for all of us. Cat's cackle breaks the spell (thank God!) with, "Damn Girl! What did you wish for?"

I whisper that, "It wasn't what I wished for, but what I am grateful for. What I already have."

We munch cake (fresh strawberry cream – Cat's granddaughters sliced the berries), and the mood gets a lot looser, which is what I had actually expected, especially from the guys. Greg (Cat's love) David (Deb's) and Norm (Nan's) are all "dudes" with whom I've had close relationships. Greg was a fellow athlete, David is a fellow creative (stand up comic and drummer) and Norm is a fellow geek (syfy, especially Star Trek, but anything like that). Yes, I am still glowing from everyone's initial reactions, but they are stepping lightly, treating me with too much respect, too quiet like I am someone other than the loud wild one they have come to know and love. I want to stop everything and say, "Guys, it's me!"

Luckily the cake did its magic for me, so I turn to everyone and say, "If you guys have any questions, please don't hesitate." And as it turns out, they have a ton and some are burning. Now, this is more like it.

David is blunt (shocker): "What about Marcy?" Like times past, whenever anyone stands to protect Mylove, I'm touched, but he has some spin on his question that is undeniable and I feel the jab as I swallow. I answer the way you would to a parent; as I've said, these friends are the guardians of our marriage. It would and will be hard to explain Mylove's and my relationship going forward. But it will never be hard explaining our love. As I wake up more and more to what it means to be a woman, I have to be open to all that entails. And as we work that out between ourselves, I know that it will always be through love, of love, for love, and because of love. He seems to be satisfied with that answer.

Later on, Nan confides in me that Norm had a real problem with my news, *at first*. He had no reference point, and no experience, with what and how to deal with it or me.

As we hug goodnight, I ask Norm about this and he admits that he feels better, but that his mind is still blown. He says he doesn't even know which questions to ask. I tell him that it's okay to not understand, I don't expect him to; I don't expect anyone who is not transgender to ever understand. That's never our point. Our point is just to love us. And treat us as a human. I make him promise to never stop talking.

After everyone leaves, Cat, Greg, Mylove and I sit by the fire pit taking stock of the party. I am able to dig a little deeper with Cat about the cake experience. She says she felt the immensity, too, and we all agree that this was not only necessary for us all, but a wonderful celebration of our friendship and life.

The next morning we meet with Cat's daughter Janine, her husband James, and her wonderful daughters Jewels, Jemma, and Jade. I've watched Janine grow from a child to amazing mother, and throughout last night's party, we connected on a new level, as girlfriends. Her daughters are at the age (5, and the twins are 4) where you can get lost for hours in word games, and we laugh and laugh as they accuse me of being "a circle." To which I counter, "No, you're a circle!" Which of course, went around and around for hours and actually picked up right where we left off the next morning as soon as we got to the restaurant.

It isn't until I excuse myself to go to the ladies room that it hits me. The circle is the symbol for the ladies room (with the triangle for the boys) was that what they were saying? They are too young to remember my boy look, so they only know me as a woman. I decide to take it as that and when I tell Janine and Cat, they both squeal with excitement. (Well. Let's be real. Cat squealed. Janine, as her daughter, is the more centered one and doesn't fluster easily. But she did grin excitedly.)

This is our San Diego; ocean breezes off the marina mix with the smell of hot tater tots and joyously relaxed laughter. Could it get any better?

Yes. Cuz there's my Big Sis, Katrina walking across the dining room to us. The first person I wanted to be there (besides Cat) may have missed last night, but she wouldn't miss her new lil sis <u>now</u> for love nor money. It was a comedy of errors that started weeks before as Cat was setting the invite list for my party. My Big Sis was the first person I wanted and Cat (who's besties with my Big Sis Katrina) said, "Yes of course, she's probably going to want to help with the food." So as we went back and forth about the other guests, I never thought another thing about it.

Until the night before, when I texted Cat that I hadn't seen Katrina's name on the final invitee list and she texted back: "SHIT!!!!!!!!!! I TOTALLY SPACED! IS IT TOO LATE TO CALL HER? I'LL TEXT HER AND CALL HER IN THE MORNING!!!! SHIT!!!!"

But that's not what happened. She called her right away (difference between women and men, I suppose: a woman would never be able to sleep). Katrina was already booked, but would try to come if she could. We were all bummed, Cat most of all.

But she is available for brunch this morning and walking in the door as we speak. She looks around for us and sees Cat. I'm the first to hug her, and she is gracious and unreadable.

That's my big Sis. She's so gracious that if she can't say anything nice, she'll go all "Thumper" on me. So, I'm worried.

But really, it's just early for her and soon she has her coffee and warms up. So I tease her a little and she admits that she is a little blown away, but it's because I'm so pretty.

Got me there. Why would I try to break that spell? I'm kidding, I tell her my now standard line, to those I love only: "If you have any questions. . . " But she confesses that right after our initial call back in January, she had been doing research on girls like me. She has studied pronouns, descriptions, even what to ask and what to leave alone – but she also confesses, "I still don't understand. But who cares what I do or don't get, I love you, that's all that either of us needs to know, right?"

It must be the water down here.

After more hugs, more laughs, and more teasing, "You're a CIRCLE!"

Mylove and I have to pack up before I dissolve into a puddle of love and tears.

And we head back up the coast with one last stop – my sister Kimm's. Normally, I wouldn't hesitate to snag a drive by hugging. . . so why would I start now? Deep breath and go.

What's strange is that you'd think we both would've planned this better, but maybe it's better that it snuck up on us. That we wouldn't let the first opportunity pass to be together, shows who we are. And maybe it's our way of dealing with huge things: we're both so poker-faced that we won't allow ourselves to even think this is huge.

It is supposed to be "no big thang" since it is spontaneous and on our way home. Don't make a fuss. But COME-ON GIRLFRIEND! ITS THE FIRST TIME YOUR SISTER WILL LAY EYES ON YOU!!!!! Yes, it will be the first time Kimm will see her new older sister. (Big sister? Not sure which one I like better or which one she'll like better, I guess we have some working out to do.)

I'm still trying to be okay with how she feels. Her confession caught me off guard. Hearing that she had had any struggle was, well, both enlightening and disheartening. That I was her model for the ideal man was only to get her through until her husband (of twenty-five years) and now her son could take over.

And really, what's the real point? Because if she had used me as the yardstick to divine the love of her life up from the wellspring of love, it worked! Her husband is an exemplary man who loves my sister and takes fantastic care of her. We get along great and he knows that not even the loss of upper body strength will keep me from killing him if he does anything but love the heck out of my Kimmberly, and he appreciates and respects that. Their son, Dane, is going to be an amazing man. Smart and caring, he's everything we want and hope in our next generation.

As we knock on the door, I realize that since neither of us has had time to prepare, we also don't have time to get weird. And the hug that greets me is all I need.

My family knows that if you don't get your hug in before the two of us start, you'll be waiting for a long time. I'm serious – our hugs last a good ten minutes, no exaggeration. It's like the Vulcan mind meld and our hearts are downloading into each other the truth that our mouths are too clumsy to get right. Knowing this, my niece slides in between her mother and me, without any words and hugs me, while the getting's good. She winks at me as she steps aside to allow her mother to get hers. God, I love that girl!

And my sister's hug tells me that, no matter what her challenge with me might be, it's never going to get in the way of what we have. What we always had, and always will.

Even though this is supposed to be a drive-by, my 18-year old nephew has made sure he's here. That he gave up skating with his "posse" (he's pretty incredible on a skateboard, watch his videos on FB, they're totally sick, dude) is all I need to know. And Kimm's husband Mikey is here, too. We haven't had a quorum like this in years. The only one missing is my eldest niece Kaylee, away at college. And it hits me, they're here because... because, you know, they love their uncle, er, *aunt*.

But let's be real, all this is going on in my head. They took it all on face value when they were first told, and now they're just here cuz we stopped by for a hug.

And all the speculation and worry and curiosity are gone instantly. Our lil drive-by lasts for three hours and, after laughter and selfies to Kaylee, it's time to get our last hugs. This time, everyone gets theirs in quick so Kimm and I can have our hug in peace. She's been saving up apparently, and hits me full force, point blank as we embrace, whispering in my ear, "Your Facebook picture doesn't do you justice."

I don't remember much after that. I must've been able to walk to the car because I came to somewhere near the Orange County line.

As we drive, Mylove asks me how I feel. I'm almost hung over, so drunk on the tidal wave of love and acceptance and heartache (it's under there a little, as we all examine our collective past) but mostly I'm just right. Wonderfully, beautifully right.

So you'll understand why Kimm's words, which came by text as we crossed the LA County line, were so dear to me:

"I figured it out! It's weird, cuz it's not weird. Am I right, Ladies?"

She has always been able to do that – take me out at the knees with a smile, hug, or a word. I don't know if she knows she has this ability, I'm just glad that she uses her powers for good.

26
BUYFOCALS

I just got the biggest compliment from Mylove. We were going to go for a walk, and you know how it is. . . one thing leads to another, one side track takes a fork, and suddenly an hour has gone by and you still haven't left the house.

What's compounding this is, when you're new, and there's just no easy way to say this, being a girl, you can't leave the house without earrings, and you can't decide which ones will finally free you to leave. Not these, these? No! How about these? YUCK! Not those either. Shit, just put something on and get going, she's waiting! By the time I finally emerge from the house, I swing around and pull a "U-ie" in mid-air; forgot a scrunchie for m'ponytail.

*I bound back out and stand before her and she sees that I've gone back for a hair tie????
She shouts at me:*

YOU. ARE. THE. WORST. CHICK. EVER!!!!!!!!!!!!!!!!

Mylove really knows how to make my day!

This is called karma folks, we're both getting back what we put in for years (twenty-eight for those keeping score). The shoes are now on the other feet.

It was I who was the impatient one, waiting for her. And I deserve her ire, having never mastered the art of gracious patience. I always let her know how she was torturing me with her "one last potty" or a list of honey-dos that were suddenly more important than us being on-time.

And now she knows what it feels like to have to wait all the time. Hang on, this is isn't really my intention; I am genuinely trying, but I can barely get my lip liner straight (figuratively speaking). That I don't look like bozo the clown each day is a minor miracle and I try not to care, but let's be real. It took me a lifetime to get here and I'll be darned if I'm gonna screw it up; and I, for darn sure, am not going to miss an opportunity to be pretty. I have no idea how many days I have left and I have to represent!

And I am finally, for the first time in my life, liking what I see. And just like my reflection in the mirror, I keep getting surprised by my projected image. Not to be confused with the projection of my image – shoot, what I am doing? Use your words.

Okay, I was trying to be specific and it painted me into a corner. But forgive me if I just step back across the painted floor and start over.

My shadow is that of a woman! It's a tickle I get on our morning walks as we take our beloved angels in fur coats, Zuzu and Aria, along the world famous "Dirt Mulholland Drive." Locals here differentiate between our stretch of LA's famed border between Hollywood and the Valley (the dirt fire road between Topanga Canyon and Havenhurst) and the rest of Mulholland. Hint: If you need a map on this portion and there's dirt, you've come the wrong way. Go back down to Ventura Blvd. and head either west or east and then turn back on to the highway – BUT you cannot get there from here and, BTW, slow the heck down we're walking our dogs here!

What I am not prepared for is actually appearing like a woman in my shadow! I'm mesmerized as I follow my shadow as she walks before me down the wide dirt patch. I'm not making this up! I've got hips and slender shoulders and when I turn, a curvy silhouette.

I am speechless. I promise to stop (after this paragraph) trying to make you understand how mind blowing and exhilarating this is. I had thought myself handcuffed to the body of a middle-aged man, doomed to be heavy, clunky, and sad but I'm free! And it's working, I am starting to look on the outside like I've always hoped I looked [OR FELT?] on the inside. But hoping is one thing and seeing is another.

I'm dropping weight like there's no tomorrow. Forty pounds in four months. Riding my mountain bike every day and no carbs until the weekend is making the hormones' job easier. Even Mylove is loving my new look and she confesses, "I can take this gender changy thingy, but if you were fat, I would be out of here."

It's intoxicating, this going from Scott to Scottie.

But I think that's God's plan. The changes when right, feel so good, that the mind re-learns to believe itself – and girlfriend, this takes work. It's been discredited by itself for so long.

There is no fast way – you have to be willing to confront everything you thought you knew.

There's been a lot of talk lately about the difference between the way a man thinks and the way a woman thinks. Mylove reminds me that for a period in our marriage, I spent a lot of time making this distinction myself. And she thought at the time that I was crazy (this was before coming out) but now thinks me uniquely qualified to have a perspective.

I can remember testing everything against a metric that asked a simple question: would this be how my mom would see it?

Now how would I know how or why my mom was thinking? All I can say is that there was a gut feeling (more like my heart) a purely visceral response, that I had a shorthand name for, calling it "a girl thought" when I was younger and "a woman thought" as I grew up.

Not only that, I would also know the exact molecules that formed the border between a "boy thought" and a "girl thought." This was something I spent some considerable time on with my therapist, who was fascinated by my ability to articulate this. The fact that I had mapped these regions of thought showed the depth of my desperation and, ultimately, my failure to suppress my true identity.

So yes, I also know how men think. If we've learned nothing else in 2015, it's that individuals can be unique, we all have our gifts, skills and strengths and weaknesses; but none of the 50 (how many are there?) genders can do anything as a whole, *better* than the others. Show me a place where you want to make that distinction, and I'll show you the exception.

Thank God! Right? Still, as I come out, everyone asks what I am.

I have to learn to describe who I am, cuz for the last four months, it's all coming out parties all the time and each has the interview portion of the show. I'm having two distinct experiences:

First, I never know how to boil down a journey of fifty years to a cocktail party answer. I vacillate between the transgender activist constantly correcting someone's question before answering it, and the gushing tell-all newbie.

Second, is being corrected on the ride home by Mylove for the answer I gave earlier (some things just can't be solved with lipstick).

And I should be able to be better at both activist and newbie because the questions are all the same.

I'm finding that especially with those close to me, the third question (right after, "are you going to have surgery and how is your Love with all this?") is:

"So are you gay?"

And, at first, I would say (as I did with Kimm) technically yes. I'm a lesbian. Because I love and am only, and have only ever been, attracted to my wife.

But Mylove pulled me up short one night as we drove home from yet another coming out party; and remember, the following is from the woman who's trying to deal with reality, our reality, the reality that was foisted upon her, the reality that defies words and socialization and education and can only be solved with the heart and the mind working at their best:

"Seriously, do you need another label?"

She's right (usually is) for two reasons (at least):

1. The label Woman is better than good enough (I don't need to declare more than that, do I?)

2. It makes her a lesbian by default. She has no issue with homosexuality of any flavor. What she's taking issue with is being labeled something she's not. (We've had enough of that in our family, thank you very much!) Now, among my sister and our close friends who are lesbian, some prefer the term "gay women" (pesky labels again!). So it's not that we (and by we, I

mean she) don't have role models for this kind of relationship/lifestyle. But as of now, it's not how my wife identifies herself. And since she's helping me define my identity for myself, the least I can do is support her with hers, yes?

So when inquiring minds demand to know and I feel like telling them, I steal the label I borrowed from Bina Rothblatt; Bina is the wife of trans woman, Martine Rothblatt, the highest paid female executive (CEO) in the U.S., who, BTW happened to work on the Human Genome Project. Bina and Martine have four children and, when asked to describe her sexual preference, Bina declares, "I guess I'm a Martine-sexual"

So when people ask, and they are deserving of an answer (again, this is our own business, right?), I now say, "I'm Marcy-sexual."

And Mylove is cool with that.

But the original question is telling because I'm usually asked if I'm gay by men so they can wrap their heads around learning that I am a woman. And… wait for it… they're not asking if I'm a lesbian; they want to know if I like boys! The women I come out to either don't care what my sexual preference is or have other, more pressing questions. Whatever the reason, women hear me when I say I'm a woman and they know who I'm attracted to when I admit I'm gay. It's natural for them to see that I love Mylove.

As I discussed earlier, many people confuse sexuality with identity. And vice versa. It's our own fault, faced with adversity and prejudice, the LGB (sexually oriented) included the T & Q (identity oriented) communities under one umbrella. We had to band together. We could, at least, relate that *each* had their struggles – facing a world that looks for any opportunity to discriminate against anyone. We're not dumb, nor are we hallucinating; we have to work together, or we will perish.

Even the most socially aware people can get it wrong like everyone is reading from the same bad script. I'm not kidding, and this is from a control group of some of the most enlightened, creative, open-minded people on the planet (my friends).

And it doesn't matter the level of enlightenment. My world has also taken me through pockets of major conservatism.

And, occasionally, I have slammed headlong into the swamp of full-blown rednecks.

But, guess what, aside from the level of respect in the way all three groups asked . . .

. . . the questions are the same.

I'm not naïve. A huge portion of the world looks at life through the binary lens. And I would be lying if I don't admit that I do, too. Since I have to play the cards I'm dealt, for me, there are two genders: the one I had to be, and the one I wanted to, but never could be.

I don't want, nor do I think I ever will want to be a "third gender." Now that I've worked this hard and come this far, and have been loved, supported and embraced as a woman, I want only to be that. I don't need any other prefixes, qualifiers or adjectives in front of my noun.

But just because I look at my own life through a binary lens doesn't mean I look at the world that way. It's how I want to see myself in the world; it does not cancel out how others want to be seen in this same world. I was raised in a binary world, and, as we know, how we're raised is unbelievably powerful stuff.

My mother and father were perfect role models of the binary system during a time when women were able to enjoy the fruits of their labors (pun intended). Mom was the classic, what we would now call (we didn't have the phrase back then) "stay at home mom." Then came the 70's, "You've come a long way baby," Helen Reddy roaring for equality (unbelievable that we are still having to fight for it!), and women finally "having it all" – a family and a career! Oh BOY!

In fact, this was when my dad refused to call my mom a "housewife." "I married her, not some house," which BTW my mom kept well and took pride in. She had no problem being in charge of the house, it was not a career she had to apologize for. Dad made the money and Mom was steward of it. Dad loved his "Cakes" (his pet name for my mom) and would push her to lighten up. And Mom protected her "Gordon" (her pet name for him) from even the devil himself. Dad worked 12-hour days and Mom had supper for him when he walked through the door.

Okay, maybe this will paint the picture better. My mom didn't drive and refused to learn. She had a family, why did she need to drive? She didn't feel dependent because she had us for her mobility, and we didn't make a move unless she decreed that it was necessary.

This would be unheard of today. No woman would want to give up independence and mobility. But my mom was a native New Yorker who never needed to drive. Many New Yorkers still don't. My mother was queen of her castle and had a family of chauffeurs – namely me, and each of my sisters when we came of age. As native Californians, driving is our birth rite.

My mom was also the epitome of the strong, independent woman who was an honor student from the time she entered Catholic grammar school to the time she graduated Catholic high school with perfect attendance, perfect 4.0 GPA – never anything less than an "A" every flippin' report card. AND she paid for my delivery (ding dong, Scottie's here) with the cashed-out retirement earnings of her short-lived secretarial career. She was not only the foundation of our family, she defined it.

So, though it may have seemed to the outside world that my parents conformed to the binary system of the times, that's not really what was going on behind our front door. My sisters were actively indoctrinated to be Modern Women who would go to college and were expected to be anything they wanted. Anything.

But, as forward thinking as she was for her children, my mother followed an invisible map for herself that still traced the rigid path of traditional gender roles. For example, Mom dreaded the days when a "horse thief" would come steal her son's heart and I would wed, and leave the nest. Yes, she would be mother of the groom, but under an expected show of reluctance that would disappear when I presented her with her first grandchild, right after I got out of the seminary. (I never said this map made sense). I think it tracked a mother's heartbreak... They know they have to give up their first-born son eventually, but nobody said they have to like it.

You think I'm kidding. When I was growing up, my mom loved my girlfriends until it got serious. I was her "pride and joy," her "*Baldy*" (don't ask). "No woman would ever be good enough for her son," explained my dad, as I was trying to thaw from the icy chill I got after every relationship passed the three month mark. This is no exaggeration. And it gets worse. I dated the same girl for three years in high school and my mother loved her. But, when we moved to college, we were going to live together. Suddenly, I was a pariah in the house, and my mother announced she wouldn't be visiting me at school. When I confronted my dad, he said, "You can't be that thick; in her world, you're going to live in sin." I protested, flabbergasted at my own mother, who meanwhile had absolutely no problem with every one of my unofficial "aunts" and "uncles" shacking up on the couch with their mistresses and boy toys.

The truth was, I really couldn't believe that the double standard was alive and well and living in our house.

I had no intention of not living with my girlfriend, and I told my mom that, if that was how she wanted to play it, so be it. And she never did come, but we talked for three hours by phone every week and, when I came home for the weekend, I would be in her hug (usually in the doorway, still holding my dirty laundry) for hours. She hated that she had to impose a Catholic law on her Baldy, but even here, I knew instinctively <u>why</u> she thought this way.

My mother taught me very well that women know the difference between "want" and "need." Though they may *want* many things: to hear how beautiful they look, to see their children happy and grown up, romance, someone to listen, someone to laugh with them, someone to dry their tears and someone who always always, always wants to hug them; they don't *need* any of these things. They are complete without them. They are whole.

It made sense to me. Still does. Because, as a woman, that's how I would want it to be, so I would want that for the woman I loved. I saw no conflict in that whatsoever.

Dad taught me that a man is only as good as his word to those he loves. The Madden coat of arms (which, by the way, is the most badass in all of heraldry) had the inscription: "Here's to those that love us, and to those that don't, fuck 'em." That means wife first, family next, friends after that, the rest had better have a damn good reason for hanging around. A man is loyal, doesn't take any shit, finds his own way, kills for his friends, takes no prisoners with his enemies, stays on it no matter how shitty he feels, never blames anyone for his failings, always rewards his team for his success.

My dad made me live by the code, "Lead, follow, or get the hell out of the way." Lead with respect and skill, follow with the same (for those rare occasions when a Madden is not in charge), and when the leader makes a turn and you cannot follow because your heart tells otherwise, graciously step aside, no need for judgment or grandstanding.

And that also made sense to me.

It was how a man should be and I lived that way (what choice did I have?) and I can say I made my father proud (cuz he told me).

So yes, I am proud that I'm the best I can be because of my parents' example, including being strong enough to know when to step off their path (despite all signs screaming "dude") to become the woman I am. I got this strength from them.

Yes, I relate to the world as a woman. And call myself that. I will, if pressed, admit to being a Trans Woman. But here's the deal, I don't do this lightly. I cannot speak on behalf of, or for the whole trans experience, only my own. I draw this distinction out of respect and love and support for my "sisters" who do identify as trans, without question or debate, because that's how they have asked the world to regard them.

And I admit that, for the strength and growth of society as a whole, having a binary view of gender is cumbersome, misleading and causes too much heart ache, break, and attack.

I cannot deny that I have benefitted from the victories of my brothers and sisters before me, who have crowbarred laws and common sense into our society that affords me the protections I have enjoyed: my gender identification has been determined by my doctor, not a clerk or bureaucrat (subject to whims or money or religious nuts), decreed by a superior court judge and changed on my birth certificate; which made social security, the U.S. passport office and the DMV, without argument, discussion or debate, follow suit. Why?

Because the LGBTQ legal advocates have been fighting for years to change arcane and outdated laws and policies. So, yes. I will stand up on our behalf alongside them.

It does seem odd that this had to be a fight. I don't understand why anyone believes they have a right to discriminate. I have never been less because someone else is more. I am more because they are more. So I don't understand why there are those who try to put anyone down. It doesn't make sense.

In our diversity is our strength and wisdom and survival.

So, what am I? I will take my place beside my sisters and brothers of the diversity community, pull my weight in the movement to end prejudice and discrimination, mentor the youth in their growth, and represent . . . as a woman.

27
MEANWHILE, OUT IN REALITY

Okay, a note is in order here: this was written before, during and after Caitlyn Jenner came out. I've left it as I wrote it because I don't want to taint my thoughts and feelings along the way by editing them. As her story is one of the biggest "news items" of the year, I find that this chapter is one I have to monitor every sday.

Case in point. The bomb dropped this weekend by Rachel Dolezai's parents "Our daughter is not black," and it took weird turns:

1. That she resigned as head of the Seattle NAACP is no surprise. What is, is it that she is now on the talk show circuit.

2. Rachel is being compared to Caitlyn Jenner. I don't know what to make of that — I can't tell if that's a Hail Mary to deflect the scrutiny, or someone's twisted idea to sell more dog food.

Okay, I hear you asking. "Selling the dog food" is a term that we all have to keep in mind when we're in the biz, or as a consumer of it. It means that nothing is done without first considering how much money is going to be made by featuring a story in some way. It's an advanced form (some might say more cynical) of "Let the buyer beware."

Whatever the rationale, please gimme a break! Without getting into Rachel's psyche, sorry girlfriend, but don't drag us into your fight. We have been struggling to change society's perception that we have anything (and we mean anything!) to do with misrepresentation, falsehood, or integrity. Also, to imply that we have a choice, as Rachel did, to be who we want to be, also misses the mark by light years. Ours is too many times a choice all right. . . between life or death! And rarely is it a career move.

So with that little pre-mumble out of the way, we now *return you to our regularly scheduled diary entry.*

It's the little things . . .

I'm serious. My cousin was calling or texting me at least twice a day after I came out to him, (as written, I'm very close to him, the retired NYPD detective) and when the news was leaked about Bruce Jenner, speculation went off the charts, as did my cousin.

I wasn't sure how to feel about being upstaged by the guy who went from World's Greatest Athlete to world's biggest punchline as part of the

Kardashian media machine. Cardboard cereal box hero to cardboard reality character. That's not fair. As a member of the reality TV tribe, I can tell where he got the short end of the edit; but even I ran out of excuses for him after the seasons wound on and when the "hush, hush, not telling" veil came down about "his" big announcement (prior to the ABC "special" Interview). I could tell it was right out of the TV 101 playbook, not designed to protect his privacy but rather the money that ABC had poured into the show.

I get it. I would do the same thing as an Executive Producer. Of course I do everything possible to protect my product, and the only way to do that (and trust me, there's no guarantees) is to keep control of the promotion for my product.

Speculation continues but, at least, we now know that Bruce IS one of us. That "he" (pronoun preferred by Brucie) is coming out didn't need even a minute of the hour, and the "why" that the world supposedly craved was presented with dignity. There will be those who squawk (haters gonna hate hate hate) about Diane Sawyer's line of questioning but, as I watch, I see Mylove and my brother-in-law Macky nodding with realization. His story has a familiar ring.

I've often been compared to Bruce Jenner.

How many girls are actually going to be able to say that with a straight face? According to Diane Sawyer, there are nearly 500,000 of us (we outnumber our trans brothers two to one). But even as I say that, our trans brothers will have more of a right to say that than even the world's most gifted athletes.

This is an issue which people have been dying for and because of. And I've been worried (justifiably so) that the tabloid media, even ABC will erase the strides we are currently enjoying, thanks to Jill Soloway (Creator and EP of "Transparent") and Laverne Cox (a force of nature on "Orange is the New Black"). We had no role models before Chaz Bono softened everyone's hearts, Janet Mock proved we were intelligent, and Kristin Beck showed that "all bets were off": the most heroic, decorated man that the conservative right should respect was a *woman*.

Transgender truly knows no boundaries, no clichés, and no boxes. It was like we were human or something.

So as you can imagine, I watch it all with guarded skepticism. Okay, that's not exactly accurate. I watch through my fingers, bracing to be disappointed at best, and horrified at worst.

And I can say I am relieved about Bruce. His story turns out to be just like all of ours. His telling of it is seasoned by almost four decades under the media microscope and yes, we're all entitled to hang onto our accomplishments and the success that come with them. He (I will school him later; he may have set us all back a decade), yes, *he* will have a tough row to hoe as they say. A truly private transition will not be had.

And that's sad, cuz the introspection, and the inner experience of freedom are the things I crave most. Even the writing of this book (although valuable for helping me see how I saw and see things) sometimes keeps me from growing up and forward as a woman (since I spend so much time going back to my thoughts of my past). Just imagine trying to figure out the day-to-day with cameras all over your every move. Still, he seems to want it and nobody will talk him out of it. But hey, Bruce, just a thought: ring up Alexis Arquette. She, too, had a reality show poised to follow her transition and pulled the plug at the last minute. So maybe you might want to know why? Invasive doesn't begin to describe the experience. Then again, there I go trying to tell you what TV Kameras really mean.

But back to present time, which is actually the morning after Bruce tells us all. Before we go any further, let's get something straight: we rarely "get it all" or "get it right" in reality TV, sawing off the edges of being human to make a story fit into a 45 second message arc, and repeating it several times every hour because some yahoo taught a course on communications which every soulless executive at the networks took, believing the audience is too_____ (insert your favorite excuse here, the top 5 are: distracted, unsophisticated, unintelligent, saturated, restless) to hear your message. So pick one point/message (called messaging) and repeat it at least twice during every act. Sad but true.

News flash! This sad little technique takes away the opportunity in a commercial hour to tell you more or deepen your understanding or present opposing views. So why Bruce feels that coming out publicly will be the source of his own healing at age 65 gets undermined by the (described above) demand to hear him say something trivial and stupid, like he can't wait to wear nail polish until it wears off (which, interestingly, is actually a good way of getting into the more complex concept of straddling two identities – but you'll never hear that. It takes too long to illustrate if you are on a network show).

And it's a new day. Thanks to Diane and her Team, Bruce got it out there. And then Laverne Cox and Janet Mock, who are now the go-to Girls for Trans issues (BTW I love them, both are articulate, intelligent and TV perfect, they can speak for me any day) are analyzing the show and saying all the right things.

So far, the circus is cowed by love and support. What? Wow! Even the haters are getting shushed by a society that seems ripe for this. Kris (Jenner's Ex) got spanked (talk about off her game; at this point, if she can't read the tea leaves then who can?). But seriously sister? Who would've ever thought you, Kween Kris of the Kardashian K, eh Clan, would "decline to comment" to Diane ABC Sawyer? Yes, a bad move. Both of Bruce's other ex-wives (BK Before Kris) sent love and blessings. Okay, let me back off a sister who's never gonna look good here. Bruce's other exes should come off as saints, their wounds are old and have healed – it's all too fresh for Kris.

Okay, it's a full twelve hours since Diane lead The Divine Ms. Jenner out of the closet, and obviously, during the night, Kris' managers have given her the Oops sorry your highness, we counseled you wrong speech, and she later tries to get in front of it on social media. She joins the chorus.

As I stand in the shower this morning, I watch the spring sunshine glint off the leaves in our backyard and I realize it is spring and I do feel a quantum shift in the force (hey, I know lots of girls who are Star Wars geeks; we make better Jedi, no daddy issues, and we wouldn't have hesitated, Luke!). But honestly, winds of change are rustling the leaves outside in a cool and refreshing breeze. And once again, I have to pinch myself. I grab the side of the shower as I'm almost overwhelmed. I never thought I would ever be here. Certainly never thought there'd be a TV show, about. . . well, me.

There's an old adage in "issue TV" (shows that dedicate themselves to presenting a subject head-on with no apologies, to foster a national dialogue) that, if even one person is helped by the airing of a show, then as producers, we've done our job well. As I've been writing to you all along, I have been enjoying almost nothing but love and support from everyone with my transition; but you can never be sure what everyone is really thinking when you leave the conversation (as was the case with my sisters, for example).

But the phone just rang and it's Morgan, my brother-in-law, who BTW has never shown anything but the highest respect and love for me, the husband of his only sister. But what he really thinks about me, I've never known.

Although he's the black sheep of the family, he's also the dyed in the wool, southern Republican (who was raised in Massachusetts, I know, I know), and we've blown up a few family gatherings with epic political debates). Full disclosure: I was a California state debate and speech champ. I can argue ANYTHING and, as a car salesman's daughter, if I can't dazzle you with brilliance, I will baffle you with bullshit; and so will Morgan. He's in timeshare and is legendary for his ability to talk and for his unabashed right wing pseudo-libertarian, tea party crap, which I'm still not convinced he actually subscribes to, so much as he knows that it's a galvanizing perspective which will reign down fire on any political discussion. And I take the bait every time.

But, he's not calling this morning to argue. Mylove and I gave him the news about me over the phone at Christmas, which he was totally laissez-faire about at the time. "To each his own," he remarked, "who am I to judge?" I wasn't sure if that meant he was cool with me or really didn't care. But that was then.

Today, He's calling to say that he saw the Bruce interview last night, and he wanted me to know:

"My heart went out to you. I feel like I understand a little better how hard it must've been, how much it must've hurt, and I want you to know that I love you, I support you, and if you need anything, my wife and I have got you covered."

Through tears, I thank him. It's always the harder they are, the harder they fall, I suppose. And really, if his heart is melted by my story, then Bruce and Diane did their job. Which dawns on me as I hang-up:

I'm the "if even one." That's it. Bruce's show helped me. The world's greatest athlete won my brother-in-law over on my behalf.

I'm speechless.

Bruce's story plays out with the next act not coming for another month – but the tease starts right away. I don't envy him a bit. I am hopeful he'll be okay as he becomes "her." And as Laverne and Janet both remind us, her story is so much more than a public transition and the attention, hopefully, will swing it's focus to the countless trans women and men who don't have millions to spend on their physical transition but need jobs and love.

Now, before this, I had only ever watched one full episode of "Keeping up with the Kardashians," and as you can imagine, it's not my cuppa', but I try to watch everything because at some point every show becomes the reference point for something else. However, Mylove and I did watch one of the two episodes devoted to "Bruce's" coming out.

And the more I watched (sorry girlfriend) the more I had to exercise emotional and intellectual restraint. I can say that his family is actually amazing! Compassionate and beautiful as they fumble with their feelings on camera. I hope and wish everyone gives themselves to understanding diversity in all its forms, as the Kardashians are doing. I don't CARE if it's all a ploy to get ratings, they are still beautiful. But Bruce, ah Bruce, you need to follow your family's example! As a sister, Bruce can count on me to protect his/her/their rights always. But girlfriend, please!

As well-intentioned as the producers are, the scary thing is that they are (by default) suddenly steering the national dialogue. I don't know who these producers are personally, but their rep is what you'd expect (and can glean from their show). Like it or not, the show IS who they are. The dirty little secret of reality television is not that the "stars" really are the way they are portrayed (good or bad); but rather that the network and producers believe you want them to be the way they are portrayed. That the network thinks you are that simple/crass or mindless is the actual crime.

And that they are the ones right now with the biggest microphone in the national dialogue is a little scary. As Bruce tries to figure out what the rest of the community is also figuring out, his successes, stumbles, and turmoil will be the impression that society will use as the "takeaway."

But there it is. As we hash this out in our love nest, Mylove, who has been telling our story almost as much as I have, makes it so clear:

"Bruce has said that he's not there yet, he has some things to do before he can be a woman. But you have always been a woman, and your struggle has been to stop having to live and act like something you are not."

And there it is, the beautiful shaft of sunlight that spears the clouds and illumines the mountain top.

I finally realize why I did not relate to the word "trans" in the first place. It's not accurate. It's a name that others have labeled "us."

Trans implies "going to." As in, "not there yet." In context, it's why we face misunderstanding and we allow others to keep their hands on the steering wheel of our happiness and fulfillment. When all we've struggled with our entire lives is the expectations of "other" why would we once again, turn over the keys to our kar. To take it further:

Trans-ition: was something else, now becoming something different.

Again, we're "not there" yet.

Trans-formation: the act or achievement of a new and different state.

Trans-fer: moving something from one place TO another.

Yeah, sorry, "trans" – I'm just not feeling it.

Mylove suggests a new word: "reconciled," as in the accounting sense, the balancing of the books.

And with that, we have the title "Getting Back To Me." It's why it's so hard to describe. The real issue is, I've subjected myself to selling out myself by myself. I believed that I had to, needed to, was supposed to "be something I'm not."

What strikes us both is that reconciling is not just the trans experience, it's the experience of anyone, of everyone. Doesn't everyone struggle to be the you that you know yourself to be? You know which you we're talking about – the best, noble and perfect you that you are in your heart of hearts –the divine you that you are always and will always be.

Bruce's story is affecting the national dialogue, and everyone's waiting for the "act five reveal" (which includes a tease before the commercial) but the meat grinder is warming up, and oh girlfriend, what a life you have coming…

28
ROSE PETALS & FAITH

Today is my wedding anniversary! (Yes, we're back to realtime once again, sports fans). I have big plans: it has to be elegant... romantic... and not cost a thing. Money's tight with no work. But money's a crutch to the true romantic. For this sorcerous? Piece o' cake.

This year, for all the right reasons, is truly different. And to celebrate it, I am wearing the Claddagh, a Celtic symbol especially dear to Irish-Americans. My Grandmother once told me that it's given to girls to show the world that they are "one who is loved." I haven't ever seen that description anywhere, so thank you, Grandma. You're the best!

Up until two years ago the Claddagh rings I saw were rather clunky, aesthetically speaking (today there are some beautiful rings worthy of an artist's finger). It's a tough design to get right: two hands clasping in friendship around or sometimes under a heart for love, and beneath a crown for loyalty. It can look too "cartoony" for my tastes. But as an Irish girl, I want to represent; And I do believe that the sentiment/custom behind the Claddagh is rich and meaningful since it's often handed down from mother to daughter. An Irish "love spell," right?

But, rings are a risky gift (unless they're the big risk, ya know). So for Mylove, I found instead a necklace that is a sweet representation of the famed talisman; and this one is worthy of our house, with a Celtic love knot to balance the design. Mylove wears it proudly and loves spreading Grandma Madden's message, whenever anyone asks.

When I started developing a sense of feminine style, I didn't have much in the way of accessories. Mylove looked at me one morning as I struggled to make the few pieces work, none making any design sense. Without a word, she placed her Claddagh around my neck and kissed me. I cried. Since I had given it to her, I wasn't sure how I felt about taking it back (even if only temporarily). But I was so touched by her whole gesture, I didn't want to trample on her loving offering, so we agreed we would take turns wearing it.

So today is my day to tell the world I am one who is loved!

And what a day it is. Twenty-six years – wow!

I'm looking at the silver bracelet (I never take it off) that Mylove gave to me just a year ago to celebrate our silver anniversary. Was it only a year ago? Silver, as in quarter of a century. Silver, as in half of my life (so far). It could've been a century for all of the life we've lived in the last 365 days.

To illustrate a quirk of how deep our love goes – I gave her a silver bracelet, too. And neither of us knew the other was going to do it. *Yes, we're that couple.*

I have always been the gift giver, the bearer of spoils of war. I've said out loud to all who ask, that the wealth of our kingdom should adorn my wife.

But for our silver anniversary, I was freaking out. I was on the road and running out of time to get her something worthy of our quarter century accomplishment. It had to be silver – and not any old silver something would do. In fact nothing was doing it – nothing looked good enough. You'd think silver would be a no-brainer!

I explained this to a dear friend in Denver when I visited her for Easter. Abby is a wonderful woman who, together with her amazing husband, Giddee, practically adopted me while I was working in Colorado. Hearing the distress in my voice, she slipped away and returned almost instantly.

"I want to help you and your incredible wife. I am the same way about jewelry. I would be honored if I could give you any one, or all of these."

She laid before me an antique silver bracelet first, an exquisite weave of silver strands tied in delicate knots to form the links of a chain. It had a sense of timelessness and beauty. It was Abby's mother's and Abby never got the chance to wear it but would feel so much better if it was on someone's wrist who is so loved. Done.

It was the perfect gift for her to wear to an intimate surprise party featuring 35 of our closest friends.

Over our decades together, I have gotten used to her line, "I hope it's okay, I ran out of time to get you anything." Which was always true, and always okay. I didn't want anything upstaging the gift I usually had which usually involved as much backstory as the bracelet I described above. But tonight is different. Mylove set me up.

I put the box on the table in front of her. She smiled and "saw" my box and "raised me" a velvet case. I needed sunscreen to keep from being torched by her! I stopped. Thank God some of my husband training was still there. My gift would have to take a back seat (for the time being). I opened the velvet case and inside was a gorgeous silver bracelet – exquisite strands of silver tied into delicate knots to form links. It was a modern take on the antique one I was about to give her.

That's what I mean when I say, we are *that* couple. It's a joyful version of "Gift of the Magi," except that with us, neither loses in the giving.

I haven't taken my bracelet off since then. I've argued (and won) with the various doctors and nurse techs who try to insist. It's stayed on through cenotes in the Yucatan, and Norwegian woods.

It was the bracelet that we both wore proudly as we walked into our favorite little Indian Café to hear "SURPRISE!" from 35 familiar and yet, totally out of context, beaming, loving faces staring back at her. Including her brother and her niece and her matron of honor?

She broke into tears and turned to me "What did you just do?" I hugged her and whispered, "Loved you like I will, forever." And then I let her float out into the tidal wave of love. It was amazing and wonderful and soul nurturing and hilarious and life affirming

It was love.

Oh, and delicious.

And as I gaze at my silver bracelet, a year after all of that, I think nobody, not even God, could've told me then that I would be wearing that same wonderful, beautiful, ring of silver on my wrist a year later... as a woman. A woman. Now, you know why I wear the Claddagh. I am, undeniably, the "one who is loved."

My head spins as I flutter quietly, preparing our bedroom love nest... I'm still dumbfounded – that was only one year ago? But this year, times aren't bad, they're just a little stretched. My challenge as I've said is this: Mylove is waaaaay too practical to have a good time when she knows what bills she isn't going to be able to pay, because her Holly-Golightly serendipitous Love (me) doesn't know the meaning of pause, quit or even back-up.

But, and maybe this is the hormones talking, or better yet, an experienced married woman who is actually learning and growing along the way; I have learned that giving is a fine art that can go south quickly when the ego is invited to the party.

Over the years, I've finally learned what I call the girl's way of giving (again don't shoot me, this is my code!). Giving like a girl is really taking a person into your heart and holding her there and if/when your heart still hums without reservation that the gift will enrich someone's life, even for a second (don't get lost in the weeds here, even a hug at the right time to the right person, is the best gift), then the Give Light is on. I didn't always know this and her closet is stuffed with "things" from me that were given before I developed this skill.

And so, when Mylove hears me ramping up for an anniversary extravagonzo, she lets me know that we can do anything we want as long as it doesn't cost any money. Which pretty much eliminates an overnight in Cambria, Palm Springs or any other romantic getaway. It even takes a fancy dinner off the table.

If you're an amateur!

We love our "honeymoon suite" (the master bedroom). The previous owners knew what they were doing: the whole downstairs of our hillside house is the master suite with French doors, fireplace, and Jacuzzi tub in a two-woman bathroom. Weekends here are magical, so why not an anniversary?

I've got it all worked out – references to past "honeymoons" will create the perfect evening to celebrate 26:

*a trail of rose petals leading her down the stairs; Mylove left just such a trail for me on our third anniversary…

*a supper of grilled & chilled shrimp with homemade cocktail sauce (bottled? Puhleez, you should know me by now); our dear friend Maura had just such a cocktail waiting for us in our wedding night suite.

*a fresh half papaya stuffed with red cherries, papaya, and mango – our original dating aphrodisiac. We used to eat them in the shower (okay that's enough for that picture).

* the long stem champagne flutes that my aunts gave us for our wedding toast, which we use for every New Year's stroke of midnight toast.

Mylove follows the trail of petals to our love nest, to find me smiling with love. Let number twenty-six commence! We toast and nibble and luxuriate. Together we are able to dream and reminisce and cuddle enjoying the sacred bubble of our love; it's like being in a diving bell, the outside world ceases to exist and we're able to breathe in each other in a world all our own.

I take a moment to tell Mylove that last year at this time, I was taking my final bows as a man. And that truly, now more than ever, I know that without her, I am nothing.

She looks at me with such love and confidence and says, "You had way more faith in me, than I had in myself. I'm so glad that I was as big with all of this as you believed I could be. I'm so glad I chose love. I chose you."

I am still vibrating.

Could it be any better?

Nope.

Now you know why we Irish women wear the Claddagh.

29
GOD SAVE THE QUEEN(S)

Okay, this is not as extraordinary as it sounds, but that doesn't make it any less exciting. My beloved Aunt Phyl and my Aunt Mish are due in three days, and my beloved sister Keira and her partner Jordyn are due in from the UK in four days. Karmic forces are working because, well, we forced it!

Yeah, this isn't the coincidence it looks like. That we're all coming together at this stage of my "blossoming" is more my taking advantage of forces already set in motion (HA!). And these forces of nature are strong women, opinionated women, beautiful, intelligent – and not too happy to have a new big sister, women. They loved their big brother and blame her for his… well, Keira already called it a death, so death it is. With all that to set the stage, they've gotten on planes to fly across the country and across the pond we call the Atlantic.

My Aunts have this time blocked out at the timeshare they maintain to stay close to their west coast nieces (and their used-to-be nephew). But we all know the truth – they're really here for their nieces' *children*. It is amazing, really. They could have picked any cool place in the world for a vacation destination (they travel all the time), but being in the lives of these kids (and their adult nieces and used-to-be nephew) is invaluable to them. And we're grateful, beyond words. We all feel the loss of both Mom and Dad, and my aunts are doing their best to fill that void. At one point, San Diego was the capital of House Madden, with three of the four Maddens (Keira moved to England 10 years ago). But with Shane gone these last three years to South Carolina, and Mylove and I in LA for the last twenty years, all that's left is our "used to be oldest" sister Kimm and her soon to be "empty nest" family. The Aunts' time-share is not long for this world…

When Keira's ill-fated (in her words) trip didn't happen last Christmas, it was put off until now and everyone dialed it in from there. We'll miss Shane. But she's gonna miss…

"Estro-fest, 2015." Will 'She' be able to go from Patriarch to Matriarch? Will "four of a kind" lose to "three Queens?"

It isn't looking good. Keira's email volley sent me for a loop. But there is a faint glimmer of hope, either because Jordyn talked sense into her, MyLove's email shamed her,

or my pouty whining – did it matter? We talked it out. Now all we have to do is hug.
Still, why did it happen in the first place?

Are you with me? It's like a Nora Ephron movie (or if it goes bad, a Michael Bay monster mash).

My aunts are already at Kimm's house in San Diego. The Brits are due that same evening. Huge east coast hugs greet us when we come through the door and my aunt Mish is actually first. She hugs me tight and holds me at arms length (while still pinning my arms to my sides) to get a better look at me. She says I am gorgeous and kisses me. I'm… okay, I admit it – stunned. Is it "two down, three to go?"

My Godmother is next, already talking over a second helping of hug with Aunt Mish, saying that I have my mother's glasses – *my glasses?* How about how I look? Am I pretty? Did you expect me to look this good? Or maybe, I don't look good and this is the best she could muster? That's the way she is and really, she has said everything already on our now famous phone call. Okay, I'll take it. Three down, two to go.

Now that we're here, we get to work and start helping make brunch, and the laughter begins, and it's the best "ab" workout ever.

My sister Kimm confronts the elephant in her room. "I've got three sisters. One is gay, one is transgender and one is Republican. Guess which one I'm embarrassed by." And she brings the house down.

And the newest lady (moi), shoots coffee through her nose. The mood grows even lighter. And I think to myself, I might just make it.

And I am watching myself. I am much quieter, and where I would normally jump in with an anecdote or a joke, I hesitate. I don't want to talk and I wish I could say why. Maybe I'm hesitating to take my rightful seat as a woman among the great women in our family? It's going well, so what am I afraid of?

It's my mission today, and I'm sure Aunt Phyl is watching me. After all, I promised her.

I would be lying to myself if I didn't document how weird this is starting to feel for me.

I am, and have always been *respected*.

As the first born son, and when dad passed, the rightful heir, the "patriarch" of this clan. Everyone <u>wanted</u> me in that role, and I loved every moment of it. It's the only way I knew how to be. I took it seriously, did a good job. I hope. But stepping back into that position now, as a woman, will require an adjustment of perspective – for me. Again with the me. Sigh.

I am the one who needs to switch gears. In just the last few months, I have already been turning to my sisters as mentors, and the roles that we forged over 49 years of love and life's trials have been reversed in mere months.

I liked being the one they would call when they needed help or encouragement. I liked sharing a language and an ethic that had been created in our childhood and nurtured through four life tracks to grow into the beautiful tree that now protects the ones we love.

So yes, it's important to get this right. To make my mother and father and grandparents proud; to be the love that they started.

So much of a person's transition is figuring out how to let go of the familiar, the millions of minuscule tendrils of the past that make us who we are, even as we embrace an equal amount of seemingly inconsequential strands that will eventually add up to doing and living . . . and becoming who we are meant to be.

And all of this is going through my head as the beauty of my family plays out before me.

And then it's time to head to the airport to pick-up the Brits. My sister Kimm and I are elected. Mylove and brother-in-law Mikey will stay behind with the Aunts and kids. (This proves to be a good thing.)

At Lindberg Field, Kimm and I circle and dodge the TSA officer who will not, under any circumstances, allow us to hang-out at the curb. While the Brits make their way through immigration and customs, Mylove is back at the ranch, learning some very interesting things:

First: all agree that Mylove is a saint.

Second: Mylove is the Shell Answer woman, holding court about all she now knows about transgender life. All present are actually cool with the changes we're all going through; this is, after all, a family matter. Mylove, with the help of my 16-year-old niece, is able to help the Aunts understand the basic permutations of gender classification that are becoming part of the nation's vocabulary, getting the answers they didn't want to hurt my feelings with the asking.

As a footnote – I didn't hear this until we went to bed that night because remember, I'm back at the airport.

I am standing in front of a pair of sliding doors, having followed Kimm's suggestion that we do this old school. While she circles the airport terminal (making TSA officers everywhere watch for real terrorists), I stare at the reflection of a rather tall woman, who's actually looking pretty good today, despite the coastal fog, waiting to greet the Brits when they are finally released from bureaucracy. Each time the mirrored sliding doors open, I have seconds to crane my neck and look over the lucky souls who've been granted entrance to our country, looking for any sign of my sister and her partner Jordyn. And then the doors slide shut, and I get to scrutinize my fashion choice for this momentous event, yet again.

And it dawns on me: I am being given a gift here. With nothing to do but wait, I'm forced to reflect on how I got to here: the trail of tears that lead to me ripping down the veil. I am dumbfounded how close I came to accepting a life of mediocrity and compromise, where the dull throb of depression would welcome the chasm of despair, if for no other reason than a blessed change.

But no. It wasn't meant to be. That woman, that one right there staring back at me from those mirrored doors, wouldn't have it. And the one person who would and should understand how hard my journey has been is minutes from my arms. My Bud, my sister Keira, with whom I shared sports, writing, and a not-so-secret brotherhood. She was the little brother I never really had and I was the big brother… who never really was. But I loved being her role model.

And it suddenly hits me: that's what she is afraid of losing: that special connection the two of us had. She looked up to me. I was a lot of what she wanted from life. But this was all unspoken. I always assumed she was more butch than lipstick, but whether she identifies now as more masculine, we've never discussed. I know only that she likes the company of men as friends, but she loves a beautiful woman, Jordyn, and has only been attracted to women.

An ache from being on my feet this whole time (getting to be almost an hour now) in three-inch heels shakes me out of that cloud. Will she even recognize me? I can't even call to tell her that it's me waiting on the other side of these sliding doors for her. Ah, the TSA and cellphones.

And the doors open again nope, not yet. And then…

Hey, is that Keira waving at me? She recognizes me instantly!? Yes, she does! Smiling and waving. I am washed with love, and smile and wave back excitedly. The doors slide shut. She's merely in queue and it'll be a few more minutes waiting for them to stamp her passport before I am able to hug her.

But she recognized me instantly, no hesitation. Either I look less like a woman (and thus more recognizable) than everyone is telling me or…

Blood recognizes blood. Bud recognizes Bud.

Who cares! At this point, all I want is that hug.

I wait for another 20 minutes. Keira's partner, Jordyn, is literally the last person through customs. But here they come. Now I'm hugging Keira and everything is cool. Everything is all right. We've forgiven each other and the hug is the handshake that seals the deal.

But Jordyn's hug sends me reeling. Because it's not there. And neither is she, not really. Something's wrong. Then Kimm pulls up and as I start to load the suitcases (hey, I still have more upper body strength than all of them put together). Jordyn gives Kimm a HUGE hug. It's almost to make a point. Does Jordyn have a problem with me?

The ride home is bumpy. My excitement at having them here is body checked by Jordyn taking offense when I suggest a better schedule, "It's our fucking vacation, and we'll spend it as we like." I try to smooth the ruffled feathers, but it's clear. Jordyn is not happy with me.

It continues through dinner – Jordyn is the light of the party with everyone but me. She's trying to make a point. Rejecting my every attempt to include her and welcome her.

After Chicken soup and more laughter around the black hole created by Jordyn's obvious (and embarrassing, and frankly, I'm doing everything to stay gracious here) silence, it's time to clear the dishes.

I ask Keira what's up with her girl. Keira is giddy at being home and I'm sorry to be Ms. Buzzkill – but this is her partner, and she's on our turf. She can, at least, be civil and follow house rules – don't bring that shit in here.

Hmm… looks like the Matriarch may be starting to stand?

Keira is embarrassed and apologizes, but I can tell it's not just jet lag – and here's where I use my superpower on my little sister. I can, just by waiting, and oh yeah, *staring*, make Keira tell the truth – she's the worst poker player on the planet. She confesses that Jordyn only heard her side of the three phone calls it took for us to kiss and make-up, and was really angry with how I had made her feel.

As asinine as this sounds, I am actually really happy for Keira. That my slightest actions had poked the bear is a good sign. It's how I would expect – actually demand – that my sisters are treated by those they chose to love.

Not all of my "big bro" DNA is being washed away by the Spiro. Jordyn, as f'ed up as her approach is, made me realize, I had taken my eye off the ball. It brought me back to thirty some-odd years ago to Keira's junior year of high school.

Back then, my father demanded that, with any of the boys my sister dated, I was to "check the schmuck out." I took this seriously. Every boy was on notice: the Madden girls were to be treated with the utmost respect. And they had to pass through me.

Any boy who didn't pass my sniff test would never get past my dad. But Keira never got into the dating thing. She was a jock. No boys. So she never had anyone for her big brother to "check out"– and thus never felt the protection of her honor by a big brother and a father. That was something for her sisters (no surprise, now). They always feigned disgust, but we all knew they loved being loved and protected. They were proud of it.

BUT… One Friday night in the spring, I was home from college and jogging up the long staircase to our house – this staircase was a monster (75 stairs) and had to be assaulted. I would get into a nice clip and not really watch where I was going – and I passed Keira and "some guy" as I huffed up the beast. Keeping my pace, I grunted a hello to my sister, as I caught a faint whiff of perfume, then was assaulted by men's cologne. I stopped. And it hit me. Keira's going on a date?

I stopped. "Hey, where are you going?" Without turning around, Keira answered, "Sadie Hawkin's dance." I could see she was clenching her fist. She was slightly embarrassed. But she was my sister, and I had a job to do. Even if it was her first time for this, she deserved the deluxe package; a thorough shakedown. "And…?" Keira turned; that the boy didn't turn until she did was not a good sign of his character, but we know our selection criteria is rougher than most. Keira stared at the ground as she answered my inquisition, "And… this is my date, Ronny." I continued with the playbook, "And is this 'Ronny' gentleman enough to introduce himself?" The kid took a breath (shit, her brother's serious!). His intro was wobbly, but he figured it out quickly (good sign) and as I kept up the third degree, Keira feigned impatience. But I wasn't going to stop short, "Hey Ronny, I know other families might do this a little differently, but I want you to check in with me after you drop off my sister, clear?" Silence as Ronny looked to Keira for guidance, and Keira nodded, "Yes, sir." Keira turned to leave but then ran back up the stairs to give me a hug. I whispered in her ear, "I love you, have fun." She wiped a tear as she ran.

So here we are in the present again – and though I'm elated that Jordyn is protective as she should be with Keira, she hasn't yet asked me, the matriarch for my blessing. Not a good idea.

Keira defends her partner, "You two need to talk this out." And as annoyed as I am at her disrespect, I make myself take the high road. I sit beside Jordyn to chat it out, but Jordyn is a… well, let's just go with, "not gracious at all," and leave it at that. She says she has jet lag and is too tired to talk tonight. It takes incredible self-control for me to let it go, but I say goodnight. So Keira & Jordyn trundle off to bed.

Jordyn obviously has no idea who she's dealing with. But… I will fight this battle anther day.

I find myself with just us girls: Mylove, Kimm and her daughter, Hana. I have to admit I'm not really sure how to change roles with my niece. We're just a few years into a real relationship and I'm not sure if she's capable of understanding what's truly going on. But Kimm is a graceful and wise mother, and I'm following her lead. It's small talk until Hana decides it's time to speak:

"Aunt Scottie, I haven't been able to say how proud I am of you. I cannot believe how hard your life must have been. I was always wondering why you were so, I dunno, intense. You must have been really sad. But now, look at you, you are so happy. B-T-Dubs (she actually speaks this way) I think you are a far cuter woman than you ever were as a man."

I'm floored! I hug her up off the couch. And I have nothing but really sweet tears as an answer. They almost wipe away the fog of Jordyn's black cloud.

As we drift off to bed ourselves, it's been a huge day for the new reigning Queen. If we can just get that upstart British colony in line, we'll be perfect.

Mylove steps in once again to save my day. As we brush our teeth, she asks what's up with Jordyn. I say that the most troubling aspect of it all is how insulted I'm allowing myself to feel. I am mad at myself for not being gracious and forgiving; for not being more feminine. Mylove grabs me by the shoulders, "Being feminine doesn't get you out of being mad. We can be downright evil when we want to be." And she reminds me of her mother's famous credo, "Ain't bitches, women?"

It hurts me to admit it. I thought I had higher standards, thought I was immune. But yes, OK, the bitch light is on.

30
TOUCHED BY A MOTHER

It's the next morning, after brunch, and we're on a field trip with the Aunts. We had to divide into a caravan, and, since this is my godmother's last day, I will ride with them, and Kimm will ride with Mylove. Keira and Jordyn have opted out. Which means I have the Aunts all to myself.

This will be great: if they have heard anything from Keira, we can address it here in the council of elders without putting anyone on the spot. But it seems that Keira is fine, and Jordyn is the only problem. Okay, so, I'm not crazy.

After we get through their observations of how everyone else is doing with me, I'm able to get them to open up about their own feelings. Aunt Phyl is never shy with her opinion, which is always presented (as most opinions are) as fact. Aunt Mish is the far better politician, her opinion reserved for calm discourse.

Both opinions matter to me, and I can tell that they aren't quite there yet with transgender as a big thought; but for little ol' me, they are loving, supportive and want only my happiness.

Even so, I still detect a veil of doubt or let's just bail to a generic here and say, "discomfort." And let's face it, though their opinion won't change any of my feelings, I would like them to like being with me. And I need to respect that they liked me as a boy, as their godson and nephew. I was usually the only gentleman when we saw each other, opening doors, helping them into their seats, jumping to treat them like the ladies they are. And they are admitting to sadness and grief.

This may be one of the biggest obstacles that anyone transitioning faces – we were LOVED by great people. That it was for a lesser, or in some cases completely different person, doesn't matter to their love. This is the point. And when everyone takes a step back to breathe, we can all see that the love was the source – it wasn't anything else. BUT – we have to allow everyone to come to this conclusion at their own pace. Yes, it's painful when it doesn't happen overnight, but everyone must be able to switch gears – even if that means they have to grieve. Because the pain will eventually heal.

Like now, as a ray of sunlight peeks into the car, Aunt Mish hands me…
what? Lipstick?? "I think this color will look good on you."

I can feel the tears loading themselves into their launch tubes. Lipstick?
From Aunt Mish, really? This is freakin' huge! And I don't want to scare
away this delicate bud of real acceptance, so instead of trumpeting this
gesture as a milestone, as a shift in human consciousness (settle down, girl!),
I open the tube and see the bright pinkie-purple-magenta-ish shiny crème
wink at me. I read the color, 'Raspberry Glace' and I put it on instantly.

Nothing says acceptance like "L'Oreal."

Okay, it's a hat trick: Keira and I back to being buds, Hana loving me as
her aunt, and Aunt Mish speaking with lipstick. I'm speechless. As for
Jordyn, she can either be an ambassador or a citizen (an outcast?) in my
Queendom, the choice will be hers. I'm done worrying about her. If she
wants to live in the exile of her own ego, who am I to stop her? But she'll
have to leave her ego at our borders.

At lunch, the Aunts, my sister Kimm, Mylove and I talk of nothing and
everything; it's the full quorum of the council of elders, plotting and fixing
the lives of those we love. They are well cared for, let me tell you.

I'm suddenly swept away by a warm wave of love that seems to be
coming from the center of my chest – I know this feeling . . . *It's my mom.*

She's sitting here with us as we nibble Italian food. It's the only regret I
have as I step forward as her daughter, her firstborn. Her baby. I do wish
that I could have her arms around me. I would love to have had the
conversations with her then, that I have with her now in my heart. I do
know that I am the woman I am because of her.

*I always thought that she did know that I was her daughter. She made a few
comments along the way that seemed wild at the time. Made me blush and stop. But I
never had the strength then to talk about it. And yet, I also knew that if she "ever found
out," we would both be relieved of a burden we shared.*

*She sits with us laughing and enjoying each other, and I tip my iced tea to her, "We
got this, Mom. Your girls are gonna be alright."*

31
VERTEX

I have a dear friend named Annie. We met years ago in production. Her handheld camera work is legendary, and most of it was in a dress. Annie is one of the role models I've been studying for years. Athletic, smart, a little bit sassy and strong.

We haven't seen each other in years but Mylove has spoken to her a lot. They share the cancer thing. Annie has been battling breast cancer for three years. She's a yoga instructor and mother of three. She's here in town from the Northwest for a radiation treatment. We are not only too happy to see her (any excuse) but honored to be able to offer her a retreat spot to get a hug and some companionship.

I wasn't prepared for this – oh sure, I've been cooking all morning, we'll be having breakfast salad. (Stop hiding behind the food girl, get to the point!) Yes, the point.

Well, when Annie first saw me, she burst into tears.

She confesses that it's not because she was sad, merely overwhelmed. She didn't expect to meet a woman. She was expecting a guy dressed as one instead.

I would be flattered, I think, if I wasn't so. . . unglued by her reaction.

Face it, I have always been in awe of her. Annie doesn't mince words. As a mother of three, she's seen and heard it all by now. I've always loved her straight-forward approach and her ability to operate a handheld camera running backward in a tight skirt (another reason she's a role model)! But when that unflinching honesty is pointed right at me, it's, well, a little harsh. However, I'm trying to be flattered.

Annie and her husband, Louis, quickly recover (wish I could say the same). Louis is down from their home to visit his bride, and that they would make time for us is amazing, even if it's. . . well, yes, freakin' uncomfortable.

I am still chopping kale and fresh basil as Annie says, "Well, Scottie. . ." Oh no, here it comes, that unflinching honesty again, "I gotta be honest, I am not sure if I accept you yet as a woman."

Did the air just get sucked out of the room? I don't even have the composure to say "ouch."

Louis must feel the vacuum, too (who wouldn't, the oxygen is gone); he immediately pipes up, "Well I'm cool, and happy, and and, and, and…"

And, *anything* to divert the energy away.

But Annie continues, explaining that she had really liked Scott, he had made her laugh, and she isn't sure she can let that go.

Which catches me off guard, no trans woman wants to think that she won't be accepted. But once again, I'm torn because, as close as you may imagine us by my description above, I am blown away that she has that picture of my former self. I had no idea, she felt that way. I thought we just, you know, clicked. Louis finds his voice and, still trying to clear the air, asks the question that girls like me have to confront every day, *"Does it matter what others think?"*

Yes (sigh) it does matter. To strangers it makes everything smoother if you aren't questioning what I am, so that we can get down to *who* I am. If you take me for a woman, then we'll each know how to interact. If you think me trans, suddenly you are fumbling with your own inner self and we're not relating. It's why a lot of women who transition fully go into stealth mode – life in the binary world just is (and will be) easier if we can remove the question mark and the discrimination. (We can get into why this is not a healthy, long-term solution for anyone later, but each girl has her own journey.) It's hard enough trying to re-integrate ourselves into our own lives, it takes constant feedback – some of us have over fifty years of neural re-wiring to do.

And while we're on the subject, it's why most of us have manicures. It's the one part of the body that we're always able to see. We can't see our hairdo and make-up job without a mirror, but our hands are constantly within eyeshot and when they look feminine, it's a cosmic tickle worth every penny and the tip we left. A feedback ping that says it's real.

But as I chew on Annie's disbelief, I realize the deeper pang. I don't want her understanding – I want her sisterhood.

After brunch, we sit in our living room, Annie and Mylove on the love seat to my left and my brother-in-law and Louis to my right. I am the vertex of a triangle whose sides angle away from each other… by gender. Annie and Mylove have their heads together, whispering gossiping, giggling, while the men talk sales and computers and bikes.

I keep getting dragged into the boys' conversation. As a gracious host, I politely listen as Louis keeps including me in his stories, but all the while I feel the girls' chit-chat is leaving me behind.

And the seating arrangement's irony is not lost on me.

Eventually, I am included in the girls' circle and I can relax. I guess this is what happens when you have to mature in days, not years, without a parent or peers. What else can I do? Do other girls think this much?

Of course, as you can imagine, Annie almost forgot she had said anything, and like all of these incidents, it's I who makes it bigger than it probably is – I say "almost," because, as we hug goodbye, she whispers, "Okay, now that I've had the chance, I get it. I get you. You are beautiful. I like this version too. Maybe better. Yes, better."

What? Deep breath girl! Hug her and take yes for an answer! I squeeze her tight. And they leave.

My heart is on a seesaw . . . I have got to get this wired before I lose my mind.

32
CHOPPED LIVER

Okay, we have to talk. Mylove is a saint. That we all agree on. As the world welcomes its newest ~~Princess~~ *Queen, she has been watching graciously, generously, patiently ignoring the slights and afterthoughts about her.*

Here's the dirty little secret: The "but what about the wife?" question has sunk many a trans marriage. The new butterfly's wings overshadow the "other woman" in too many coming out stories. She's the spouse who is suddenly thrust into a territory not of her choosing, the former queen dethroned by the center of her universe and forced to rise above her own marriage being changed beneath her own feet. It's not fair – I admit that.

But . . . and here's where it gets messy. Just like coming out – it may never end. It may require a constant readjusting – for us and our marriage of close to three decades. It took us that long to get here, it might take at least that long to figure it out.

Everyone asks, and I tell them, "Mylove is amazing." This never satisfies those closest to us. They lean forward and whisper conspiratorially, "How is she _really?_" (as if I've been lying up to that point, but since that "really" word got used, I am now compelled to confess – sigh). No one trusts that anyone could be amazing with this "life change."

I do try to make it known that Mylove has not had an easy time with this. She got here by constantly adjusting her grip on our love. She does the work. And I want her to get the credit for that.

Our marriage and life together have had more than a few rocky bends in the river. We get through them like all couples: some yelling, some crying, a lot of talking, a lot of laughing and never ever, no matter how mad either of us is, going to bed without a kiss.

But today we hit the wall. Today, a dirty frying pan kicked off the nuclear threat. Months of pressure, no work, and a dying beloved Labrador against the backdrop of lipstick and lace transformed a simple frying pan into a detonator. We've been airing two points of view at levels that bring the entire neighborhood up to speed with our current feelings about each other.

Everything can be boiled down to the black tar of fear. Mylove is afraid that I will never stop moving the finish line. Whereas . . . I am afraid that she's right.

To translate: the finish line is the boundary of "never" that I keep promising I will never cross. With hormones, with officially changing my identity (and no, I haven't brought myself to change our marriage certificate, yet.) Each was a negotiation that I hadn't intended. I confess, each time I asked for something, she asked that it be the last thing, the finish line. She wanted a stopping point so she could try to wrap her head around her new normal. I get that. But how could I know how I would grow?

Heck no, it's not fair for her to ask. And I buck against it every time . . . *in my mind.* But I hear my mouth strike a deal, to ease her into a compromised state for both of us.

Today, though, she laid it all on the line. She went all upfront on me. Screaming with tears and fears, "I KNOW AS SOON AS WE GET MONEY, YOU'LL WANT SURGERY!"

Even when she's blowing snot bubbles, she's so unbelievably gorgeous. But . . . I can't deny her words.

She's right, partly. Yes, I want it. I'm feeling so free having busted out of the dungeon, that the only thing left is not having to ignore parts of my body. Not having something that I have to look past, forget is there, while not compromising my health.

It takes more energy than you can imagine. Even more lately.

But what hasn't changed is the need for sexual intimacy. Unless. . . that too is changing and neither of us is brave enough to say that out loud.

We calm down. We are getting really good at dousing the flames before the whole house burns down. We are rational. I'm not making deals this time. As I'm listening to her reasons for the dirty frying pain being an issue for her, a huge pain wells up inside my heart. I choke on the sob, this has to come out clear, and I can't let emotion mess this up: "Mylove, you aren't touching me."

She freezes. "I don't know how to touch another woman. I don't want to know how to touch a woman." I'm too shocked to celebrate the joy of being truly regarded as a woman by the woman I love. I am breathless. A chasm suddenly opens up and the updraft is deathly cold.

And she's on the other side . . .

Up to now, I've been able to hold back from this area of my consciousness. The momentum of the great strides we've been making with my transition had cooled the fire within me. Our marriage has never been stronger. Our life never more joyful. But her questioning has stoked this fire in my heart and it's a roaring blaze!

For now, we come to a truce. Love brings us back to who we are. But love is not the answer to this most fundamental of questions. Yes, my identity is being solved with hormones, acceptance, and her love. But what about hers?

My coming out is her coming out as *something she's just. . . not.*

And I don't have any answer for her. The fighting we can fix, we always do, but what do we do about this . . . chasm?

33
THIS IS OL' WHAT'S HER NAME

We've stumbled, mumbled and actually fumbled many times in the past few days. We both are carefully building bridges from our sides of the chasm. I think we scared each other. We're stepping lightly, but still we are getting "post-it notes" from the Universe to wake-up! Some are friendly little tickles of our new normal (like, what to do when we both want to wear the same lip gloss on the same day, or the debate about my skirt being too sheer ends with Mylove letting me borrow one of hers).

But others are seismic jolts of what Donna Rose called "the tomorrows that will never come. (Like, what do we call each other? How do we refer to each other to others?) Seems small until you take it all the way through. Although I always wanted to be someone's wife, I never thought that one day. . .

I wouldn't be Mylove's husband.

There it is again. These jolts are white hot bursts that arc right over the breaker box of the mind and hit the heart at high voltage.

One reason that we cling to what we call each other is if for nothing else, to let the outside world know how to enter our magical world.

As I painted with bold strokes at the beginning of this journey, I am very proud of our marriage, as is Mylove.

And as we roll with the changes, we've had to "revise and update" several things that we created together and I guess every day we get reminded of the words that aren't working anymore.

I confess to loving the girlie end of the fashion spectrum. I brave heels when most girls would opt for flip-flops, but hey, I've got a lot of catching up to do! Clothes don't make the woman, women wear whatever they want, whenever they want. I choose to get my flair on, and it's usually pink and girlie.

So when Mylove introduces me to a new person and turns to me and says, "This is my husband, Scottie," well, let's just say it's getting some interesting looks.

But we're not that way, we're not trying to make a statement. We don't want to be a social experiment. I don't want to have any negative energy swirling around our sacred marriage, we've had enough lately. I don't even want to have to muster the "I don't care what you think" shielding. All of my energy is reserved for positive waves when it comes to our union.

Not that two happy women being married would even get a second look in our hood. After all, this is 2015, and although Same Sex marriage is still waiting for its day in the Supreme court, this is still *SoCal.*

So, we've been experimenting with alternatives:
Significant other – too non-committal (we're married, damn it, and proud of it!)
Partner – too dry, sounds like a business deal (never got why anyone in our LGBTQ community stood for it).
Spouse – too clinical (we're talking LOVE here).

Nothing seemed to be working. We also tried (I can hear you, yes it's obvious), My Love (with a space and a comma) as in, this is My Love, Scottie. People already know I'm calling her this, until they hear me refer to her like that in the third person, and then the confusion comes.

But finally, we came to: *My Honey.* It's sweet and warm and tells the world that we are that special one to one another.

But it doesn't carry the gravitas of being married for 26 years, and although I would blush and gush if she called me her wife, I have to agree that we *both* must agree on it 100% or it just ain't us, right? And we both know how she feels about having a wife.

Right. So, at least for now, it's My Honey.

We just got off the phone with Carmen, our new best friend. She's our BK (bankruptcy) attorney, who's helping us through the last dregs of the economic meltdown of 2008.

This woman is so cool – a high voltage powerhouse herself, who's another great example of the woman I can be. (Quick aside, it's not lost on me that God has put me in the company of inspiring, amazing women – the upbringing that I never got, maybe?) Carmen is sharp, sweet and level headed.

Our first meeting was over the phone and I did all of the talking. It was a few weeks after my big Christmas, when I was in the beginning stages of shaking off my chrysalis. Of course, I still sound very masculine on the phone and no, silly, I don't introduce myself as trans *anything.*

But our second meeting was face-to-face. Mylove and I waited in the conference room of her office as she returned from some other business. She strode right in to see two well-dressed women with piles of bank records as requested. She never flinched.

And by flinched, I mean about me. At that meeting (post Christmas), I was ecstatic to be walking in the world as a woman, but my steps were still a bit tentative, unsure what people saw when we interacted. Carmen made my day when she looked at us and said, "Now, is this a legal marriage?" She said it with the air of a lawyer getting the lay of the land.

Mylove looked at me, a bit confused by the question, but I winked at her and smiled. *She's asking if we're in a "same sex" marriage.*

I was on cloud nine! She took me for the woman that I am.

But our business over the next three months would require letting her "all the way" into our life, and as she got the full story, she was respectful and supportive. Our case was happening simultaneously with my legal identity transition. So what to do? Should we change my name on only the new forms going forward, or wait until the whole shootin' match was over?

As you know, I worked too hard for that F and all that went with it. Carmen saw how important this is to me, that it is more than emotional. But I didn't want to blow our case either. I was really torn, and a little mad at myself, for getting ensnared in my emotions. Carmen was better than great. She was *Gracious.*

She walked us through the last details to sign the final papers. This would make all of this BK business go away, in our favor, once and for all (I told you she was good). I told her, "And since we sent the updated license (with my glorious F) should we tell the bank to lay off the sir and Mr. stuff?"

Carmen thought that we should take our settlement and run. I agreed, here's a place where I don't need to stand on ceremony. But she could tell I did it with a heavy heart. I cannot stand to lose or back down. She dropped her attorney voice and said as a woman and friend, "But Scottie, how would you prefer me to address you?"

I was so touched. She was truly being thoughtful. I could feel my eyes welling up. I looked at Mylove as we heard Carmen say, "I mean is it Mrs. and Mrs. Madden?"

The pros & cons ripped through my head like lightning.

Mylove is 26 years married. I am proud of her, our marriage, and the fact that she married me. She loves being Mrs. Madden, She IS Mrs. Madden, at the legal and business levels, and has been for almost three decades.

And though we've settled on "My Honey," it's hardly a legal term.

I blurted out: Ms. and Mrs. Madden.

Mylove looks at me like the RCA dog (the look I get when we haven't discussed something that we would've, should've, better've).

Carmen knows Mylove too well, she waits for <u>her</u> approval before responding. The silence fills the air but Carmen doesn't know that we've been on either sides of a frozen chasm this past week. Carmen doesn't know that Mylove has confessed her very real fear that she won't ever be able to really love being in love with a woman. And Carmen has no idea, when Mylove looks into my eyes with such love and revives our wedding vows, repeating, "Ms. and Mrs. Madden," why I am crying.

All Carmen knows is that she got what she waited for, "Ms. and Mrs. Madden, it is. Perfect." We thank her again and say goodbye and let our new names float in the air. They land on the table like eagle feathers. Done.

We're reminded every day that twenty-six years ago, the shared vision, promise and prayer of a future was made official one sunny day in April. The power and strength of those words carried us through sicknesses and "healths," deaths and births with the golden light of Grace. It won't let us down. . . with any challenge.

Almost like we planned it.

34
MY DINNER WITH ANTHONY

My love and I are sitting in our car, ten minutes early to a dinner with Anthony, wife Lydia and her mother Marie, that has already been postponed three times. I have already come out by phone to Anthony, and we promised to get together. In recent years, every time we've gotten together, it felt so weird to have been apart, and I guess I just don't want to screw this up.

Anthony is my former partner and, together, we made our first Hollywood dream come true.

In this partnership I've been the brash one, the loud one, the spokesperson; but even when we didn't always agree on the "how," we shared an unquenchable desire for the "what" – to tell stories.

We created a children's series that was everything our "little dream" demanded, right down to puppets, science fiction and comedy. It was the culmination of a thousand prayers said every weekend in my childhood, over a bowl of cold cereal in my lap, as I knelt before the altar of "Saturday morning cartoons."

We put everything we had and then some into our little show, won national awards, turned some heads; but we weren't able to pull our company out of the dive before we both had to pull our ripcords and parachute our separate ways. We were a great creative team and could've been good as business partners with something called experience.

As a partnership, we complemented each other, and although we both were the Executive Producers and Creators, we each had aspirations of directing. But I directed our show and Anthony was one of our puppeteers. We co-wrote each episode: I would write half of the episodes, Anthony the other half, then we would swap and edit the other's half. We were fast! I've only found one writing partner like him since.

Anthony is scary talented as a performer, writer, director, and craftsman, having had his own specialty make-up effects and prop company. His credits are amazing and A-list to be sure, but he is his own storyteller first.

But for years (at least ten?) he made the props, puppets or effects for every one of *my* crazy ideas. We both started our careers in San Diego and it seemed we were the only ones in the whole production community that wanted out, wanted to "go to the show" of Hollywood, just up the freeway. So he gave and gave and gave and one day... *I hit.*

I sold a show. I sold our show. We both had moved to LA by this time, and he was very successful with his SFX and prop shop, and I was making a decent living as a freelancer (producing and shooting). But when I hit, he dropped everything, including his shop, and we started our four-year journey that would solidify our friendship forever.

No, it wasn't all peaches and roses; we also couldn't be further apart as people. For all my yoga and vegetarianism and liberal "freakiness," Anthony was the one with two kids, the suburban marriage to his high school sweetheart and stability.

What neither of us knew was just how similar we both were – we each had a secret that was slowly, quietly, destroying us.

Anthony's came out first, as a victim of child abuse. It cost him his picket-fence marriage, and a few years of therapy, to recover. He was inspiring and relentless with his recovery, and Mylove and I were there for him. But I had yet to fully understand my secret, let alone disclose it to him.

Our orbits remained strangely, spookily parallel. I had taught him to edit and he jumped in with both feet, making a name for himself in this game called, are you ready. . .?

Reality TV. Huh, no kidding, me too.

He couldn't take not doing his own thing, worried that his big dream might pass him by. So he bit the bullet to produce in order to direct his own independent feature film.

His was a period love story co-written by his father called, "Kings of the Evening." Mine was a vampire love story called "the kiss." His film became a festival darling. Huh! No kidding? So did mine.

I thought I had broken away, becoming the showrunner for adventure documentary, running Discovery's survival hit, "DYS." Anthony started working on, guess what? A Discovery show called, "Naked & Afraid." You mean the show that was our lead-in? Huh. You gotta be kidding me.

When you write it all down, it seems like I'm making it up.

Anthony was quick to point out where Mylove and I had influenced his life for the better – in a healthy lifestyle, in open minded thinking (having an intention, thinking positive thoughts, etc.), and, when he married the star of his movie, Lydia, that true love could not only be possible, but his. He wanted us to know that despite his pessimism at the time, he had been listening and was smart enough to look for love.

So. . . that's what's on my mind as Mylove and I arrive at Anthony's house. Am I this anxious to see him? Heck yes! I love him, and as nervous as I am (this is the third outfit I tried. Only three? Girlfriend, so decisive tonight!), I want to let him "in" on another chapter of our life.

Dinner is amazing. I can tell that even though he's seen my Facebook picture, Anthony is a little (okay, a lot) blown away with me (I know him – very bad poker face). But he's very sincere with his compliments. He is an artist, so I trust his eye. I did for over 20 years.

Lydia, his new bride of three years, is also an artist. She was born in Brazil and raised in Pennsylvania; and her Brazilian mother Marie is here too, a gracious and doting grandmother to their precious 18-month old, Lulu.

We nibble chips and guac as I say, "If you guys have any questions, you know you're family and have a right to ask things I wouldn't tell anyone outside of us."

Lydia wants to know how I was able to be such a happy person with all that pain. She has known me for four years now. I'm flattered, and we get to talk about things she's witnessed with her other friends in the theatre side of the tribe. It's always kinda cool to be speaking with someone who knows more about my new world than I.

Anthony has had time to settle down and tries to step lightly as he quenches his curiosity. He asks about, well, my plans for my body. This invasion into my privacy is followed with a compliment, "I mean, you certainly don't need it, do you? You're beautiful, and not that that's what this is about, but you know."

I smile. He's such a guy. Lydia is looking for a hole to crawl into. But he's also so respectful and innocent with his question. Mylove jumps in, likening it "to the same bizarre way that people feel they have a right to rub a pregnant woman's tummy! They wouldn't dream of touching a non-preggers woman without asking, so what suddenly makes it okay?"

Anthony shrugs, saying something about a ton to think about, but not the answer to his question. I borrow from Laverne Cox's, "Three things you should know about transgender" to see if this will work:

1. Please don't ask about our genitalia unless you are a health care professional or are seriously interested in dating us.

2. Genitalia is not a destiny. Please don't reduce a transgender person to what surgeries they've had or haven't had.

3. Pronouns do matter.

I decide to tell him. This is one of those questions that is usually off-limits, but "You're family. I don't have a 100 grand or a year to devote to myself." It's true, enough. And that seems good enough for him.

The answer hasn't stopped echoing off the kitchen wall, when he says he has one more question. "Do you sit down to pee?"

I laugh with relief. "Of course." He grins with satisfaction, he knew it. But presses the question, "Why?"

This is my partner – he knows that I would have an answer and that I would take the extra effort to help him understand. I can't disappoint now.

I tell him that it doesn't feel right to stand, and that "after you feel what it's like to be dry down there for once, you never go back." This is what boys call a brushback pitch. (Borrowing from baseball, a pitcher will throw a warning pitch at a batter who's getting too close to the plate.) Anthony nods and smiles. Luckily I still remember how to speak "Dude." He reserves the right to tease me (there it is again, dude-speak for, I still love you, man, I mean woman). We're going to be okay.

After a lovely dinner and homemade ice cream (all of my friends are great cooks – I never thought it was a requirement) then it's time to say goodbye. After a huge hug from Anthony and Lydia, I turn to Lydia's mother, who's been very quiet all dinner long. I admit I've been watching her, wondering if her conservative Catholic Latina world has room for women like me. She hugs me tight and whispers in my ear, "You are beautiful and so very brave. And I wish you and your wife only happiness!"

It's not what she says but the force with which she says it. I feel my knees buckle. I am too struck to reply with more than a tighter hug in return. But I hope by pressing my heart as close to the surface as I can, she'll feel how deep her words touch me.

On the way home, both Mylove and I wonder: is the world really changing, or was it always an open and loving place? Is it a parallel universe to the one the media wants us to believe is so dark and backward?

We can't tell anymore. Everyone I meet has been loving at best, and, at least, kind at worst. This is what being upfront does.

35
THE "C-WORD"

I just got called the "C-word" by an angry, white (I think he was white, although he was red when he spit his venom at me), middle-aged guy! I'm so mixed up, I don't know what to even think! On the one hand, I wanted to reach through his window and yank him out onto the street to give him a story that he would never forget ("This crazy woman went all Terminator on my ass!"). On the other hand. . . well, at least he got my gender right!

Okay, there's still some testosterone floating in these veins, which is creepy enough. And I hate feeling it, let alone admitting it out loud. I'm still shaking from rage roaring through me like a lava flow. Here's the scene:

I'm waiting at a 4-way stop and, as the saying goes, "minding my own business." The car to my right looks to me and I wave, and the car takes off. Then it's my turn, and I start into the intersection. But the car that had been second in line to my right roars in front of me, cutting me off. I slam my brakes and honk – and he flips me off!

This is where the dregs of testosterone still left in my veins sees its chance for a little action! It had been sitting back, feeling neglected, watching as estrogen has the floor (practically turning it into a runway!) until now, when it "scratches in" to ride the wave of adrenaline.

I instantly turn left and follow the offender, who continues to flip me off as he drives. Suddenly, he pulls over. So I pull right in behind him. This is where it gets weird, and it's also the place where Mylove would've been freaking out. This is, after all, La La Land, home of the drive-by shooting and road rage Olympics.

I'm sitting like a serial killer watching its prey stare back at me from his rear-view mirror, waiting for the next move.

I have no idea what the heck I would ever do with this a**hole. I haven't been in a fight since high school, and every other angry encounter I've been in since, has been solved with Zen-like calm.

So really, girlfriend, what the heck are you doing?

He revs his engine and I stay in the car doing my best impression of Steven King's "Christine" (the killer car), *knowing* that my silent menace is driving him to wonder if he's picked the wrong fight.

He drives off suddenly, flipping me the bird as he roars back into neighborhood traffic. So I follow. He stops again; I stop again. This continues for two more blocks until he stops with a screech of tires, jams his white Mercedes SUV (you know the one, for people who can't drive a real Range Rover) into reverse and skids up beside me.

I watch as he spits out vitriol at my closed passenger window. I can't hear his venom as it ricochets off the safety glass. Not only is he mean, he's an idiot.

Now you should know that I'm not dressed up, but my hair is in an up-do and I'm wearing big gold hoop earrings and my stylish Audrey Hepburn sunglasses. I'm not dressed to kill, just to stun. I lower the passenger window.

Veins popping in his forehead from rage, blood vessels already firecracking across his nose, overweight by at least fifty pounds, gray frazzled hair, *and that white Mercedes SUV...*

He lets it fly...

"You stupid C**t! You think you're tough?"

Did I just hear what I thought I heard? He did NOT just call me the c-word?????? And my blood pressure SPIKES!

But testosterone loves this and clears my head, and drops me further into serial killer mode. My rage implodes into a black hole of evil as his words echo through my head... Tough? I see his wife trying to vanish into the passenger seat. Did he just say tough? Does he really want to fight a woman?

So I put on my best, sugary sweet, sixteen-year-old blonde voice and look past him to his wife and say,

"Does he kiss you with that mouth?"

Bull's eye. She can't even look at me. Which gives him time to reload and fire the c-word again (I guess that's all he has in his quiver?). Then he jams the SUV into gear and makes an illegal power turn into the elementary school parking lot and disappears.

Usually in the aftermath of such situations, I burst into laughter. But, I admit, I am too stunned. "Stupid C**t?" Really?

And then something goes off in my gut, and estrogen and testosterone must've both jumped to battle stations, because the evil calm vanishes and a supernova bursts forth from the black hole and I am suddenly convulsing with rage. I am righteously rationalizing a need to protect the sisterhood and wanting to see his head on my trophy wall. I am capital L livid.

But why I'm still shaking is becoming clear. I realize that this has nothing to do with some old man trying to fend off challenges with his bark because his bite ain't what it used to be. I turned into an alpha wolf with no more provocation than an opportunity to squash a beta. I can turn on my switch way too easily. And this haunts me.

I confess that with five months on hormones, I can feel the cool breeze of reality sweeping away the clouds of fantasy and doubt – femininity is to be my permanent state. Yes, testosterone can be cleansed from my system, but can you take the He completely out of the She?

This is probably what my life journey is about, and several women I love have counseled me so. They are a wise group of women that includes Mylove, who coach me to be open to taking some things from my boyish past with me.

Which is good, because, if it were up to me I would throw the baby boy out with the old bathwater. Even that image makes me tear up, not just because it's cutting off a part of me, but the image is atrocious. The point is, I'm trying so hard to make sure I "present" myself to the world as a woman, I won't let any lingering trace of "boy" cancel out my F.

Yes, it's silly, a bit immature, a whole lotta crazy for sure, but there it is.

My male ego was pretty good at being an alpha because I had a secret advantage; I didn't care. My life didn't depend on being the alpha, it was just better when it was.

I'm calm enough to drive home, albeit much slower, and when I tell Mylove why I'm late, I lead with, "You're never gonna guess what some guy just called me..." And her answer? "The C–word? Congratulations. You've made it."

I'm speechless. How did she know that? Because it's obvious. Because every woman HATES that word so much, it's the only possible answer. It is designed to cause the reaction it gets. And that's what we hate. If a dude launches that word, he's looking for it to cause damage. It's the cipher for a slap across the face.

Mylove wants to know what *I* did to draw fire. When she hears, she flushes with passion. "As a woman, you can't invite that kind of confrontation – you'll need to keep your head on straight, girl."

This is something little girls are taught at their mother's knee. And I can almost hear my mother whispering under her wing to my sisters.

Mylove and I meet Audrey (our dear friend and realtor) as we walk our dogs this morning. Mylove can't wait to have me tell Audrey what happened and she congratulates me, too. We laugh with the timbre that rings with a sigh of resignation, of irony, and of pity.

Why, as women, are we okay with men and their anger? How can we be okay with condoning madness?

When did it become okay to be an asshole?

Audrey smiles that knowing smile and says to Mylove, "They're so cute when they're young." She hugs me "welcome" to the world of women.

As much as I never want to be in a man's body again, I have great love and respect for the men in my life. But I have nothing but revulsion and disdain for those who call themselves men and act like the cretins mentioned before.

The men I know and love are like my father.

The men I know are men. And they enrich and make my life infinitely better. They make up a huge part of the world that I love being in, and the men I know and love, love me. They've accepted me. They harbor no ill feelings that I walked in their world for the better part of my life because I upheld their standards and I earned their respect.

The men I know would never call anyone a stupid C-word nor flip anyone off while they themselves are doing the very act deserving everyone's middle finger.

No, that's a boy. A boy who's given up the right to adult respect, privilege or honor.

I hope he hasn't had a chance to multiply.

36

SPINNING ONIONS

It's May, holy sh*t! No gigs yet and I'm trying to keep focus. In other words, I ain't worked since December. I'm writing every day, and pounding the pavement while trying to ignore the wolves that bray at the doors of my mind. But whenever I start to feel that "ignore" is not working and my blood pressure is on the rise, it's Mylove who reassures me.

Say that again, sister? *Your* love? *Your* wife is reassuring *you?* To be fair (and maybe it IS the hormones), our roles, like everything else, are shifting. For the last 28 years, I'm the one who would take Mylove into my arms and reassure her, yes we'll get work, or a loan, or a something to make it through.

These are the roles we've developed and they've worked. I'm 14 years younger than my bride. But age doesn't explain the sometimes diametric views of the world; we were born on mirror image planets. We know we were born for each other.

She's the only girl with three brothers. I was raised the only boy with three sisters.

She was raised a Yankee blue blood (her father was born in Tuxedo Park – the birthplace of, you guessed it, the Penguin suit itself – and the country's first gated community. My wife's clan had a generational family summer home on Martha's Vineyard).

I was raised a So Cal liberal, my dad hustled for our money, and I mean *hustled*, feeding us with his pool cue and charm; and we never knew how close we were each month to even more drastic measures. The army of "uncles" that would come at the slight raising of my dad's eyebrow was our perimeter of security; we didn't need no stinking gate.

But as different as we are on paper, nurtured, and raised by almost polar opposites, we are the perfect match; each tab has it's companion slot. In the roles we've created, it's obvious when you meet us why we are hopelessly in love.

And it's clear from the romance and respect, right down to the most mundane: she keeps the books, I make most of our money. I do the cooking, she washes the dishes. I take the chances, she keeps us legit. I am the dreamer, she is the practical one. I'll know that the only real answer to a problem is ice cream for breakfast. She'll know that I'm right, this time.

She's the worrier and I'm the poker player – I never let anyone see us sweat.

But none of my Zen skills are working. I'm… vulnerable.

Which is why she's the one reassuring me. I'm really starting to sweat, I can't get over the feeling that maybe I've upset our apple cart this time. I have to be honest here, it's been half a year since my last gig, and I've only been on a few interviews, and these have been as full-blown Scottie. Every once in a while, I feel a ripple of fear shudder through my body. What if the biz isn't as cool with transgender people as they all say they are?

What if my experience and skills don't really matter?

What if the people looking to hire me say they're okay with me, but choose to pass it off on their crews or their clients as the ones with the problem? (Who wants another hurdle in the sea of obstacles that makes up every show?)

But no. Mylove won't let me go there. She has a different take on the lack of wind in our sails…

In a classic case of life imitating art, I've been reading chapters of "our book" (as it's being called in this house) aloud to Mylove before bed each night. And I'm not lying, sometimes it's not been easy, reliving the eyes of the needles that I've pushed us through.

We're in our sacred place, love nest bedroom. We sip fawkey and look on as the fire in the fireplace makes this the perfect Saturday morning. And Mylove suddenly hits on why she's happy and grateful for "this time": we've both needed to completely devote ourselves to being the new version of "just us" – two women, two lovers, two souls – who have been tumbling in a cosmic journey from lifetime to lifetime with a grand and mysterious purpose.

She is proud of me and my courage. And grateful that I've been relentless in preserving our love. And proud of our book.

It's hard for her to relive the pain and suffering I've endured alone. In fact, it breaks her heart that she was happy while I was keeping a hell from consuming us. The conundrum being that "it" *could* occur during our marriage.

A picture flashes in my head, giving me finally a way to describe this mystery: I can see an onion, as big as a planet, with separate layers that spin slowly, independently, of each other. The layer of depression can spin of its own accord within and next to the layers of work, joy, love or marriage, without tainting or poisoning them in any way. Life can have dichotomies, simultaneous parallel tracks of opposites and similar incongruences, *without falling apart.*

I describe this image and Mylove smiles and says, "Yes, that's it." I can articulate these very tricky realms of being human because I am inside them. This is the why of our book.

And as I look at the woman I love across the still warm fawkey in our hands, I realize that we have needed this time to get to "here." If work had come immediately when we both felt the pinch, I wouldn't have had the time to write and examine all my feelings, to mature as the woman I am to be.

This time has been the chance for us to really examine our love and marriage so that it, too, will mature to be what we dreamed it to be, instead of what we feared it might become.

But… I am itching to get out into life as Me. I need to see that I'm the capable woman I profess to be. Will I be graceful under pressure, lovely and warm under fire? Will my crews follow me now that they know me? Will they regard – and respect – me as a woman?

And what if I never get those answers?

This is the test of my state and attainment: can I weather the doldrums (heck, anyone can weather chaos, all ya gotta do is hold on). So, I chop wood; I carry water. I need to be ready to be ready when the wheel stops and I need to be grateful that we've had this time to integrate.

And even though life on the outside looks slow, on the inside, I'm going through puberty at warp speed and I have love.

I'm good, so far.

37
VANITY, FAIR?

Yesterday it felt like the earth really did shift on its axis. Caitlyn Jenner's Vanity Fair Cover Photo dropped, and my first reaction was a tsunami of conflicting thoughts. I knew I had to revisit my journal entries that I am coming out at the same time as Caitlyn. Okay, it needs to be said: this is too freakin' weird to ignore.

As we go to bed, Mylove asks how I feel and it takes an hour to list all of the feelings ripping through my head and heart. Love, Compassion, Envy, Jealousy, Bitchiness, Support, Worry for her, Worry for Us. And blown away. Can I really feel the world changing?

We've just come from dinner out, just the girls, our niece Ace and her mom, Tamsin. Tamsin hadn't seen the new me, so we got dressed up and went to a lovely outdoor cafe under the trees in the canyon.

We were driving home when I took out the thought of Caitlyn Jenner and turned it over in my hands, examining it from all sides, and it hit me. Growing up, there were more than a few times when a transgender person made the news; I grew up in the Dr. Renée Richards era. With each story, I was spun for a loop for days and I would be locked in an endless cycle of: How did she? Why can't I? Is that what I am? What's wrong with me? Can this go away? WHY DID GOD DO THIS TO ME?"

I learned over time to avoid these news items – strange to admit that now. But I just couldn't take the feedback loop. Still, I would get blindsided every so often and the gate I built to keep the dragon in the dungeon would be blown to smithereens from the outside.

But not with Caitlyn. So much so, that even my memory of how a mere picture like this could ruin my life for days, seems like a story I read once, rather than an experience of my own. An experience that once ruled my life. Claimed my life. Derailed my life.

Hijacked me.

Not this time. This time, I'm a allowing myself to be the woman that I was born to be, and I'm strong. Caitlyn Jenner's debut on the cover of Vanity Fair does not remind me of a world I'll never see, but rather an anecdote in my world.

Hmm.

I look to the full moon and an owl strafes across our path. I am flooded with gratitude, dropped to my knees (thank God Mylove is driving) in humble appreciation. My deepest prayer has been answered and was answered a while ago. I'm on the other side! I have been on the other side for long enough to almost forget I wasn't always already here. Almost.

I explain this in the litany of answers to Mylove's question as we lay back on our pillows. Yes, "Ms. Jenner" is drop dead gorgeous. Mylove reads me a text from our friend Weezie saying that I'm not to worry, I'm prettier than Caitlyn. It's a sweet attempt. They're family, they have to say that.

But once again, my hero Laverne Cox is the first to raise the whole convo up a notch, reminding us all that we can't make trans all about how well we're able to achieve what the world currently believes is how beauty looks. Or we're all doomed.

Jon Stewart brings it all home, saying, "Congratulations, Caitlyn. You're now being treated like every other woman: objectified and dismissed. You have a shelf-life. Forget your accomplishments, your gold medal, all we're gonna talk about is your hair."

But there is a shift in the earth's rotation. We're talking about it and trust me, my own Facebook page blew up with mostly positive remarks.

It's not an issue for anyone to decide. It's not up for a vote. It's not even really a discussion. The issue is how are we going to correct the situations that impinge on anyone's rights? How are we all going to live together and flourish?

I am overjoyed that Caitlyn's debut has been handled with so much effort and class – ABC News, Diana Sawyer, Vanity Fair – and as a moment of history, rather than a tabloid fad or fancy. I really believe life and my country are changing and, like me, growing up and discarding denial.

So I take back most (not all) of what I wrote earlier about Bruce.

But Caitlyn? Caitlyn is changing my mind little by little.
Go girl.

38
DEFYING GRAVITY

My stomach hurts. . . my face is salty. . . my eyes are still burning. . . I have been laughing for a half-hour solid. It almost got scary. . . I couldn't stop – didn't want to stop.

I've been trying to find an ending for this book. Another ending. You see, I'd planned on landing a gig: upfront with everyone – check; hired – check; successfully "doing what I do" as a full grown woman – check; after which I'd report back to you on my Happy Ending – check. All meant to inspire us to reach for the stars, dream big and, above all, be true to ourselves.

It hasn't exactly turned out that way.

But my laughing fit this morning was a little more earth shattering than maybe I'm letting on. . . once again, to myself.

The setting is our magical, never-ending honeymoon bedroom. We've both been on edge for the last four months. Despite love and growth and acceptance, the phone has failed to ring and weekly calls to my agents get me five minutes of hollow reassurance that results in only one deep breath that evaporates as reality descends again. Yes, we're panicking. I made over 200k running three different shows last year and it's almost all gone paying bills. We've barely had even a dinner out or a movie, as we hold onto faith that the world wants a transgender showrunner on their show – I say we, because Mylove is even more helpless than I, trying to stay patient as my agents' empty words fall flat. I stay sane by writing but, to her, that's not "finding work." However, as a testament to her resilience and love, she's supporting my creativity – ever faithful that I will, once again, bring home some bacon (turkey bacon, but whatever). She's watching her whole world get tossed into a blender – rolling with every change with grace and patience and love and strength – bucking me up when my grace gives way to a good old-fashioned tantrum over a computer glitch or burnt toast. Her whole security has been swept away by some eyeliner… And yet, she's the one to dry my tears.

How much do I love her? More than life itself.

We wipe the sleep from our eyes this morning, awakened by the snoring of our beloved Zuzie, who's lying between us on the bed (neither of us had enough room to actually sleep). Zuzie's not got a lot of time left here on this plane and we're both making the most of every moment. We talk of the things I have to accomplish today – I joke that Mylove is my manager – all ideas and no follow through (not fair – but when we get into the financial doldrums, she has millions of ideas for me to sell myself, all of which require me to sell me rather than do what I do, which takes me away from doing what I would be selling – it's a vicious circle that has caused many a fight). But as I start to contract, I'm grateful for her, and her care, and her ideas. I need to listen to these, I say, which suddenly sparks her to illustrate this point. She picks up her iPad (wonderful addition to every American bedroom – not!) and scrolls through her Facebook page for something somebody posted that she just has to show me now. As she scrolls, anticipation builds – this must be the holy grail – the one piece of a wisdom that will kick it all loose – that will unblock the dam – that will release the dogs... but she can't find it! It was just here, she says! She's taking way too long, and I've got work to do – we've still got to walk the dogs and I've got a laser appointment (once you start, any interruption is money wasted), and I'm trying to stay interested. I can't even remember the point she's trying to make (bad move – call it up girl, before it's too late), and... and, and I try to let her off the hook, saying "well, why don't you just tell me what it was – after all this anticipation, there's no way it could be better than your description."

But she's a dog on the scent and won't back down, until, until . . . scrolling, scrolling . . . "Here it is, here it is!"

And with great glee, she hits "play" and we watch a video of ...

a cow playing with a soccer ball!

I stare at her.

"That's it? THAT'S IT?? All that for... for a ...

a cow playing with a soccer ball???"

Mylove blinks at me. Yes.

And before she can say any more, I suddenly can't feel the bed underneath me.

I explode into gales of laughter. I'm crying, can't breathe, choking on my own spit, and laughing more, and she joins me too, and her high pierced shrieking giggle rides over my roar with utter abandon, and we're both gasping for air and then laughing again, riding wave after wave after wave (will it ever stop?)... Our other dog is licking my face with concern – then finally gets tired of the noise and leaves, and still I laugh...

I have no idea why I'm laughing so hard at this, but I have absolutely no control. This laughter and these tears are coming from so deep inside of me that the last vestiges of an ancient dungeon are blown to smithereens by the simple act of the most incredible woman on the planet, Mylove. This is our life. This is our love. And this is both our present and our future. And I still can't stop laughing.

Finally, I have no more, except those little ripples of giggles that bubble up between the sore muscles, and my pillow is sopped with tears and drool... and Mylove of 28 years says, "I have NEVER seen you laugh like that <u>ever</u>."

Wait, what just happened?

Oh, not much really, just a major shift in consciousness – a breaking off of the last vestige of dross, that accumulation of ash and impurities from the crust that covered my heart. We kiss and I get up from the puddle and realize that Mylove is right, I have not laughed and cried like that for over forty years – yes I laughed, yes I cried. But not like that. I'm free.

I shower and dress for the day. On the radio comes the news, The Supreme Court has spoken: same-sex marriage is a dignified and just act already guaranteed by The Constitution. Same-ssex marriage is the law of the land. Wait, what just happened? It's a new America.

And as I write, President Obama's grand eulogy for Rev. Pinkney reminds us all that we get God's Grace whether we are worthy or not, and it echoes through our house. His words are not about race, and yet they are. They are not about divisions and yet they are. But more than anything, they are about Grace. And how we live together and grow together.

Grace. Yes, capital "G" -race (wow, I didn't intend that but. . . well, wow. Anyway). It's Grace I want to live in, and offer, and be. Not that Grace is the sole domain of women, but it's *my* domain. I want to bring Grace, in my own way, to my part of the world.

And right now, my part is adventure television. I can't deny that I'm optimistic enough to look forward to driving a truck through that infamous glass ceiling. Am I crazy? Foolish? Naïve?

My friend, Valerie, an African-American writer, producer, and all around formidable woman, answers me this way. *"Glass ceiling? Well, you're an over-fifty woman trying to make it in a Hollywood ruled by its isms. You are three layers thick, Scottie: ageism, sexism, and transphobic-ism. You didn't make it easy on yourself; but hey, welcome to the team."*

So I set out to tell a tale about how a girl grows up as a boy to become a woman. To show how the little whispers of doubt and fear can either be your stone cold prison or, once you realize how strong the human heart really is, the guiding light.

And yet, I do feel that the winds of change are in my favor. And it's here that Pollyannaism suits me perfectly. Because I can feel that the biggest change from my "trans" formation of these last six months – from M to F, from brother to sister, from son to daughter, from nephew to niece, from Husband to Honey, from Scott to Scottie – has been from *denial to acceptance*. From sadness and fear to overwhelming joy.

Without huge fanfare or fireworks, my prayers to one day wake up as a girl have been answered –

I got back to me.

I can't wait to see the woman that I will become, as I take my place among the great women of my family and my life. I owe it to them, to Mylove and to myself, to step out into this world with my best foot forward. Only now, (thank God!) it'll be in a tasteful three-inch heel.

Four inch for *special* occasions.

ABOUT THE AUTHOR

Scottie currently lives with her love in a treehouse in the shadow of LA's
infamous "dirt Mulholland," with their black dog, Aria. When she's not
pretending that developing, writing and running television shows is
anything other than a dream come true (if they find out it isn't hard at all,
they'll make us work!), she is cooking up some wild adventure in food for
her friends and family.

CPSIA information can be obtained
at www.ICGtesting.com
Printed in the USA
LVOW04s2228050616

491342LV00008B/82/P